LIVING WITH

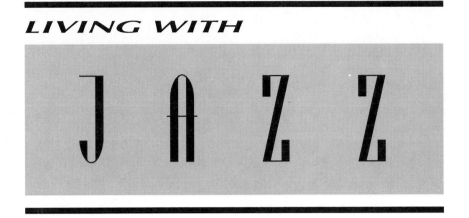

LIVING WITH JAZZ

AN APPRECIATION

FRANK TIRRO

Yale University

HARCOURT BRACE COLLEGE PUBLISHERS

Fort Worth Philadelphia San Diego New York Orlando Austin San Antonio
Toronto Montreal London Sydney Tokyo

Publisher	Ted Buchholz
Editor in Chief	Christopher P. Klein
Acquisitions Editor	Barbara J.C. Rosenberg
Developmental Editor	J. Claire Brantley
Project Editor	Sarah Elaine Sims
Senior Production Manager	Kathleen Ferguson
Art Director	Scott Baker
Photo Editor	Cheryl Throop

ISBN: 0-15-500318-6

Library of Congress Catalog Card Number: 94-74260

Address editorial correspondence to:
Harcourt Brace College Publishers
301 Commerce Street, Suite 3700
Fort Worth, TX 76102

Address orders to:
Harcourt Brace & Company
Permissions Department
6277 Sea Harbor Drive
Orlando, FL 32887-6777
1-800-782-4479 or 1-800-433-0001 (in Florida)

Printed in the United States of America

5 6 7 8 9 0 1 2 3 4 039 9 8 7 6 5 4 3 2 1

for Charlene, John, Cyndi, and Misty
the rhythm section of my life

Preface

The primary goal of *Living With Jazz* is to excite readers and listeners with jazz by offering and explaining selected masterpieces from the repertory of this magnificent American music. *Living With Jazz* will reveal some of jazz's inner workings and point out a few details of its extraordinary beauty, but the most eloquent spokesman for the music is the music itself. It is hoped that this textbook will open the magic door and help students become jazz lovers, fans, and perhaps even dedicated members of the jazz community of musicians and listening connoisseurs.

A college education is not, principally, about collecting facts, but learning to think. *Living With Jazz* has been written with that in mind using a concept referred to by educators as "the spiral curriculum." Throughout the text many important subjects are revisited, each time with an increasing degree of sophistication. A given subject in American history (the American Revolution, for example) might be introduced to first graders, fifth graders, eighth graders, tenth graders, college students, and graduate students with increasing levels of complexity and detail. In this book, the development, recognition, and understanding of jazz styles occurs in the first lesson, and continues almost without interruption through the last. Other basic ideas are treated similarly.

In brief then, the plan for *Living With Jazz* is based on the method by which we learn to speak our own language and learn the other basic subjects of our education. We begin to learn English by listening and speaking, not with lessons in grammar or etymology or through exercises in noun declensions. I have attempted to do the same with this introduction to the music of jazz. In this book and in the recordings that accompany it, I share some of my personal favorites, music and musicians that I like, hoping that others will like them, too; I also explain what I hear and find exciting—or soothing or inspiring—in the performances. As the text proceeds, I ask students to remember and relate things they have heard and read. Gradually, I try to stimulate them to question what I have said and even question what they know and have heard. In this way, students, too, will become part of this evolving music.

Throughout the text, questions have been provided at the ends of the units and in the review sections that go beyond remembering names and dates, requiring serious thought and informed interpretation, mostly about the music but also about art, life, and society as well. Thus it will be seen that an equally important purpose of this book is to help students learn to think critically while gaining a sophisticated level of aural ability.

Living With Jazz is addressed to college students who need a guide to their introductory voyage in jazz. After all, we are dealing with an incredible amount of music, about one hundred years of creative activity by some of the world's most extraordinary and prolific musicians. Students have the rest of their lives to continue learning about this ever growing and constantly changing art form, and this book hopes to entice the student, to build the basic vocabulary, and to offer an attractive introduction. At the end, each student will have internalized a collection of pieces that broadly represents the greater world of jazz.

And although this is a jazz appreciation textbook and not a jazz history, students cannot help but learn a fair amount about this music's history. After listening to the music, interacting with the teacher, reading the text, and discovering interesting facts about the musicians' lives, the history of jazz will naturally begin to take shape.

Experienced teachers know how to energize their class presentations by projecting beyond the parameters of the individual reading and listening assignments. They will surely want to present Miles Davis, John Coltrane, Louis Armstrong, Thelonious Monk, and others of equal stature in a fuller display of their stylistic, philosophical, compositional, and historical impacts on the jazz community and the entire music world.

To this end, a reasonably extensive survey of jazz recordings has been selected and prepared in compact disc (CD) format to accompany this book. None of these pieces duplicate those available in the *Smithsonian Collection of Classic Jazz*, the recordings for Frank Tirro's *Jazz: A History*, second edition, or the *New World Anthology of American Music*. By not duplicating these works, this textbook and its

CDs clear the way for instructors to select from a second large repertory of recorded masterpieces with accompanying commentaries. Of course, instructors will also want to bring to class a few cherished items from their personal record collections, and this fresh material can reinforce the sounds of the introductory pieces first presented in the text.

Throughout *Living With Jazz*, I have tried to be reasonably informal, not because jazz is not a disciplined art—it is—but because most jazz musicians, their music, and their patrons, are usually relaxed, both during performance hours and after. Actually, when a musician is playing an up-tempo solo, he or she only gives the appearance of relaxation, for the jazz improviser is working intensely. But if the artist cannot make the music sound effortless and relaxed, he or she is probably not playing very well. There is also an amiable, fun-loving, and humane aspect to this music and its practitioners that refuses to stand on pretense and formality. In jazz, it is not the price tag and label of a musician's instrument that counts, but the quality of his or her tone, the interest of the musical ideas he or she plays, and how well these ideas are expressed.

I enjoy depicting jazz in its social context rather than in the sterile atmosphere of a commercial recording studio. Very few of the cuts included on the CDs were recorded "live," that is, in concert rather than in the studio, but the best studio recordings strive for the spontaneity and presence that improvising musicians experience while playing for a responsive audience and in the company of respected, competing musicians. So, partly to lure students to hear jazz live, and partly to dispel the false impressions that jazz is primarily found on records, cassettes, and CDs, I invented the Chez Imagination, a big-city nightclub that features jazz and hosts musicians from any era, even on the same night.

I have also gone to great lengths to avoid placing obstacles in the way of any well-intentioned reader who has no preparation in music and no experience in jazz. There are no footnotes. There is no apparatus at the back of the book that a diligent reader must refer to constantly in order to understand the text. If a word or concept is important enough to merit inclusion in the book, a definition or explanation is placed right where it belongs, in the text. There are no examples of musical notation. Many nonmusicians find written music intimidating, and I do not believe that a person must be able to read music or play a scale to enjoy music. *Living With Jazz* uses only as much technical description as is necessary to talk intelligently about the music and as much technical vocabulary as will give an aspiring jazz fan a sense of belonging to the jazz community. Enjoy!

Acknowledgments

I wish there were a more satisfactory method to express gratitude to my students who, over a 32-year span in the classroom, have taught and continue to teach me more than I pass on to them. Some are very special, and I swell with undeserved pride when I think of their accomplishments, but the list would be long and the omissions painful. Also, I wish it were possible to individually thank all the musicians I played with at home and on the road. The gig is the best classroom, and the band bus or leader's car is an institution that cannot be duplicated. These musicians are the real experts of jazz and life, and they know you learn best by doing, just as you prove yourself by doing, not talking.

Because *Living With Jazz* is unique among college textbooks of this kind, I wish to specially thank the decision makers of Harcourt Brace College Publishers for their support and willingness to risk breaking the mold of historical, chronological presentations. Barbara J. C. Rosenberg, acquisitions editor, kept the project in motion, and the developmental editor, J. Claire Brantley, brought great skill to the process of editing and shepherding a manuscript and all its appendages through the complex tasks of book publishing and compact disk production. She brought the enthusiasm and knowledge of a real jazz lover to the process of reading and criticizing the manuscript. The Harcourt Brace production team—Sarah Elaine Sims, project editor; Scott Baker, art director; and Kathleen Ferguson, production manager—has been a joy to work with.

Living With Jazz benefited from the advice and criticism of many reviewers who looked over the manuscript while it was still in preparation; special thanks are due to Charles Blanq, University of New Orleans; Susan Cook, University of Wisconsin; Scott DeVeaux, University of Virginia; Tom Everett, Harvard University; Antonio García, Northwestern University; Jeff Hellmer, University of Texas; Chuck Israels, Western Washington University; Tom Knific, Western Michigan University; Jon Lindsey, Nicholls State University; Charlotte Mabrey, University of North Florida; Larry Panella, University of Southern Mississippi; Jeff Stout, Berklee College of Music; Russell Thomas, Jackson State University; Steve Wiest, University of Wisconsin, Whitewater; and Father George Wiskirchen, University of Notre Dame.

If anyone had a direct hand in the creation of this book, it was Charlene, my wife. It takes time to write a book, and she gave me time. It takes nights out, concerts, and many costly recordings, and she allowed me these. It also takes moments of frustration and irritability to complete any major project, and she ignored them. So, what can I say, she's a great wife.

Contents

Unit 12 Improvising Brass I 126

Louis Armstrong, Jack Teagarden, and Bix Beiderbecke
New Orleans and Chicago

Unit 13 Improvising Brass II 144

Dizzy Gillespie, Miles Davis, J. J. Johnson, and Ray Anderson
Bebop and Avant-garde

Unit 14 Improvising Brass III: The Women 158

Tiny Davis, Melba Liston, and Rebecca Coupe Franks
Swing, Ballads, Modal Jazz, and Modern Bebop

Illustrations

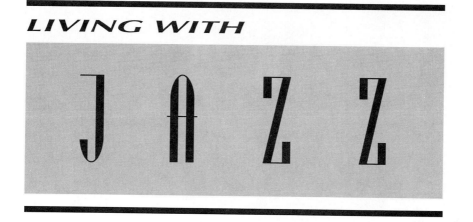

LIVING WITH

JAZZ

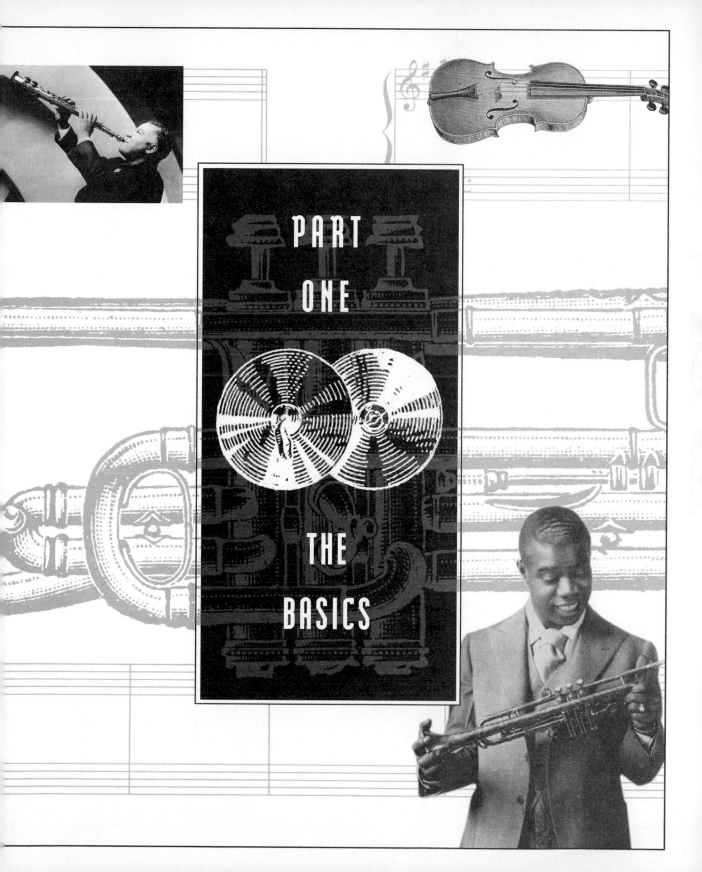

PART ONE

THE BASICS

Identifying the Sounds

Welcome to the world of jazz! No sense wasting time. Let's get started with a quick trip back to the "Jazz Age," the Roaring '20s and the early 1930s, when all the American cities, but especially Chicago, Kansas City, and New York, sported a profusion of night clubs, speakeasies, dance halls, and theaters that featured jazz and dancing as entertainment. If you think you are not ready because you don't know a thing about jazz, don't worry. Neither did most of the patrons who frequented the jazz clubs and had a great time. They learned by listening, and so will you. By living with the music they heard and danced to, they learned the instruments, the players, the bands, the tunes, and what was happening with the music. They also learned to separate the good from the bad. They learned about jazz just as you learned to speak your own language, through total absorption, a little at a time. Use your imagination and your intellect as you read this book and listen to the recordings, and I'll show you a good time while you learn about jazz.

Let's turn on that imagination right away. As you read these words, come with me to my favorite Manhattan nightclub, the "Chez Imagination," and let's check out whoever is playing there tonight. Follow me up these stairs, past the bouncer, and follow the maitre d' to that table in the corner. See how easy it is? No sense being tedious about this project. The sound of the room is great, no smoking is allowed (bad on the players' lungs), and people stop talking when the music starts. If you are settled into your chair, it's time to get to know some players, a tune or two, and what the instruments sound like when they are used to play jazz.

We are in luck, for this evening a classic band calling themselves the **Chocolate Dandies**, a seven-piece group from one of New York's most celebrated large jazz ensembles, the **Fletcher Henderson Orchestra**, is being led by the great saxophonist **Benny Carter**. There's a dance floor over there near the stage, and the musicians are warming up in that room back of the bandstand. This **combo**, short for "combination" and meaning a small group of musicians rather than a big band, will play several **sets** tonight, groups of pieces played one after another. Then they will stop for a few minutes, take an intermission to rest, give the patrons a chance to talk, and give the management a chance to serve food and drinks. Then the players will get back to work.

Now, there is one very nifty detail about our imaginary night out. We will be able to listen to the same performance more than once (one of the advantages of recorded sound) and focus, during each successive listening, on new and different features. You'll hear all the sounds of the performance every time you listen, of course, but we are going to focus our attention and isolate certain important characteristics each time we listen. That will give you something to think about every time you hear the group. If you get tired, just listen for fun, and when you are rested up, listen again and pay special attention to the particular aspect of the music you are reading about. This way you won't get confused, and you will systematically add more understanding to what you already know. The basic concepts will quickly go into that intellectual toolbox we use to understand and appreciate the more

One of the most popular night spots in 1930s New York was the Cotton Club in Harlem. This photo of a typical floor show was taken in 1934 at the original location on Lenox Avenue (now Malcolm X Boulevard). In 1936 the club moved downtown to West 48th Street. Both Cab Calloway and Jimmie Lunceford served as Cotton Club band leaders during 1934.

complex aspects of music, and we can pull them out and use them as they are needed to eventually become a connoisseur who discerns and truly savors this great American art music.

The musicians are coming on the "stand," the bandstand, that is, and we should check out the instruments they are going to play. We need to know what they look like, so we can recognize them by sight, but more importantly, we want to know what they sound like. If you ever played in a band or orchestra, you may think this is a waste of time, but in jazz, the sounds can get pretty tricky, so bear with me a moment. In jazz, each player likes to develop "his or her own sound," his or her own unique musical voice. That's the first major difference between jazz and "classical" music. In classical music, the players strive for a more or less agreed-upon standard of perfect sound; in jazz, the players want their own identifiable voice. The musicians in this band are no exception, and with a little practice you'll be able not only to tell a trumpet solo from a trombone improvisation, a clarinet sound from the tone of a saxophone, but one player from another just by his or her sound.

If you look on the bandstand again, you will see that the **Chocolate Dandies** use a trumpet, a trombone, and two saxophones in the **front line,** and a piano, guitar, and brass bass in the **rhythm section.**

Fletcher Henderson's band from the late 1930s featured a small group, The Hot Six, just as members of his earlier band formed The Chocolate Dandies. In this photo, we can see a rhythm section of piano, bass, and drums; a brass section of three trumpets and two trombones; and a reed section of five saxophones.

We will talk about the **rhythm section** later, but for now just notice that the single-note melody instruments group together up front, the **front line,** and the piano, bass, and guitar form another cluster in back slightly to the side. One other thing: notice that the leader, **Bennie Carter,** "doubles," that is, he plays more than one instrument. On this number he is going to play both clarinet and alto saxophone.

No drums, you ask? I am glad you noticed, and that's right! Most jazz groups have a drummer who plays a set of drums. A few bands don't, and not every band uses drums for every number. On this recording, you will see that these musicians can create all the rhythm they need for this performance without even touching a drum. The tune they are going to play is called *Bugle Call Rag*, and they recorded this number in New York back in 1930.

BUGLE CALL RAG (CD SELECTION 1.1)

Now that you've heard it once, let's talk a little about the music and then listen to it again. The piece opened with a **trumpet** solo. No, it wasn't a bugle as the title suggests, but that's not important. What is important is getting the sound of Bobby Stark's trumpet fixed in your mind. Bobby Stark was the player, and his trumpet sound is that high brass tone that cuts right through the ensemble and provides the lead, or most important melody of this piece, at the beginning. You probably noticed that *Bugle Call Rag* featured a succession of solos, and that will make it easy for us to identify and remember the sounds of all these instruments. After the trumpet solo, Bennie Carter played a solo on his **alto saxophone.** The "alto," a common abbreviation and nickname for the alto saxophone, also plays in the same range as the trumpet, but its tone and **articulation,** the sound and the sharpness of the attack on each note, are different from those we heard from the trumpet. Then, Jimmy Harrison takes a solo on his **trombone,** a brass instrument that sounds very much like the trumpet but plays notes that are in a lower range. Also, since Harrison's trombone uses a slide to change pitches where Stark's trumpet uses valves, you will notice that there are many subtle differences in pitch and articulation (again, the attack or beginning of each note) between the slide trombone and the valve trumpet. Coleman Hawkins follows Harrison with a **tenor saxophone** solo, and in addition to sounding lower than the alto, his

This montage of jazz instruments includes (clockwise from top left) brushes on snare drum, piano keyboard, slide trombone, trumpet, tenor saxophone, clarinet, guitar, and bass. Some of the musicians are George Wettling (percussion); Jess Stacy (keyboard); Jack Teagarden (trombone); Bobby Hackett (trumpet); Artie Shapiro (bass); Eddie Condon (guitar); Bud Freeman (tenor saxophone); and Pee Wee Russell (clarinet). All of these musicians played Chicago style jazz and were featured at the New York club called Eddie Condon's.

"tenor" sound has a different **vibrato,** the wobble or shake of the pitch up and down, from that of Carter's alto sound. Then an interesting thing happens in the music. For a brief time several instruments take the lead together, playing a synchronized set of notes that work in a coordinated fashion. That type of playing is called a "soli" passage, as opposed to a "solo." **Solo** and **soli** are both Italian words meaning the same thing, but "solo" is singular and "soli" is plural. Next, the **tuba,** or brass bass, gets a brief moment of glory in John Kirby's solo, which is interrupted and followed by Benny Jackson's **guitar** solo. You'll notice that on the guitar solo, Jackson plays the instrument melodically, one note at a time, where elsewhere in the music he strums chords on the beat, quickly passing his pick over several strings to help lay down the rhythm with the piano and bass. Horace Henderson, Fletcher Henderson's brother, enters with a **piano** solo next, and he is followed by the leader, Bennie Carter, again, but this time on **clarinet.** The clarinet, although related to both the alto and tenor saxophones, is made of wood instead of metal and has a different shape and construction. Thus it sounds quite distinct from

Bennie Carter, who led a distinguished 60-year career in jazz and the movie industry as leader, saxophonist, arranger and composer, is shown with his Savoy Play Boys band of 1928. Notice the rhythm section of Sousaphone, piano, banjo, and drums with the brass sections to the right and the reeds on the left.

the saxophones even though it is a member of the reed family. The tone of all the reed instruments is produced by vibrating a shaped reed on a mouthpiece, while the brass tones are produced by vibrating the lips into a cup mouthpiece. How the sounds are produced is of no real concern now; we are primarily trying to remember what each instrument sounds like and how these sounds differ from one another. So, listen again, and focus your ears on the trumpet, alto sax, trombone, tenor sax, section soli, brass bass, guitar, piano, and clarinet solos in that order. On this second trip through the recorded music your only job is to learn the sounds of these particular musicians playing the **trumpet, alto saxophone, trombone, tenor saxophone,** [soli], **tuba, guitar, piano, and clarinet.**

THE MUSICIANS SPEAK   SIDNEY BECHET

I wouldn't tell all this in a story about the music, except that all I been telling, it's part of the music. That man there in the grocery store, the Mexican, the jail—they're all in the music. Whatever kind of thing it was, whenever it happened, the music put it together. That boy having to play for those people to dance there in his own house; that man wanting to scare me down by the railroad tracks, getting a pleasure out of wanting to scare me; and when I was in jail, playing the blues, really finding out about the blues—it was always the music that explained things. What it is that takes you out of being just a kid and thinking it's all adventure, and you find there's a lesson underneath all that adventure—that lesson, it's the music. You come into life alone and you go out of it alone, and you're going to be alone a lot of the time when you're on this earth—and what tells it all, it's the music. You tell it to the music and the music tells it to you. And then you know about it. You know what it was happened to you. . . .

But ragtime, that's no history thing. It's not dead. Ragtime, it's the musicianers. *Rag it up*, we used to say. You take any piece, you make it so people can dance to it, pat their feet, move around. You make it so they can't help themselves from doing that. You make it so they just can't sit still. And that's all there is to it. It's the rhythm there. The rhythm *is* ragtime. That's still there to be done. You could do that to all kinds of numbers still being played, still being composed today.

That rhythm goes all the way back. In the spirituals the people clapped their hands—that was their rhythm. In the blues it was further down; they didn't need the clapping, but they remembered it, it was still

BUGLE CALL RAG (CD SELECTION 1.1)

If you are a rock 'n roll fan and think the guitar sounded different from what you are used to, you are right. Remember, there were no electric guitars in 1930. Also, after the clarinet solo finished, I hope you noticed that there were three more solos. What were the instruments, in order, and who were the players? Right! Jimmie Harrison on trombone, Coleman Hawkins on tenor, and Bobby Stark on trumpet. Now that wasn't hard, was it?

there. And both of them, the spirituals and the blues, they was a prayer. One was praying to God and the other was praying to what's human. It's like one was saying, 'Oh, God, let me go,' and the other was saying, 'Oh, Mister, let me be.' And they were both the same thing in a way; they were both my people's way of praying to be themselves, praying to be let alone so they could be human. The spirituals, they had a kind of trance to them, a kind of forgetting. It was like a man closing his eyes so he can see a light inside him. That light, it's far off and you've got to wait to see it. But it's there. It's waiting. The spirituals, they're a way of seeing that light. It's a far off music; it's a going away, but it's a going away that takes you with it. And the blues, they've got that sob inside, that awful lonesome feeling. It's got so much remembering inside it, so many bad things to remember, so many losses.

But both of them, they're based on rhythm. They're both of them leading up to a rhythm. And they're both coming up from a rhythm. It's like they're going and coming at the same time. Going, coming—inside the music that's the same thing, it's the rhythm. And that rhythm and that feeling you put around it, always keeping the melody, that's all there is to it. That's nothing that's dead. That's nothing that could die: 1910, 1923, 1950—there's no difference in that. And to give you what this Jazz is—all you need is a few men who can hear what the man next to him is doing at the same time that you know your instrument and how you can say on it what you gotta say to keep the next man going with you, leading one another on to the place the music has to go.

REVIEW   1

Primary Goal
of Unit 1

Recognize the characteristic sounds of:

trumpet
alto saxophone
trombone
tenor saxophone
tuba
guitar
piano
clarinet

Study Questions

1. When was "The Jazz Age" and where did it take place?

2. Who was the leader of the Chocolate Dandies and what instrument or instruments did he play?

3. Who are the sidemen, the other musicians besides the leader, who played in this recording of the Chocolate Dandies and what were their instruments?

4. When and where was *Bugle Call Rag* recorded by the Chocolate Dandies?

Other Concepts

1. What is a combo?

2. What do musicians do when they play a set?

3. What does a musician do when he or she "doubles"?

4. What is the "front line" of a jazz combo?

5. What are some of the differences between the reed and brass instruments used in jazz?

6. Which instrument uses a slide to change pitch?

7. What is the difference between "solo" playing and "soli" performance?

Individual Voices

We are in luck! Tonight the "Chez Imagination" is featuring the King of Swing himself, Benny Goodman. He is here with his **sextet** (a combo of six instruments), and this will give us an opportunity to compare his clarinet sound with that of Bennie Carter's, which we heard last night (Unit 1). Also, we'll have an opportunity to compare his front line and rhythm section with that of the Chocolate Dandies. Then, we can listen to the two piano solos and see if we can hear a difference between the playing of Goodman's pianist, Mel Powell, and that of Horace Henderson. Wait a minute, pianos are mechanical instruments. You can't bend the pitches or vary the tone or vibrato like saxophonists and trombonists can. Shouldn't they sound the same? No! Pianists have different touches, use the pedals differently, grab clusters of notes or play running passages differently, and they also play in different styles. We'll talk about style later, but for this evening's listening let's continue to concentrate on identifying the instruments and seeing if we can recognize Benny Goodman's and Bennie Carter's clarinet sounds as well as Mel Powell's and Horace Henderson's piano techniques. As for identifying the instruments, we have three new ones in this group which were not used by the Chocolate Dandies—**drums, string bass,** and **vibraphone.**

While the waitress is bringing us our drinks, let me warn you about the variation in quality of sound you will hear tonight. Goodman's sextet recorded this number right after the Second World War, more than ten years after the Chocolate Dandies recorded theirs. During these years there were striking technological improvements made by the recording industry, so the sound of Goodman's music is cleaner and has more presence. You will have to direct your ears to use their imagination too, for they must ignore the technology factor when comparing one recording with another and concentrate on the music. Both were recorded in monaural, as opposed to stereo, sound, but there were considerable improvements in the microphones, recorders, and recording studies between 1930 and the time this side was cut in September of 1945.

The men are moving onto the stand, and here comes Benny Goodman accompanied by a thunderous applause. He is one of the best known and most celebrated figures in the world of music, classical as well as jazz. Through tours and radio broadcasts, he popularized his style of jazz, **swing,** to an immense, worldwide audience. Everyone is thrilled to hear him play in person, and his fans are letting him know they are in the house. He is known as the "King of Swing," and in 1945 he is riding on the crest of fame and popularity. Isn't it great that at our club, the "Chez Imagination," we can hear whomever we choose whenever we please for the same low price? That's what I like about the place. Also, it is clean and efficient. Notice that at our club the musicians move on and off the stand without wasting any time. Morey Feld set up his **drums** in nothing flat. And that red-haired guy set up his **vibraphone** and plugged it in before I noticed. Yes, that's

Three members of the Benny Goodman Sextet of 1945 are shown here in the background: Goodman, clarinet; Red Norvo, vibes; and Morey Feld, drums. The neck of Mike Bryan's guitar can be seen on the left, but pianist Mel Powell and bassist Slam Stewart are not shown. The man pictured in the forefront is Lawrence Tibbett, famous bass-baritone of the Metropolitan Opera.

Red Norvo on vibes. Let's see, what else is new? Mike Bryan is tuning up his guitar, and notice that it is similar to the one we heard before. It is an acoustic instrument with six strings, and it is used in a jazz combo primarily as a rhythm instrument that strums chords on or off the beat to accompany the other musicians. Among the instruments of jazz, it is one of the quietest, so unless its sound is amplified its presence is often more felt than heard.

Slam Stewart is standing there with his bass viol, a **string bass,** or **double bass,** or just **bass** for short, rather than the brass bass, or tuba, we heard John Kirby play before. And rounding out the group is a very young man, Mel Powell, on piano, certainly one of the finest pianists and arrangers of the swing era. Swing Era? Isn't that the late 1930s and 1940s? I thought we were in the Jazz Age, the 1920s! Well, we were, but with a little artistic license our club moved effortlessly through time. Right now we are concentrating on the sound of the instruments, so forget about anything else and give a listen to *China Boy* as performed by the Benny Goodman Sextet in 1945. Notice that the front line consists of two instruments only, clarinet and vibes, and the rhythm section has four—piano, bass, drums, and guitar.

CHINA BOY (CD SELECTION 1.2)

There is no question that virtuosity is Goodman's strong suit. As soon as one hears the short, solo introduction the listener knows that he or she is in for some up-tempo excitement. Benny Goodman flies over the notes, keeps an even tone, and takes charge of this piece from the first moment on. When the band comes in, notice that as Goodman plays the tune, Norvo improvises a countermelody, or a different tune that fits with the main melody, in the background on his vibes. The drums lay down a soft pulsating beat by using wire brushes dragged and patted on the snare drum; the bass plays a plucked rhythm pattern on every beat, unlike the 2-beat or every-other-beat performance of John Kirby's tuba on the Chocolate Dandies recording; the guitar is almost inaudible but is playing a rhythm-guitar pattern, regular strumming of chords on the beat; and the piano is both accompanying by playing chords rhythmically and interspersing improvised countermelodies along with the vibes. Also, during the first chorus when Goodman was playing the melody, vibes and piano filled up the spaces when the clarinet paused at the ends of phrases.

Let's take our first look at the drums. Although Morey Feld has a full set of drums—bass, snare, and tom-toms, cymbals, sticks, and brushes—his playing on this number is restricted to an unobtrusive background pulsation of brushes on snare. Occasionally there will be a little flurry of percussive activity at the end of phrases, a process called "playing fills," but on this recording the drums do little more than lay down the beat. Still, his roll is vital. He is the **timekeeper** and is responsible for holding the beat steady. Now it is true that these outstanding musicians would probably keep the beat rock solid if the drums were absent, but it is also true that the background pulsation is one of the characteristic sounds of this style of jazz. We grow accustomed to its presence and would miss it were it absent.

Benny Goodman first brought his swing band to New York's Carnegie Hall in 1938. As they did for most performances, a smaller group of musicians (Goodman's quintet) performed while the rest of the band took breaks between sets. In 1973, the quintet returned to Carnegie Hall for a special performance; pictured are Goodman (clarinet), Slam Stewart (bass), Gene Krupa (drums), and Lionel Hampton (vibraphone). Absent from the photo, but at the piano, is Teddy Wilson.

Slam Stewart plays his bass in two different ways on this number. He plucks the strings, plays "pizzicato," when he is accompanying as part of the rhythm section, and he plays the instrument with a bow, bows the strings or plays "arco," when he is soloing. Also, Slam Stewart developed his own special bass-solo technique—he sings in octaves with his instrument as he solos. This manner of singing vowels to carry the sound and consonants to articulate the notes but not singing words is called "scat singing," and it has a long tradition going back to the early days of jazz in New Orleans. It was later popularized by Louis Armstrong and others, and we will deal with it later when we study vocal jazz. But to sing simultaneously while playing a bass solo was new; in fact, it was unique at that time to Slam Stewart. One could not easily identify Stewart's string bass playing when hearing him perform in ensemble as part of the rhythm section, but one would always recognize his solos. He achieved that personal musical identity that is so precious to jazz musicians.

The vibraphone is an interesting instrument that generates sound when tuned metal bars are struck with mallets. It uses resonators beneath the bars to amplify the sound and uses motor-driven rotating butterfly valves in the resonators to give the tone a vibrato. A pedal allows notes to be sustained, and several types of mallets allow for a variation in tone. When Norvo plays here, he uses soft mallets for a mellow sound, and he plays primarily in a melodic style by playing successive notes with two alternating mallets. He can play chords by striking three or four mallets at once, but on this piece he primarily concentrates on melodic improvisation, the art of simultaneously composing and performing new melodies to fit with the harmonies and rhythms played by the other members of the group.

If for a moment you can ignore the wonderful playing of the piano during the piano solo you will have your best opportunity to hear the drums and guitar in accompaniment. Then focus your attention on the piano solo and notice the whirlwind of notes Powell plays with his right hand as he improvises melodically. All the while his left hand is busy accompanying. At first it is bouncing back and forth, striding from bass notes to chords, and later he inserts a variation of this chording technique without striding up and down. While his left hand "comps," or accompanies, his right-hand fingers are flying over the keys playing an extraordinary melodic solo.

Even though there is an obvious attempt to recreate the feeling of a **jam session** on this recording, a session when musicians will gather to spontaneously improvise together, there is also a necessity for compressing those elements into a coherent three-minute recording, the maximum time span of 10-inch 78 RPM recordings in 1945. On this performance, Goodman solos the introduction, plays lead for the first chorus (plays the melody with a little ornamentation), plays a solo chorus after the bass solo, and plays another solo chorus after the vibes solo at the end. Like the recording of the Chocolate Dandies, the players on *China Boy* take their turns at a featured solo improvisation (with the exceptions of Mike Bryan on guitar and Morey Feld on drums), but unlike the practice of the former group, where the solo time was divided more or less equally, Benny Goodman predominates as the featured soloist on this number. He is clearly the star, the personality the people have paid their money to hear, and he carries this responsibility well. His ideas are imaginative and daring, he features the entire range of the instrument, he plays with a feeling of ease and grace, and his sense of swing is propulsive. That **sense of swing** is what great jazz artists give to their music. They charge their playing with rhythmic excitement, give it forward propulsion and an essential

Benny Goodman organized his first big band in 1934 when this photo was taken; in November of the same year, the group won an audition for the NBC radio series "Let's Dance." Two things during this period helped form the Goodman band's sound: Fletcher Henderson was engaged to prepare arrangements for the band's radio broadcasts, and drummer Gene Krupa joined the group.

feeling of drive and energy that is noticeable in every great jazz performance.

Now, let's listen again to *China Boy* and concentrate on the characteristic sounds of the instruments, the **clarinet, piano, bass,** and **vibes** in solo, and the **guitar** and **drums** in accompaniment. The order of the solos is:

CHINA BOY

Brief Intro	1st Chorus	2nd Chorus	3rd Chorus	4th Chorus	5th Chorus	Final Chorus
Clarinet	**Clarinet**	**Piano**	**Bass**	**Clarinet**	**Vibraphone**	**Clarinet**

THE MUSICIANS SPEAK DANNY BARKER

My grandmother. She was a hard-shell Baptist. She said, "That's no way to make a livin'. It's the Devil's music. Out all night—dissipatin'. That's no good." She was a Christian woman. She was concerned about me playin' in gamblin' houses and honkey-tonks. There were so many varied degrees of spots where music was played. So, she didn't want me to get involved with rowdy people and stayin' up all night. The old folks know what's best for you bout gettin' your rest and eatin' right.

This is what it was like in New Orleans around 1925. It is not true that nothing happened after Storyville closed. There were always, in New Orleans, both before and after Storyville closed, there were always so many musicians, so many great cats all the way down the line. . . . A lot of them would play roadhouses, and vaudeville shows and circuses and the riverboats and lakeboats, like at Lake Ponchartrain. And also—this was during the 'twenties, too, as well as before—there were so many halls in New Orleans, fifteen or twenty. And each one would have some kind of an affair going on. There was also always some kind of lawn party or parades going on.

So you never had to figure on getting work in The District, so it wasn't so important when it closed. . . . And, as a matter of fact, some of the clubs were going in the 'twenties. They would have a closing, and then a quick opening, under cover, in The District. Also, bands like Lee Collins' would be based in New Orleans but would be on the road for a while and play towns outside of New Orleans. Little towns in states like Mississippi, Alabama, Georgia, Florida, and Louisiana. Men like Buddy Petit, Sam Mor-

CHINA BOY (CD SELECTION 1.2)

Coherence is one of the key features of this performance, a smooth, seamless grace which ties phrase to phrase and solo to solo. There is an elegance in the performance of all four of the featured soloists on *China Boy* that combines an easy virtuosity with the absence of excessive material, a balance of similar phrases and well-shaped lines, and a smooth lyricism that carries the listener along in one long, continuous motion.

In summary, these first two units have introduced you to most of the principal instrumental sounds of jazz. You should be able to

gan, Leslie Dimes, Baptiste Brown, and Victor Spencer were some of the New Orleans musicians who would take these road trips. New Orleans, you see, was the center of bands, and, as way back as I can remember [born 1909], people in that area would get their bands from New Orleans, and, in fact, they still do. They would go out on the road a week or two weeks, and people in these small towns would keep you on option, according to the business you did and according to how you acted. New Orleans had always been looked on as a city for musicians and New Orleans' being an entertainment center—all the great shows played in that city, like in the Lyric Theatre. And all the big circuses would come through New Orleans. And if they needed a musician, they knew they could pick one up in New Orleans.

All the minstrel shows, like the Rabbit Foot Minstrels [Gertrude "Ma" Rainey and Bessie Smith] and Silas Green and the Georgia Minstrels, used New Orleans musicians year in and year out. You would see a cat disappear, you would wonder where he was, and finally somebody would say that he'd left for one of the shows, that they had sent for him. During the 'twenties, as before, the town had so much night life. Even now, the bars stay open twenty-four hours a day. And then there are musicians who didn't want to leave New Orleans to go up North. Even though they had offers. Some cats would meet a pretty Creole girl, and she'd say she didn't want to go on the road. So, he settle down in New Orleans because there were enough gigs. A lot of out-of-town musicians settled there, too, because there was always some kind of work, good food, and a carefree life.

identify the characteristic **brass section** sounds of trumpet, trombone, and tuba; the **reed section** sounds of clarinet, alto saxophone, and tenor saxophone; and the **rhythm section** sounds of piano, bass, drums, and guitar. You also have been introduced to a rare but important instrument, the vibraphone. There are more instruments, variations of each type, and special effects that will appear as we move along from band to band, but if you master the technique of recognizing these eleven instruments now, you will be safely on your way toward an exciting journey through jazz.

REVIEW 2

Recognize the characteristic sounds of

vibraphone
string bass
drums (brushes on snare)

and compare the

clarinet playing of Benny Goodman and Benny Carter
piano playing of Mel Powell and Horace Henderson

Primary Goal
of Unit 2

1. Who were the four featured soloists in the performance of *China Boy* and what were their instruments?

2. Why did the recording of *China Boy* sound clearer and have greater presence than the recording of *Bugle Call Rag?*

3. What four instruments comprised the rhythm section of the Benny Goodman Sextet?

4. When and where was *China Boy* recorded by the Benny Goodman Sextet?

5. What is the jazz performer's sense of swing?

Study Questions

1. If two jazz pianists were to play the same number, one after the other, what might be some of the devices that each might employ to make his or her own performance different from the other's?

Other Concepts

2. Likewise, what devices or methods of playing might two wind instrument performers use to establish their own sound and style?

3. What is "scat singing"?

4. What is the difference between "keeping time" and "playing fills" on the drums?

5. When a rhythm section pianist "comps," what is he or she doing?

6. When a string bassist changes from "pizzicato" to "arco," what does he or she do?

7. Most recorded early jazz performances are three minutes in length. Why?

The Rhythm Section

Jazz musicians do not listen to music the way most people do. That is, most people listen to and remember the melody of a composition, and, if there are words, a complex of melody and words that group together in the mind as a unit they remember as the piece. Of course, jazz musicians hear melodies, and other people, whether or not they are performing musicians, hear and remember other elements of music which catch their interest. But jazz musicians, by necessity, focus their attention first on the work of the rhythm section, and then they work their way up into the melodic, rhythmic, and tonal exterior. Much as a layman first admires the facade, landscaping, and interior details of a beautiful home, and finally, if ever, comes to inspect the basement, an architect or architectural engineer begins with the foundation and substructure of the building and works upward into a design that complements and is appropriate for the space, terrain, and geology below.

Classical performers and audiences tend to have a similar approach when relating to classical music. The best-remembered aspects of the Mendelssohn *Violin Concerto* or the Beethoven *Ninth Symphony*, for most people, are the treasured melodies that are repeated over and over in each subsequent performance. Composers, on the other hand, listen for the inner workings of the composition—the form, harmonies, orchestration—that will give them intellectual material for new music. At the same time, they see and appreciate a world of musical complexity that is hidden from view and missed by those who only perceive the surface. Jazz is a classical music, and improvising jazz musicians are, in fact, composers or musical architects. In their work they concentrate on the substructure of the piece they are dealing with and build new musical edifices of melody, harmony, counterpoint, rhythm, and tonal effects upon a substructure that is laid out for them by the members of the rhythm section.

After checking with the owner of the "Chez Imagination," I learned that a few musicians were rehearsing in the hall this afternoon.

If we hurry over, we might have a chance to catch the rhythm section at work. So, let's go! It's amazing how quickly we can travel when we are in a hurry. Since the club is empty of patrons, let's start by going up on the stand and inspecting the instruments. The three "standard" instruments of a **rhythm section** are **piano, bass,** and **drums,** and a guitar is commonly included in the group or used as a substitute for the piano. Today, the musicians will restrict themselves to **piano, bass,** and **drums.** The piano is familiar to everyone, so there is little need to explain its workings, but please note that it is a quality instrument. Some people hold the strange notion that broken-down, honky-tonk pianos are appropriate for jazz. They are wrong. Jazz pianists want the best instrument they can lay their hands on, and they want it in tune and in excellent condition.

The bass we see is the standard orchestral bass, the largest member of the viol family. Today, jazz musicians often refer to it as an

The Count Basie Orchestra rhythm section in 1947 included Basie on piano, Jo Jones on drums, and Walter Page on bass. In 1937, guitarist Freddie Green joined the band. The Basie rhythm section spent hours in rehearsal—not only with the rest of the band but also independently to develop the flexibility and responsiveness that would influence future generations of rhythm players.

acoustic bass, because electric and electronic bass instruments have been successfully introduced into jazz. "Acoustic" simply refers to the fact that the instrument has its own resonator, the hollow body of the instrument, and the sound you hear is that which is produced by the instrument, not by an amplifier or tone generator. Today, most bass players in jazz, even when they are playing an acoustic instrument, often attach a special microphone, or pickup, to their instrument and amplify the volume so that the low tones might be more easily heard, but they try to get amplification only, not a distortion of the instrument's characteristic sound.

The drums are less familiar, you say. Well, let's take a look at a **set of traps,** a combination of percussion instruments used by a jazz drummer that usually includes a **bass drum, snare drum, tom-toms,** and **cymbals** as a minimum set.

This modern trap drum set is pictured from the viewpoint of the drummer. Notice the bass drum with foot-operated pedal beaters in the center. A foot-operated hi-hat (or sock) cymbal (pair of cymbals) is on the left. A snare drum sits between the drum pedals and the sock cymbal. Suspended on floor stands, above and circling the other instruments are five ride (or crash) cymbals. This set also includes five tom-toms of varying size and pitch; they are on floor stands behind and to the right of the bass drum.

The **bass drum** has changed over the years, but in general it is the largest drum with the lowest-sounding pitch. It is stood on its side, held securely to the floor by metal pegs, and played with the drummer's foot. You will notice the bass drum mallet or beater is part of a foot-operated contraption that is attached to the bottom rim of the drum, and the drummer, sitting on a stool, can sound the drum by stepping on the foot pedal.

PEDALS

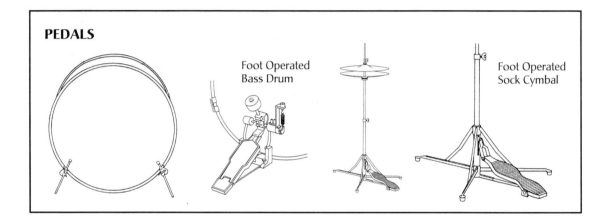

Foot Operated
Bass Drum

Foot Operated
Sock Cymbal

Slightly behind the bass drum and to one side is a foot-operated pair of cymbals called the **hi-hat cymbals** or **sock cymbals.** The pedal mechanism is similar to that of the bass drum beater, but it works a rod up and down to which a cymbal, the "hi-hat," is attached. A matching cymbal faces upward and remains stationary on a post while the hi-hat remains suspended by a spring mechanism a short distance above the lower cymbal. Step on the pedal, the hi-hat comes down, and we have a cymbal crash. Most drummers play the bass drum with their right foot and the hi-hat with their left, and a beginning drummer can lay down a simple beat by alternating foot strokes—right, left, right, left, and so on. We will see that fine jazz drummers can perform exciting and intricate rhythmic maneuvers with their feet while using their hands independently to operate sticks, brushes, and mallets on drums and cymbals.

On a drum stand between the drummer and the bass drum sits a **snare drum,** an instrument smaller than the bass drum. It is held in place by a stand which allows its playing surface, the **drum head** or **head,** to be almost parallel with the floor. It has a second head on the bottom, and a band of curly wires, the **snare,** stretched across the

Below: Lionel Hampton, vibraphonist and drummer, played in Benny Goodman's small ensembles from 1936–1940; in 1940 he formed his own group. He toured throughout the world with his own band; some of the musicians who have played with Hampton's group include Clifford Brown and Quincy Jones. Hampton was responsible for making the vibraphone (or vibes) a viable instrument in jazz.

Above: Chico Hamilton, drummer and bandleader, was a master of wire brushes on snare drum, and he raised this technique to a new artistic level during the 1950s when he led several innovative modern quintets of winds, cello, bass, guitar, and drums.

surface of the bottom head to buzz and vibrate in sympathy when the top head is struck by a **drum stick** or **mallet** or is vibrated by **wire brushes.**

Suspended from a vertical metal arm attached to the upper rim of the bass drum or suspended from floor stands, single cymbals of various sizes and configurations also are usually found in a typical trap set. Unlike the **sock cymbals** which choke off the sound when the two cymbals are closed one upon the other, a **suspended cymbal** rings with a slow decay so that one percussive attack melts into the next, or one final crash slowly fades away.

All of the cymbals, as well as the bass and snare drums, are considered instruments of indefinite pitch. Their use is purely percussive and rhythmic rather than for tonal effect. However, the **tom-toms,** usually a pair of drums midway in size between the bass and snare drums, are drums with heads that may be tuned to give a resonant pitch that varies from high to low depending on the size of the drum and the tension of the heads. Like the snare drum, **toms** are mounted with their heads parallel to the ground, but they are usually positioned to one side of the drummer. They are not often used in keeping time, the regular rhythmic activity of the drummer, but are used most often for solos and for "fills," the distinctive soloistic patterns of notes drummers use to separate and bind phrases together.

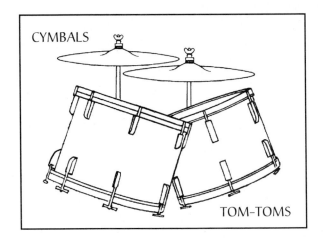

There are literally hundreds of percussion instruments that come into play in different jazz styles, but this **set of traps,** or basic trap set, **of bass drum, snare drum, tom-toms, hi-hat,** and **suspended**

cymbal are the core instruments we need to understand and listen for in jazz. Now let's hear what they sound like and observe how they are used.

The musicians of the rhythm section of **piano, bass,** and **drums** are coming to the stand to play a couple of choruses of the *Blues in F.* The blues is a musical form that we will talk about later, and "F" just refers to the key in which they are going to play this pattern. The rhythm section is comprised of Dan Haerle on piano, Rufus Reid on bass, and Mike Hyman on drums. Let's hear what they do and pay attention to the distinctive sounds of the three instruments.

FAST BLUES IN F (CD SELECTION 1.3)

Rufus Reid, playing pizzicato, used a **walking bass pattern,** a smoothly continuous line of bass notes played on each and every beat, notes that are selected to coordinate with the harmonies of the piece. Most of the time he plays the bottom notes, or roots, of the chords on the first beat of each measure and connects them smoothly with nearby notes. We will study the blues chord pattern a little later, but for now just be sure you recognize the bass's sound and the walking bass pattern. Also notice that Reid plays one fill of his own in this excerpt, a flurry of descending fast notes, in the middle of this example.

Dan Haerle, instead of playing chords on the piano in a monotonous, regular fashion, interjects rhythmically **syncopated chords,** harmonic clusters of notes which are accented and off-beat, to match, ornament, and add rhythmic propulsion, or **swing,** to the pattern of notes played by the bass. Together the two, bass and piano, are keeping time (regular beats), producing the harmonic framework of the piece (sounding the notes of the chords at proper places), maintaining the formal structure of the piece (repeating a pattern of chords that define the blues), and creating that forward rhythmic propulsion (**swing**) that is an essential element of jazz performance.

The drummer, Mike Hyman, keeps time on the sock cymbal by playing a repeated, but varied, pattern of long and short time intervals with a light drum stick on a mostly closed sock cymbal. He also occasionally taps the snare for a little syncopated rhythmic activity with another light drum stick, allows a suspended cymbal to sizzle sympathetically in the background, and occasionally taps the bass drum with his foot-pedal beater for a tasty accent here and there. Together, the three musicians supply what the improvising jazz musician needs to know, what he listens for. In this way they fulfill the standard responsibilities of the rhythm section by playing the harmonic, rhythmic, and formal structure of the *Blues in F.*

Are the *Blues in F* always played this way? Yes and no. There are certain elements of this structure that are always present, are required, but there is great latitude and freedom for jazz musicians to play it their own way. For example, what would happen if these same musicians were to play the *Blues in F* again on a different occasion? Would it be exactly the same? One way to find out; let's ask for another go around. Surprise, they agreed to do it again. Give a listen and see what's changed.

BIRD BLUES (CD SELECTION 1.4)

This time you heard that the **tempo,** or speed, was a little slower. Also, Rufus Reid varied the nature of the pattern of bass notes by occasionally repeating the same note in succession and occasionally varying two adjacent notes by making one longer and the other shorter. Dan Haerle, together with Rufus Reid, actually played more and different chords throughout this performance of the same basic blues pattern, and Haerle used a more legato, a smoother or less percussive, piano style in which he held most chords a little longer and only inserted an accented punctuation occasionally. Mike Hyman used a variety of stick patterns on the snare, sounds he did not employ in the first performance.

What would happen were we to ask a different rhythm section to play the *Blues in F?* Well, I just asked the club owner, and, surprise again, he said he just happened to have another trio in the house willing to play a few measures for us, too. Pretty neat club! This time we'll hear Kenny Barron on piano, Ron Carter on bass, and Ben Riley on drums.

The Jamey Aebersold Quartet at work in Phoenix in 1981; the personnel at this time included James Williams, piano; Todd Coolman, bass; Billy Higgins, drums; and Aebersold on alto saxophone. Jamey Aebersold has contributed to jazz education by recording professional rhythm sections for use by jazz musicians who are developing improvisation skills. These recordings allow musicians to work with accompaniment even when a live rhythm section is unavailable.

NOW'S THE TIME (CD SELECTION 1.5)

The first obvious difference is that Ron Carter plays 2-beat, rather than 4-beat, bass. At the beginning Carter does not play a walking bass pattern of one note on every beat. Instead, you can hear him playing a sustained note on every other beat, two out of four or 2-beat bass. Then, partly along the way, he and the piano vary the rhythmic pattern in such a way that they almost totally obscure the beat. You have to listen carefully and focus intently on the regularly repeated pattern of Ben Riley's stick on the suspended cymbal so that the piano and bass syncopations don't make you lose your way. Playing that stick over the suspended cymbal is called riding the cymbal, and that regularly repeated rhythmic figure of

| long | long-short | long | long-short | long | . . . . is called a drummer's **ride pattern**.

THE MUSICIANS SPEAK   JOE TURNER

I arrived in New York City, which is a three hours' train ride from Baltimore, with only a dollar twenty-five in my pocket and a suitcase made of cardboard. (I had told my mother I had a job in New York, which explained my reason for not taking more money with me. But in reality I had no job; I was just trying to make my luck in the Big City.)

I asked the first person I met where I could find the colored people in town. I was told to take the L-train to 130th Street in Harlem. There I asked where the musicians were hangin' out. They told me that it was a place called the Comedy Club.

Going there, I had a drink, set my bag down, and noticed that anyone who wished could go to the piano and play. Realizing that none of the pianists who had performed before me had done anything special, I walked over to the piano and started to play. After a warm-up number, I went into the *Harlem Strut*, and then I went to the climax with *The Carolina Shout*.

When I had finished, people swarmed around me and wanted to know where I came from. After I told them, someone in the crowd reminded me that the composer of the last two numbers I had played was in the room— James P. Johnson! Of course, you can imagine how I felt! I must have impressed him, however, since he left his table, came up to the piano, and played the same two numbers as nobody in the world could!

After it was over, someone asked me if I wanted a job, and, of course, I said, "Yes!" Then I asked, "When do I start?" To which he replied, "Right now, just come with me."

I went with him to Baron Wilkins Club (most famous piano club in Harlem, all the best pianists having played there at one time or another) where I met for the first time, and played with, Hilton Jefferson, the great alto man.

If you listen carefully and compare the playing of one rhythm section with that of the other, you will notice that both bass players, both drummers, and both pianists play their instruments differently from each other. Each gets his own sound out of his instrument, each has his own collection of devices and favorite patterns that create his own personal style, and each feels the rhythm of jazz, the blues, and this particular rendition in his own unique way.

When the boss told me he could pay me only thirty a week, I almost fainted, because until then I had never made more than twelve dollars a week.

I worked there successfully a few months, then I joined the red-hot band of trumpeter June Clark, who was a carbon copy of Louis Armstrong. June and Jimmy Harrison were known as the greatest brass team of that (wonderful) period. "Jazz" Carson (a fine drummer) completed our quartet.

During these first few months in New York, I visited Clarence Williams' office once, where I met what I considered a truly great pianist, Eddie "Blind" Steele, who played a very full piano.

This was also the time when we had the world's most exciting piano contests, night after night, with the following pianists regularly present— James P. Johnson, Willie "The Lion" Smith, Thomas "Fats" Waller, and Joe Turner. Very rarely did other pianists dare to play. Of course, there were times when Stephen "The Beetle" Henderson was getting into the contest, and he demanded the greatest respect for his perfect left hand. . . .

After my first few months in New York, I had a tour out West. . . . Benny Carter told me that when I reached Toledo I shouldn't play any piano because there was a blind boy there, named Art Tatum, and I would not be able to touch him. . . . I went there and waited for Art to come. . . . Art Tatum arrived at two o'clock sharp. . . . I played first *Dinah* for warmin' up and then my *Liza*.

When I finished, Art Tatum said, "Pretty good." I was offended because everywhere else I played *Liza* it was considered sensational, and there was Art Tatum saying "Pretty good." After that Art sat down and played *Three Little Words*. Three thousand words would have been an understatement! I had never heard so much piano in my life.

REVIEW　　3

Primary Goal of Unit 3

Learn to hear the rhythm section as the primary provider of the structural elements of a jazz performance.

Suggested Activity

The recorded excerpts are brief, so listen to each seven times.

On the first playing, listen only to the bass.

On the second playing, listen only to the drums.

On the third playing, listen only to the piano.

On the fourth playing, listen only to the bass and drums in combination.

On the fifth playing, listen only to the bass and piano in combination.

On the sixth playing, listen only to the piano and drums in combination.

On the final playing, listen to the coordinated efforts of all three instruments.

Study Questions

1. What are the standard responsibilities of the rhythm section?

2. In what way does a jazz musician listen to his or her music differently from the way most people listen to music?

3. What are the regular instruments of the rhythm section?

4. What are the basic instruments of the trap drum set?

5. Who were the bass players of these excerpts?

6. Who were the piano players of these excerpts?

7. Who were the drummers of the excerpts?

1. What is syncopation?   Other Concepts

2. How is an acoustic instrument different from an electric instrument or electronic instrument?

3. Why do you suppose the author said, "Jazz is a classical music and improvising jazz musicians are, in fact, composers"?

4. What is the difference between pitched or tuned percussion instruments and percussion instruments of indefinite pitch?

5. Why might members of a rhythm section play complicated syncopated patterns that obscure the beat?

6. What is swing?

One Soloist Plus the Rhythm Section   4

All of the rhythm section performances we heard at the club yesterday afternoon (Unit 3) were based on a 12-bar repeated pattern called the blues. We will study the blues in more detail as we go along, but there are a few things we should look at right now to help us understand the music we will hear tonight at the "Chez Imagination." Jazz has a **beat,** an unrelenting basic pulse that pumps along from the beginning to the end of a piece. This is one of the characteristics of African drumming that influenced the development of jazz, and it is one of the most obvious characteristics that you already have heard in every jazz performance we have listened to thus far. Because it is so regular, and because jazz musicians do not want the **beat** to speed up or slow down while they are improvising to the **changes,** the chords or harmonies of the piece, the drummer is sometimes referred to as the keeper of **time.** Excellent jazz musicians have good **time** (not "a good time" but "good time") and poor musicians do not. That is a fact.

If we represent a steady beat as shown below, you can see that it is impossible to differentiate one beat from another.

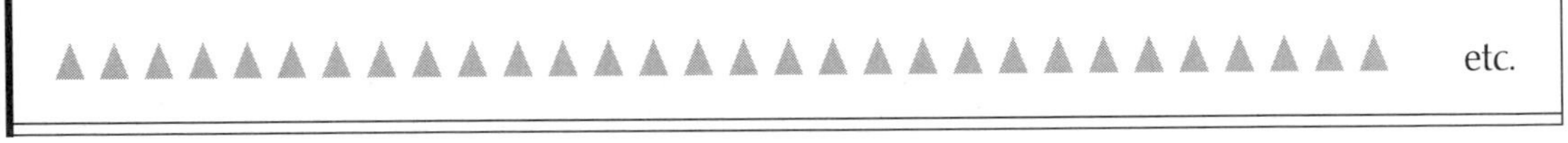

▲▲▲▲▲▲▲▲▲▲▲▲▲▲▲▲▲▲▲▲▲▲▲▲▲▲▲▲▲▲▲   etc.

Music, therefore, is divided into strong beats and weak beats; and most music, especially most jazz, is grouped into patterns of four, occasionally three, and rarely something else by the insertion of a strong beat (indicated by large triangle) followed by a series of weak beats (indicated by smaller triangles), as shown on p. 37.

1 2 3 4 1 2 3 4 1 2 3 4 1 2 3 4 1 2 3 4 1 2 3 4 1 2 3 4 1 2 3 4 1   etc.

Now we see and hear groups that are more easily managed, more easily grouped into larger units:

Along with the **beat** or pulse, there is another rhythmic concept we need to deal with. **Syncopation** is an essential element of jazz, and when we have a regularly recurring pattern of strong and weak beats, we have an opportunity to **syncopate,** insert strong or accented beats or notes where they are unexpected. For example, if the drummer lays down a regular pattern, as in the first line of the example below, and the trumpet, at the same time, inserts an irregular pattern of strong and weak notes, as in the second line below, we perceive it as **syncopated** music, irregular patterns in a regular world.

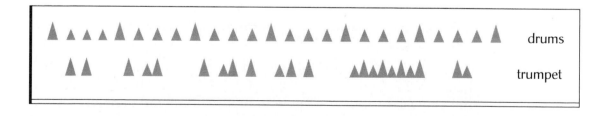

drums

trumpet

In the pieces we have been listening to, all of the music had its string of regular beats divided into groups of four, and one group of four beats in this music is called a **measure** or **bar.** The **blues** is a musical pattern of harmonies that fits into a connected larger unit of twelve measures. Yesterday, we listened to rhythm sections performing the **12-bar blues.** It took them twelve bars to play the complete pattern, and then they repeated it, and then they repeated it again, and they could have repeated it all night or until they decided it was time to end the piece.

⊢12 measures⊣ ⊢12 measures⊣ ⊢12 measures⊣ ⊢12 measures⊣

They were playing patterns that grouped like this familiar example:

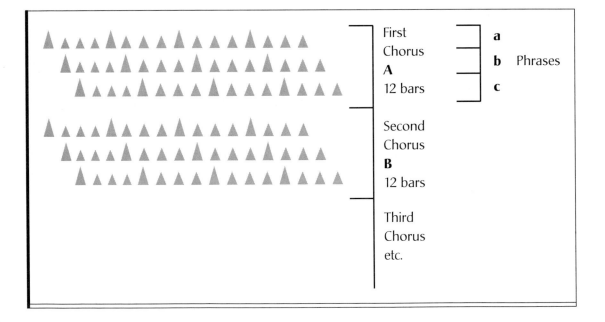

Listen to the first excerpt, and count on the beat like this:
1,2,3,4 | 2,2,3,4 | 3,2,3,4 | 4,2,3,4 | 5,2,3 . . . 11,2,3,4 | 12,2,3,4, and you will hear that the pattern repeats itself and immediately begins again: 1,2,3,4 | 2,2,3,4 | 3,2,3 etc.

FAST BLUES IN F (CD SELECTION 1.3)

BIRD BLUES (CD SELECTION 1.4)

NOW'S THE TIME (CD SELECTION 1.5)

Most improvising jazz musicians playing the blues use this information in the following manner. They play a simple tune or melodic pattern (**head** or **riff**) at the beginning and end of the piece, the first set of twelve measures and the last set of twelve measures. Since twelve measures is not very long, they often repeat the **head** at the beginning before they go on to play a succession of improvised solo **choruses.** (Each of these repeated patterns, here a 12-bar blues, is called a **chorus.**) As they play, they **improvise** (make up on the spot) solos that fit with the pattern, that express their feelings, and that give vent to their creative imaginations. The soloist listens to, and feels, the repeat of the pattern played by the rhythm section, and together with them plays through the music with notes and sounds that are spontaneously composed in the moment. Thus, jazz improvisation is like a spirited conversation among a small group of interested and informed participants. The first says something; the second reacts; the third agrees; the fourth disagrees; the second and third go at it; the first chimes in; and so on. In the same way, the sensitive and informed listener at a jazz performance focuses on the musical conversation and hears the coordination of rhythm section and soloist as this process takes place, listens for the agreements and disagreements, and especially notes and takes pleasure in the expression of new and clever ideas. Sharpening our skill at listening critically to a jazz "conversation" will be the task of our evening out at the club.

Tonight at the "Chez Imagination" one of the greatest improvising musicians of all time, Charlie Parker, will be the featured soloist with his own quartet—alto saxophone plus piano, bass, and drums. No one in jazz did more with the instrumental blues than Charlie Parker, and we are fortunate to have a front row table to hear him blow (play) the blues. We've got our drinks, we've talked about and reviewed the rhythm-section blues we have been listening to the last couple of days, and we've checked to see that the piano, bass, and trap set hold no surprises for us. Now we are ready, and here comes the band. Al Haig moves to the piano, Percy Heath quickly touches up the tuning of his bass, and Max Roach limbers up his sticks and tightens a head on a tom-tom. The club manager strides to the microphone, intro-duces the band, and waves on the leader, the great alto man, Charlie Parker. Parker nods to the audience, faces the band, kicks off the tempo (counts or taps out a couple of measures to indicate the speed of the number), and turns to face the microphone and us as the rhythm section plays a 4-measure introduction.

NOW'S THE TIME (CD SELECTION 1.6)

That was a remarkable performance. There are so many fascinat-ing things to enjoy and talk about in this one brief encounter. Parker takes so little material, a simple twelve-measure pattern, and reshapes it into fresh, coherent musical structures with so much ease, elegance, and logic. This is no mean accomplishment. To enjoy it even more, we can begin to make this particular work our very own by learning the tune, even taking part in this performance and participating at our own level.

One of the best ways to learn jazz tunes is to sing along with them just as many people sing along with their favorite popular music on the radio. The **head** to *Now's the Time* is very simple and is in a good key for singing, so let me suggest you try your hand at scat singing. You might sing along with:

> La La La La La La
> La La La La La La
> La La La La La La La La La La La La La La
> etc.

but that is a little square, definitely not hip, totally out of synch! Why not use the following set of syllables as a song sheet to *Now's the Time?* Don't be self-conscious. It is really fun and very easy. It will give you a feel for the blues that discussions alone will never impart. You will have an opportunity to coordinate with the blues pattern as you sing and learn the **head** of *Now's the Time*. Sing right along with Charlie Parker as he plays the **head** in the first chorus.

One of the premiere bebop combos performing at the Open Door Cafe in New York City in September of 1953. Charlie Parker, on alto saxophone, leads the group, and his rhythm section consists of Thelonious Monk, piano; Charles Mingus, bass; and Roy Haynes, drums.

NOW'S THE TIME (CD SELECTION 1.6)

Ba Do nn Do Be Do
Ba Do nn Do Be Do
Ba Do nn Do Be Do nn Do Be Do nn Do Be Do
Ba Do nn Do Be Do Bah
Do nn Do Be Do Bah
Do nn Do Be Do nn Do Be Do nn Do Be Day
Blee Ba Do nn Day
Bah Do nn Do Be Bop Bah Be Bah

As you are singing along with the saxophone you will probably notice that the **head** separates into three sections:

1st

> Ba Do nn Do Be Do
> Ba Do nn Do Be Do
> Ba Do nn Do Be Do nn Do Be Do nn Do Be Do

2nd

> Ba Do nn Do Be Do Bah
> Do nn Do Be Do Bah
> Do nn Do Be Do nn Do Be Do nn Do Be Day

3rd

> Blee Ba Do nn Day
> Bah Do nn Do Be Bop Bah Be Bah

That is because the 12-bar blues divides neatly into three units of 4 measures each [4 + 4 + 4], and this corresponds with the pattern we studied above.

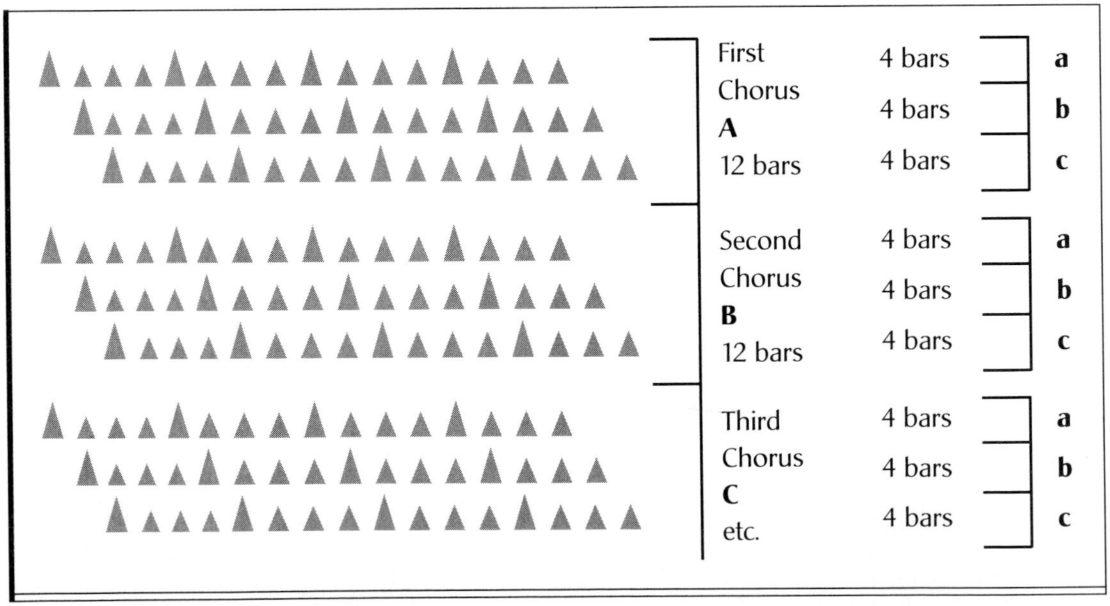

"a"

    Ba Do nn Do Be Do
    Ba Do nn Do Be Do
    Ba Do nn Do Be Do nn Do Be Do nn Do Be Do

"b"

    Ba Do nn Do Be Do Bah
    Do nn Do Be Do Bah
    Do nn Do Be Do nn Do Be Do nn Do Be Day

"c"

    Blee Ba Do nn Day
    Bah Do nn Do Be Bop Bah Be Bah

Also, you probably noticed that the first two sections or phrases, "a" and "b," related pretty closely to each other, while the third one was a little different, a kind of answer or response to the first two. This is a

Charlie Parker appeared at the Festival International de Jazz (Paris Jazz Festival) in 1949. This festival was held in 1949, 1952, 1954, with performances in the Salle Pleyel, one of the great Paris concert halls. Other performers included Miles Davis, Sidney Bechet, Dizzy Gillespie, Thelonious Monk, and Gerry Mulligan.

characteristic of the blues, a common feature of most vocal blues, and we abbreviate this form aab or aa'b.

NOW'S THE TIME (CD SELECTION 1.6)

Would you believe that Charlie Parker and his quartet are willing to play the piece over again, note for note? Only at the club "Chez Imagination" would this be possible, for in real life there are no two identical jazz performances. To help you keep track of the progress of the piece, let me give you this outline.

Intro	Head	Alto Solo	Piano Solo	Bass Solo	Drum Solo	Head
4 meas.	**12-bar x 2 blues**	**12-bar x 5 blues**	**12-bar x 2 blues**	**12-bar blues**	**12-bar blues**	**12-bar blues**

There is an introduction followed by twelve blues choruses. The first two and the last one sound the **head,** the blues melody, and Parker follows these two opening choruses with five consecutive improvised solo choruses that comprise one unified solo. In the first chorus, notice that he inserts a series of notes on the same pitch with an alternating sound. He does this by playing the same note with two different fingerings and using his tongue rapidly to articulate the rhythm pattern. Throughout he leans on, or stresses, the **blue notes,** certain notes in the scale that give the blues a special feel. He mixes in rapid notes with slower ones, intersperses clusters of notes with open spaces. Occasionally he throws in part of a phrase that is a reference to a different piece of music. These **quotes** (quotations from other compositions) usually come from the repertory of well-known popular songs or other jazz compositions that informed listeners would recognize, and sometimes they are used just to be clever; other times they actually might convey a message. It is common knowledge that Charlie Parker was not averse to throwing in a phrase from *A Pretty Girl Is Like a Melody* when an attractive woman entered the club. All the while one idea must lead smoothly and continuously to the next, and it does. When

Parker finishes his fifth solo chorus, his melodic line overlaps the beginning space for the piano solo, thus covering a seam that lesser musicians would leave exposed.

Al Haig follows Parker with two solo choruses of his own on piano, and he uses a sparse left-hand accompaniment to underpin the melodic work of his right hand. Note that his style of playing is vastly different from that of Mel Powell. Where Powell kept a steady stream of running notes pouring from his right hand while his left hand strided about or chorded continuously, Haig plays with an austere, hesitant solo piano style.

Percy Heath plays one solo chorus on bass, and there is no confusing his solo playing with that of Slam Stewart. Heath employs pizzicato, rather than arco, technique, and he doesn't sing. Max Roach, in his drum solo, gives you your first opportunity to hear the tom-toms in action. In the middle of his solo you can hear his sticks run back and forth from snare to toms. Notice too that his solo style is entirely different from his rhythm section playing. Still, also note that he is the most aggressive rhythm section drummer we have heard yet, and he throws in accents with the bass drum and keeps his snare and cymbals busy all the time. It is also interesting to hear that the pianist, Al Haig, comps not only for the alto solos, but also for the bass and drum solos. In this way, even the drummer gets an opportunity to think melodically with respect to the **changes,** the harmonic framework of the piece.

When the drummer finishes his solo, Parker takes charge and plays the **head** again, with a fair number of improvised ornamental passages thrown in, to end the performance. By 1953, when this music was recorded, it was no longer necessary to limit performances to three minutes, because the new microgroove 33 1/3 RPM long playing (LP) recordings allowed performances of almost one-half hour in length. But Charlie Parker, the recording industry, and the public were still locked into the old mode of three-minute takes. Some advantages of this layout were the sale of singles, the convenient format for radio broadcasts, and the variety of pieces that could be grouped on a single 10" or 12" long play record, but the principal disadvantage was the missed opportunity to record and preserve extended, syntactically coherent improvisations from this period, an art in which Charlie Parker was the master.

As you listen to the recording, remember that the primary object of this unit is to hear the coordination of soloist with the rhythm section work, to hear the musical interaction between and among members of the ensemble. Finally, why not play this recording again and compare the saxophone style of Charlie Parker with that of both Benny Carter and Coleman Hawkins? The style of both Hawkins and Carter changed some as their playing matured in later years, but some personal aspects remained true throughout long, productive careers. It is pleasing to report that as these words are being written, Benny Carter is alive and well in California, a very busy musician in his mid-80s. He is playing as well now as he ever did, and he is writing and arranging for the studios, touring, and leading ensembles of various kinds. His *Harlem Renaissance Suite* won a Grammy as best jazz composition of 1992, 62 years after he played alto and clarinet on *Bugle Call Rag!*

THE MUSICIANS SPEAK   DIZZY GILLESPIE

In those days we had several means of access to experience: big bands were one, jam sessions were another. I tried to get plenty of both. Musical happenings at that time were an excellent reason to want to stay around New York. Amongst musicians when I came up, we had a very close feeling of camaraderie. We were all trumpet players together—Charlie Shavers, Benny Harris, Bobby Moore, and I—and we were unified socially; not just trumpet players, other musicians too. We traded off ideas not only on the bandstand but in the jam sessions. We had to be as sensitive to each other as brothers in order to express ourselves completely, maintain our individuality, yet play as one. Jam sessions, such as those wonderfully exciting ones held at Minton's Playhouse were seedbeds for our new, modern style of music. . . .

Leaving Billy Eckstine in 1944, I recommended Fats Navarro for the job, and he proved to be an ample replacement for me in the trumpet section. I took a job with Oscar Pettiford. We became co-leaders of a group at the Onyx Club on Fifty-second Street. Of course the ideal group was always Charlie Parker and me, but the first group with Oscar Pettiford was magnificent, and that was the thing that put us on the map. The opening at the Onyx Club represented the birth of the bebop era. In our long sojourn on Fifty-second Street we spread our message to a much wider audience.

Oscar and I decided to get Charlie Parker. We sent him a telegram in Kansas City, because he'd gone back home for a while. Didn't hear nothing

BUGLE CALL RAG (CD SELECTION 1.1)

NOW'S THE TIME (CD SELECTION 1.6)

When you compare these performances, remember that a quarter of a century separates the two recordings of the **Chocolate Dandies** and the **Charlie Parker Quartet.** Still, some of the unique sound qualities that differentiate one saxophonist from another are still apparent and are part of the personal sound ideal that each man carried with him throughout his musical career.

> for months, so the initial group consisted of Max Roach (drums), Oscar Pettiford (bass), George Wallington (piano), and me. . . . Yard said later that he hadn't received the telegram, because I know he would've come with Max Roach and George Wallington in the group. . . .
>
> The height of the perfection of our music occurred in the Three Deuces with Charlie Parker. He'd gotten in touch with me, played in the big band, and finally we'd assembled in a setting ideal for our music, the quintet. With Yard and Max, Bud Powell and Curley Russell, aw, man, it was on fire all the time. . . .
>
> Bud Powell was the definitive pianist of the bebop era. He fitted in with us more than anybody else because of the fluidity of his phrasing. He played just like we did, more than anybody else. . . .
>
> Yard and I were like two peas. . . . Our music was like putting whipped cream on jello. His contribution and mine just happened to go together, like putting salt in rice. Before I met Charlie Parker my style had already developed, but he was a great influence on my whole musical life. The same thing goes for him too because there was never anybody who played any closer than we did on those early sides like "Groovin' High," "Shaw 'Nuff," and "Hot House." Sometimes I couldn't tell whether I was playing or not because the notes were so close together.

Primary Goal of Unit 4

Learn to hear the rhythm section as you listen to solo jazz improvisation.

    Charlie Parker played five continuous solo choruses. Can you hear the 12-bar pattern repeating in the rhythm section during his solo? When you focus your attention on the work of the rhythm section, can you hear the three divisions of the 12-bar pattern?

Study Questions

1. What is the **beat?**

2. When jazz musicians are playing the **changes,** what are they doing?

3. Who is the "timekeeper" in jazz? Does the bass player keep time?

4. Can you define **improvisation?**

5. Who was the pianist in the Charlie Parker Quartet?

6. Who was the drummer?

7. Can you describe the bass solo that Percy Heath played?

8. When did Charlie Parker make this recording of *Now's the Time?*

Other Concepts

1. Explain some characteristics of the 12-bar blues.

2. Can you sing the **head** of *Now's the Time?*

3. What two elements combine to create **syncopation?**

4. Are you keeping a mental record of some of the unique characteristics of various bass players, saxophonists, drummers, pianists, and so on?

The Element of Swing

Tonight we will have our first opportunity to hear a **big band,** that is an ensemble that, in addition to a **rhythm section,** uses a **trumpet section** instead of a single trumpet, a **trombone section** instead of a trombone, and a **saxophone** or **reed section** instead of individual reed instruments like the clarinet or saxophone. Of course, for a section to play together, written music must be used, so big bands have **arrangers,** musicians who transfer the elements of a jazz composition or popular song into notes on a score for band members to play. Although solos are usually interspersed throughout the performance of a **big band** number, we will notice that most of the music we hear is that which the arranger scored for the three sections of the band, the **brass, sax,** and **rhythm sections.**

We mentioned **swing** before when we heard Benny Goodman at the club, and we mentioned "swing" again on a couple of different occasions when we were talking about the propulsive rhythmic quality of jazz. And jazz musicians took this word, which also referred to a **style** (one kind of jazz prominent from the 1930s through the 1950s with identifiable characteristics that separate it from other kinds of jazz) and made it into a verb that compliments excellent music and great performances. "Man, that swings!" or "Hawk (Coleman Hawkins) swung his tail off on that number!"

Obviously, **swing** is important, but can we hear it? Can we tell when something swings and when it doesn't? I asked that question of Don Redman, a great leader and arranger, and he suggested we come on down to the club tonight where he would show us. So, that's what we are going to do right now. Redman is fronting, leading (standing in front of), a fourteen-piece orchestra. (In jazz, we sometimes like to call big bands orchestras; it adds a little class.) If you have reviewed your notes and are ready to add a little more to what we have already covered, then we are ready to zip on down to the "Chez Imagination" to hear this splendid group. It is 1931. Did you notice? The depression has been running full force for a couple of years since the stock market crash, but some of the clubs are doing very well. Redman played and arranged for Fletcher Henderson, and the last few years he took over the musical direction of McKinney's Cotton Pickers. Funny name, but great band. Just this month he formed a new band under his own name, and there is talk that he has a contract to move into the basement club on Seventh Avenue, "Connie's Inn," if all goes well. I understand the band he is bringing to the "Chez Imagination" tonight has Henry Allen, Langston Curl, and Leonard Davis on trumpets; Fred Robinson, Claude Jones, and Benny Morton on trombones; Redman, Edward Inge, Rupert Cole, and Robert Carroll on reeds; and a rhythm section of Horace Henderson, piano, Bob Ysaguirre, bass, Manzie Johnson, drums, and Talcot Reeves on banjo. That's an awful lot of names, but you don't have to remember them all. In fact, for tonight's session at the club, let's just stick with Don Redman, who will sing as well as play alto saxophone, and then pay attention to the section work rather than the individuals. It's not that they aren't important. The sidemen are crucial, and that's why I listed them here, but there is only so much we can get to sink in at one time. At least, that is the way it is with me. You might note, though, that several of them went on to make big names for themselves after they left this band, such as Horace Henderson, whom we met before, Benny Morton, and Henry "Red" Allen. Actually, Allen is the lead trumpeter with

This 1962 recording session featured Frank Sinatra (right of center) and the Count Basie Orchestra. Basie is at the piano (center); the photographer was positioned near the trumpet section. Sinatra recorded with the Count Basie Orchestra for the Reprise record label from 1962–66.

Luis Russell's band, but Redman booked him for the recording session and this gig (job) at our club.

The stage of the "Chez Imagination" is no bigger than it was when the Charlie Parker Quartet played here, and you might wonder how a fourteen-piece band can play in the same space. Somehow, they do. All these clubs just squeeze the musicians in. Since we got here early, let's watch what happens. The bandboy, the jazz equivalent of the rock band "roadie," comes in lugging big, black suitcases, some on wheels and some not. He shoves the piano to the left side of the bandstand, and then he grabs some chairs and starts lining them up starting on the back right as you are looking at the stage. Three in the back row for the trumpets, three in the middle for the trombones, and three in front for the saxes. Redman is the fourth reed player, but since he is fronting the band, he doesn't get a chair. He stands up front all night. The bandboy checked out the microphone, but that is only for vocals and some instrumental solos. Most of the horn players just stand up where they are, blow their solos, and sit down again, because the arrangement goes on. While the bandboy is opening up the library, the black music case, let's look at the chairs he set up for the **brass** and **reeds.**

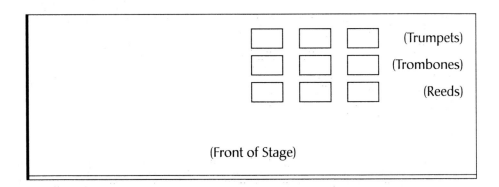

The bandboy does not set up a chair for the drums, because the drummer brings his own stool, and he does not set up a chair for the bass, because the bass player stands to play his instrument. The banjo gets one, and the piano gets a chair or a bench, whatever the player prefers. Everyone but the piano and drums get music stands, and instead of the standard racks orchestral musicians use, the bandboy sets out **fronts,** a specially devised big band music stand that has a billboard on the front with the band's name on it. The pianist just spreads his music on the piano or uses the piano rack, and the drummer usually doesn't use music. If he needs it for a particular number, he'll find something to spread the **chart** (music) out on; for example, on top of his toms. The bass might use a tall stand, because it is no fun squinting down to knee-level music all night long, but he may not. He does most of his playing by ear anyway, and his music, like the pianist's and the banjoist's, is often just a set of chord symbols. The actual sounds the rhythm section plays are usually entirely improvised to fit in with the arrangement, the notes the arranger puts on paper for the **brass** and **reeds.**

Now that the bandboy has finished, we can see that the territory mapped out for each member of the band looks like this:

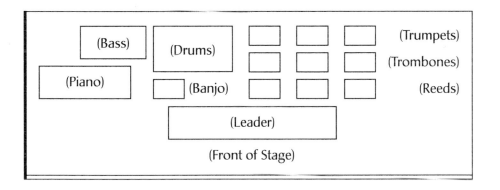

A swing band saxophone section in action. Notice the instruments being played by the seated musicians (left to right): tenor, alto, alto, tenor, and tenor saxophones. The leader of the band, Charlie Barnet, who is standing in front of the band, is also playing the tenor saxophone. These musicians "double" on other reed instruments; notice a straight soprano saxophone and a large baritone saxophone on the sax stand in the center of the picture as well as a clarinet and alto saxophone on the sax stand at the far right.

The leader has to move around, but he spends most of his time at front stage center. Also, when he plays saxophone with the others, he can stand right next to them to blend in. With a grouping like this, the rhythm section can hear and see each other, and this helps them work as a cohesive unit. The brass and reed sections hear the rhythm section as a unit on their right, and they are also grouped to hear each other. It is a toss-up whether the brass or saxophones are louder, but the brass project their sound straight ahead and are positioned in back for that reason. Usually, the saxophone sound radiates backward almost as well as forward, so you can see that there are practical acoustical reasons for bands to set up in this particular manner.

Enough of this small talk, let's hear some music. The band files in, quickly tunes up, and gets out the first **set,** a group of a half-dozen or so arrangements that will take them to the first **set break,** a brief intermission. The nightclub owner comes to the microphone and makes his announcement, and Don Redman walks on to kick off the band.

SHAKIN' THE AFRICAN (CD SELECTION 1.7)

What did I tell you? Redman was going to teach us about **swing,** wasn't he? He didn't spend much time on those "sweet band" sounds, but there was enough of an example to show the contrast of playing "sweet," which jazz musicians consider "square" or "commercial" (playing whatever someone will pay you to play), and playing "hot" or swinging. What was it Redman said?

> Well, it looks like we've picked out the wrong spot this evening, don't it, huh? You know, this "sweet" music is all right, but we always been a bunch that go in for plenty of pep and excitement. I know where to go. Let's get our coats and hats and get out of this joint, huh? Come on then, let's go from here, where we can have some fun I mean.

While he was saying that, did you hear the slow wobbly sound of the saxophones playing softly in the background with the bass bowing a slow, legato 2-beat "businessman's bounce" (old-people's music)? That was "sweet," and that didn't swing. But when the trumpet solo

The rhythm section of the Cab Calloway Orchestra is clearly pictured in this photo. Notice the piano, banjo, and bass as well as the expanded drum set. A regular trap set includes bass drum, snare drum, tom-toms, suspended cymbals, and hi-hat or sock cymbals; the expanded drum set pictured here also includes a xylophone on the left, orchestra bells and Chinese gong at the back, and timpani (or kettle drums) on the right.

Don Redman, first an arranger and saxophonist for Fletcher Henderson, soon led his own band.

started, it was more than just the fast solo that gave the music a feeling of swing. Listen to the saxophones as they **back,** play accompaniment behind, the trumpet. They are still playing with a vibrato, but they are pumping energy into their playing, putting a little rhythmic surge into the notes of the scored chords of the arrangement. At the same time, the bass changes to a sharp pizzicato attack, and the banjo and drums join in to give that series of pushes that set up the beat. When the bass played his first note on the beat, the drummer started slapping his snare drum off the beat to create a little syncopation, and all these things put together **swing** the music.

After the trumpet and alto solos, Redman sings a chorus. The "African" is a new dance that is "better than the Black Bottom," another popular jazz dance of the day. If you've got the spunk, why don't you move on down to the dance floor and give it a try? After all, this jazz is not just meant for listening; it is dance music. Did you notice the **soli** chorus after the first vocal chorus? That was a combination of just a few instruments with clarinet playing lead on top. They bounce around playing chords together until the clarinet takes off briefly on his own. Redman returns for another vocal solo that is only part of a complete chorus, and notice how his irregular placement of words conflicts, or syncopates, with the regular performance of a chordal background by the sax section. During Redman's vocal half-chorus he tells us where he is, which is where he recorded this piece in October of 1931. Now listen again to *Shakin' the African* and see if you can hear some of the other devices the jazz musicians throw into their performance to give their music that vital quality that resists a precise definition, **swing.**

SHAKIN' THE AFRICAN (CD SELECTION 1.7)

When the trumpet began his first solo, he played a sequence of fast notes to get started and to lay down a beat for the band to follow, but he also ripped up to a high, loud, longer note. That **rip** (an upward smear of pitches) is not something you find in classical or sweet music. It's an exciting device, and jazz seeks excitement to swing. Then, just a few measures later, the trumpet throws in a **shake.** The loud, long, high note gets a wide, shaky vibrato, and this effect is actually created by shaking the horn a bit with the hand that does the fingering of the valves. You'll also hear the trumpet repeating some brief little **motives,** patterned groups of notes, rapidly one after the other as if trying to generate momentum for the next plunge. And the very last note of his solo before the entrance of the alto sax to play the sax solo is a bent note that first goes up in pitch and then down. Why does the trumpet man bother with all these details? To make the music swing. A good arranger could notate most of the pitches of the solo in the right sequence and commit them to paper, but that written solo, in and of itself, would not swing. Hand the manuscript to a virtuoso classical trumpet player, and he might play all the notes, but it still would not swing. Hand it to a jazz trumpet soloist, and he might not be able to read it well enough to play all the notes in tempo. But give him the freedom to play it his own way, or give him time to copy by ear the sounds from a record, and he can create, with the cooperation of a swinging band, a swinging solo.

REVIEW   5

Primary Goal of Unit 5

To grasp the concept of **swing.**

Some music swings, and other music does not. What is the difference?

Study Questions

1. What is a **big band?**

2. What are the **sections** of a big band?

3. What are **charts?**

4. How does an **arranger**'s work differ from a composer's?

5. What were the instruments of our 14-piece band?

6. Don Redman was the vocalist for *Shakin' the African*. Did he sing a melody? What did he do?

7. Can you list the instrumental solos in the order in which they were played on this Don Redman number?

8. What are some of the elements or ingredients of **swing?**

Other Concepts

1. What are **fronts** and why do you suppose they are used?

2. What is **sweet** music? Do you suppose **sweet** music could be jazz? Why or why not?

3. Why do you suppose most **big bands** set up in a traditional fashion on the stage or bandstand?

4. We heard several solo devices used by the trumpet soloist in this recording. Are devices gimmicks? Why or why not?

Form, Meter, and the Blues Scale   6

This afternoon we are going to a concert at the college auditorium. "A concert," you say, "and not an evening out at our favorite club? What kind of jazz is this?" Bear with me, for times have changed. Today is in the late 1950s, or hadn't you noticed, and the clubs and dance halls are having a hard time. Even movie houses are having financial difficulties, in large part because television has become so popular, and people are staying home nights to enjoy free entertainment in their living rooms. Jazz musicians have been looking for other venues to display their wares and make a living, and Dave Brubeck was one of the first to find success in playing concerts with his quartet at colleges throughout the country. After two notable performances, one at the College of the Pacific and the other at Oberlin College in the early '50s, the record sales of his music from those concerts were not only a huge financial success, but they did much to popularize modern jazz among a vast new audience. Now it is 1959, just when he recorded the number we're about to hear in New York, and he has something new to show you. I'm sure you will like it. He's playing at our college today with his "classic" quartet: Paul Desmond on alto, Eugene Wright on bass, Joe Morello on drums, and Brubeck on piano.

The whole atmosphere of a concert in an auditorium is different from hearing a jazz performance in a club where the band is most often viewed as popular entertainment. The concert hall speaks of culture, imparts attitudes and behavior, and in many ways is better than the old nightclub routine, but fewer musicians are able to make a living in this manner, and young players do not have the countless opportunities they used to have to apprentice and hone their skills. Well, let's not debate the social and economic history of jazz; there are other places for that. Let's just get into the music.

I bought these tickets last month, and we've got our seats reserved here on the aisle in Row H. This Sunday concert starts at 3:30 in the afternoon and will probably run until 5:30 or 6:00 p.m. with one intermission. Not much to see; the curtain is drawn. Our printed program gives a little biography about the players, but unlike a classical concert, the pieces they will play are not listed. The lights go down, the curtain goes up, the spotlight hits the piano, and the music starts. The crowd goes wild. It is a favorite from Brubeck's newest LP.

BLUE RONDO A LA TURK (CD SELECTION 1.8)

What a superb performance. Desmond and Brubeck are in great form, and Wright and Morello are as dependable as any in the profession. Speaking of form, let's follow a pun and start with musical form. Jazz musicians love puns, and they not only pass many hours on the road sharpening each other's wit with puns of every variety, but many of the famous titles of jazz compositions are also puns (*Esthetic-Lee, Groovin' High, Take Five, Shaw Nuff*, etc.). This piece is no exception.

The Dave Brubeck Quartet with Paul Desmond, alto saxophone; Joe Morello, drums; Gene Wright, bass; and Brubeck on piano. These four players formed the classic Dave Brubeck Quartet; the personnel remained unchanged from 1958, when Wright joined the ensemble, until 1967 when Brubeck dissolved the group to concentrate on composition.

On the surface the title means "Sad or blue-colored Rondo (whatever or whoever that is) in the Turkish mode." **Rondo** is a musical song form dating back to the Middle Ages (Rondeau) as well as a compositional form (Rondo) that Haydn, Mozart, and Beethoven loved: ABACADA, etc. In a Mozart Rondo, the performers keep coming back to the familiar musical material, A, that was introduced at the beginning of the piece. Well, that happens in this piece, but how can it be blue? Also, the form is not used in a straightforward manner. Here, blue doesn't refer to a color or mood but to the **blues,** that form we've already studied that takes twelve measures to complete and divides into three phrases, 4 + 4 + 4. The **A La Turk** is a reference to Near-Eastern folk music that often uses **irregular meters,** beats divided up into units other than the common groupings of four or three such as five or seven or seemingly irregular combinations, as shown below.

Five	(▲▲▲▲▲▲▲▲▲▲ etc.)
Seven	(▲▲▲▲▲▲▲▲▲▲▲▲▲▲ etc.)
Irregular Combinations	(▲▲▲▲▲▲▲▲▲▲▲▲▲▲▲▲▲▲▲▲▲▲▲▲▲▲▲▲▲▲ etc.)

This piece starts with a large unit of nine beats and jumps back and forth between two configurations of nine, the first irregular and the second common:

2 + 2 + 2 + 3 repeated = 9	(▲▲▲▲▲▲▲▲▲ ▏▲▲▲▲ etc.) 1 2 1 2 1 2 1 2 3 1 2 1 2 etc.
3 + 3 + 3 repeated = 9	(▲▲▲▲▲▲▲▲▲ ▏▲▲▲▲ etc.) 1 2 3 1 2 3 1 2 3 1 2 3 1 etc.

If you count rapidly, as on p. 63:

```
1 2 1 2 1 2 1 2 3     a
1 2 1 2 1 2 1 2 3     a
1 2 1 2 1 2 1 2 3     a
1 2 3 1 2 3 1 2 3     b
```

along with the piano at the start of the piece and whenever you hear similar music in the piece, you will have the tricky part mastered.

BLUE RONDO A LA TURK (OPENING) (CD SELECTION 1.8)

Very little jazz is written in units of nine, so you can imagine how hard it might be to improvise at a rapid tempo in a **meter** (the grouping of beats in a recurring pattern defined by accentuation) of nine, especially when it keeps changing from three groups of the irregular pattern to one with a more simple pattern. Surprise, they don't improvise in nine! Perhaps they found it too difficult, but I doubt it. I suspect the real reason is musical. Brubeck's compositional judgment told him to mix the composed and improvised portions in the manner we hear here. Whatever the reason, we can see that Brubeck organized this piece so that the improvisatory sections were set up for your old favorite, the **blues,** in a straight 4 beats to the measure pattern. How did he do that? Actually, in a variety of ways. Take a look at this outline of the overall form:

Head	Chorus, 6 phrases 1/2 Blues, 1/2 Head, alternating	Alto solo Blues 4 choruses	Piano solo Blues 4 choruses	Chorus, 6 phrases 1/2 Blues, 1/2 Head, alternating	Head
A	**B**	**C**	**D**	**B**	**A′**

A formal pattern ABCDBA' is not a **rondo** (ABACA) at all, but then again remember that Mozart varied the pattern a bit (the A' on the end is common) and also realize that the B chorus, which returns near the end, has brief recurring elements within itself from the A section (xaxaya, where "xxy" is our familiar **blues** form and "a" is the first phrase of the **head**). Now listen again to the whole performance, and be sure you hear the main sections (ABCDBA') and the alternation of blues and **head** phrases in both B choruses. To further complicate your life, I must mention that the blues phrases in the B section are only partial, but let's not get too picky.

BLUE RONDO A LA TURK (CD SELECTION 1.8)

At the beginning of the music Brubeck starts alone in what sounds like an introduction but is not. It is the first phrase of the **head.** On the second phrase the bass and drums join in. On the third phrase Desmond adds his alto saxophone to the mix, and they all continue for the fourth phrase, a total of 16 measures, 4 + 4 + 4 + 4. At this point they have all completed the first larger section of the *A La Turk* music (all composed and worked out), and let's label this group of four phrases "X," a subsection of the **head** made up of four 4-measure phrases, where each is divided into four 9-beat motives of which two are played at a lower level and two are played at a higher level:

```
                  X (1st SECTION BLUE RONDO A LA TURK)
        ┌──────────────────────────┬──────────────────────────┐
        │                          │                          │
  A (piano)   A (+ bass & drums)   A' (+ alto)         A'        16 meas. (4+4+4+4)
    ┌─┬─┬─┐      ┌─┬─┬─┐           ┌─┬─┬─┐          ┌─┬─┬─┐
    a a a b      a a a b           a a a b          a a a b    (each 1 measure)
    1 2 3 4      1 2 3 4           1 2 3 4          1 2 3 4
```

Sounds like higher math and looks like a genealogy chart for a king or queen, but it is really not so complicated. Besides, I am sure you sensed it all as you were listening even before you intellectualized it. Now, why don't you check it out? Move your finger along the bottom of the chart measure by measure as you listen.

BLUE RONDO A LA TURK (BEGINNING) (CD SELECTION 1.8)

This pattern and similar ones are combined to make up the entire first section, the **head.** You heard that there was some variety in the orchestration, an occasional variation of the regular pattern, and an extension that serves both as a transition into the first improvised solo chorus and as an ending to the piece. You probably also noticed that there was an elision at the end of the second B chorus so that the last two choruses overlap. All these details are fascinating, and the more you hear, the more enjoyment you will experience. For me, there is a ladder effect of higher and lower phrases in the **head** of this piece, and they appear to me to sound as represented in this diagram. Each block symbolizes four measures of music. Once again, if you will use your finger to find your place on the diagram as you listen, you will keep your place and see what I mean.

HEAD, *BLUE RONDO A LA TURK*

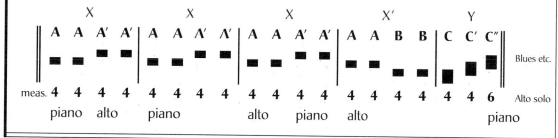

BLUE RONDO A LA TURK (HEAD) (CD SELECTION 1.8)

Yes, you are right. You did notice some regrouping of the patterns from:

    12 12 12 123 | 12 12 12 123 | 12 12 12 123 | 123 123 123

into:

    12 12 12 123 | 12 12 12 123 | 123 123 123 | 123 123 123

and you might also have noticed that the **head** had its own **rondo** effect each time the initial melody was repeated.

This composition is one of the more complex pieces in jazz, and we have gone through these patterns and their variations in some detail to stretch your ears into understanding better some of the enormous complexity that is not only possible in jazz but is frequently present. If you grasp this, there will be very little in jazz that you cannot master. Some people think that jazz players don't bother to calculate all these complex ideas; the music just miraculously appears. In most cases, these people are wrong. As a rule, the best jazz musicians are a very thoughtful lot, and they polish both their art and their craft daily throughout their lives. You cannot play well unless you understand the music, and you cannot rest until yesterday's accomplishments are surpassed today. Real artists are self-motivated and driven, and through their efforts we have the pleasant opportunity of hearing, learning, understanding, and enjoying the marvelous intricacies of a great music.

Before we leave this piece, there is one more important detail to observe—the **blue notes** or the **blues scale.** There is an African-American melodic system that is part of the jazz tradition that stresses certain notes of the scale to create a characteristic **blues** sound. This piece separates two distinct melodic traditions and makes it easy for us to hear one against the other. The **melody** of the **head** uses the European **major scale** throughout. The improvisations to the **blues** switch gears and use the **blues scale** for their melodic material, and you can hear the lowered tendency tones and bent pitches in the alto solos just as you can hear the major-minor conflicts in the piano chords Brubeck uses in his **blues** improvisation. One doesn't have to read music or know the technical language of music theory to hear these differences; they are apparent to the ears of novice and expert alike. When Paul Desmond plays the **head,** his tone is straight, his articulation precise, his phrasing classical; when he plays the **blues** you can hear bent pitches, false fingerings, stressed notes, and varying tone color. All these devices are part and parcel of the **blues.** When Brubeck plays the **head,** his melodic playing is crisp, his touch even, and his chordal pronouncements Romantic (in the classical sense); when he plays the **blues,** his melodic style is relaxed, his chordal clusters stress the major-minor conflict, and his improvisation includes riffs (notice the similarity of his fourth, or last, chorus and the Parker riff, *Now's the Time*).

Paul Desmond, alto saxophone soloist with the Dave Brubeck Quartet, was a leading influence of Cool Jazz. Desmond composed the popular "Take Five" for the quartet.

   With all the attention we have given **form, meter,** and the **blues scale,** we have virtually ignored the fine bass and drum work of Eugene Wright and Joe Morello. Though this lesson has asked you to listen to the recorded example more times than other examples were required in any previous unit, why not listen one more time, paying specific attention to their excellent contributions? One especially interesting place is the alto solo when the piano lays out and the bass and drums alone do all the work of the rhythm section.

BLUE RONDO A LA TURK (CD SELECTION 1.8)

Primary Goal of Unit 6

Learn to hear a complex **form;** identify and respond to a complex **meter;** and differentiate the melodic style that uses the **blues scale.**

In this composition with its ABCDBA' form, which sections use the following:

1. the complex meter of nine beats to the measure?

2. the simple meter of four beats to the measure?

3. Rondo or Rondo-like form?

4. Blues **form?**

5. **major scales** in the melodies?

6. the **blues scale** in the melodies?

Study Questions

1. Who are the members of the "classic" Dave Brubeck Quartet?

2. When and where was *Blue Rondo A La Turk* recorded?

3. What is the meaning of the title of this piece?

4. What is Classical Rondo Form?

5. What does this formal outline, xaxaya, have to do with the **blues?**

1. What are some of the differences between hearing jazz at a club and hearing jazz in a concert hall?

2. Can you count the irregular *A La Turk* rhythm in time with the performance?

The Harmonic Structure and Popular Song Form

7

When jazz musicians get together for a **jam session,** they often play with musicians from other bands whom they may not know or young players who want to show off or test their skills. A **jam session** is a totally unrehearsed, almost totally unprepared performance by almost any combination of jazz musicians who, through their improvisatory skills, are able to make excellent and often exciting music. Why did I say "almost totally unprepared"? That's because in order to play at all they must be proficient on their instrument, and in order to play together they must know certain conventions, the ground rules, and a **basic repertory** of **blues heads, popular songs, and jazz tunes.** They learn this **basic repertory** by playing jobs (gigs), listening to records and live performances, and reading from music collected in **fake books.**

A **fake book** is an accumulation of pieces jazz musicians have found to be interesting or useful in their work, and it is different from most printed music, because it does not tell the performer the precise notes to play. A piano sonata by Mozart has every note the pianist should play printed on the page. All the **fake book** contains for any piece is the **melody,** the symbols for **chords** which can accompany that melody, and a little information that is of interest to the musician and may be useful in announcing the piece at a performance, such as the **title, composer,** and (recorded) **source.**

When certain **blues, popular songs,** or **jazz tunes** become well-used favorites and stay in the repertory for a long time, they are called **standards,** and it is a basic knowledge of a large group of **standards** that a jazz musician must bring to a **jam session,** pieces such as *I Got Rhythm, When the Saints Go Marching In,* and *Somewhere Over the Rainbow.* If he or she can play well, can improvise, and knows the same music other musicians know, they can improvise a performance together. When it is a spontaneous gathering of musicians, it is a **jam session;** when it is a booked engagement, it is a **date,** or **rehearsal.** What the musicians all understand and rely upon in these circumstances is the convention of the **rhythm section,** usually piano, bass, and drums, who will be there to play the **changes,** maintain the **form,** and keep **time.** The **rhythm section** can be as spare as bass alone or as full as piano, guitar, vibes, bass, drums, congas (another type of drum played by another percussionist), synthesizer, and theoretically even more. The piano and bass play the **changes,** the chords of the piece in their proper order and in their right places in time, over and over, and the drums keep **time. Horn players** at the session, usually saxophone, trumpet, and trombone players, along with members of the **rhythm section,** take their turns at **improvising to the changes.** That is where we, the listeners, come in. If we know the tunes and can hear the **changes,** we can tell whether the performer is doing a good or bad job, whether the improviser is coming up with brilliant ideas that magically fit into the pattern of the piece or whether he or

A fake book is the working musician's one-volume library of standards. When a fan or patron walks up to the band stand to request a particular song, the improvising jazz musician can turn to this book to find the necessary melody line with chord symbols notated conveniently on one page.

Composer, band leader, and pianist Duke Ellington was born Edward Kennedy Ellington on 29 April 1899 in Washington, D.C. During the 1930s, when this photo was taken, Ellington's orchestra had grown to include a four-person rhythm section, four reeds, and six brass instruments. In 1939, pianist Billy Strayhorn joined the ensemble as arranger and composer.

she gets lost, plays wrong notes, or rehashes worn and dull ideas. That's what this whole book is about, really, how to listen to jazz, how to hear what's going on, and how to get the most satisfaction from your listening experience.

Take the "A" Train is a **standard** by Billy Strayhorn and Duke Ellington that was composed in **popular song form.** Ellington first recorded this piece with his big band, Duke Ellington and His Famous Orchestra, in 1941. It became a **standard** almost immediately, and over the years has become a **classic.** Certain recorded performances of this work have become **classics,** as well, and these recorded **classics** are the preserved masterpieces of the art of jazz. If you can't read music, it doesn't matter because we will learn what we need to know right here without referring to any notated music. If you can read music, you will see in the illustration from a **fake book** page that *Take the "A" Train* is in a simple form we call **popular song form** or **pop song form**—AABA. The first phrase of a piece (A) is repeated once. A new phrase (B) of the same length follows for variety. The original phrase (A) returns at the end to round out the piece and give it unity and stability. We already know **blues form** and **rondo form,** so let's compare the three:

POPULAR SONG FORM:	A A B A
BLUES FORM:	A A' B
RONDO FORM:	A B A C A

It's all really quite simple. As you may have guessed, popular song form got its name because virtually every popular song from the 1910s through the 1960s was composed in this form: *What Is This Thing Called Love* (Cole Porter); *Over the Rainbow* (E. Y. Harburg and Harold Arlen); *Yesterday* (John Lennon and Paul McCartney); and thousands more. **Pop song form** and the **blues** take care of the vast majority of all pieces performed in jazz, probably 90 or 95 percent, so if you can handle these two and recognize them when you hear them, you will know what's going on and understand the inner workings of nearly every jazz performance. The remainder you can pick up as you go along.

At a **session** or on a job, the improvising jazz musician knows that a certain pattern of chords will be repeated over and over, the harmonies of the piece. If it is a piece in **popular song form,** he or she knows the first phrase (A) will be played first and then repeated once (AA). A contrasting set of harmonies (B) called the **bridge** will follow. This **bridge** or **release** is interjected at this point to give variety to the first pattern, to give the listener release from the sameness of the first phrase. It also bridges the beginning and end of the piece. Finally, the original phrase returns in its specified place at the end—AABA, and the players and listeners know this in advance. Then, for the performance at a **jam session,** the players usually start together by playing the original tune at the beginning both to warm up and to let the audience know what the piece is. They usually take turns playing solos on those same changes as they are repeated over and over until it is time to end. At that point, the musicians play the tune again and quit.

TYPICAL JAM SESSION PERFORMANCE OF A TUNE IN POPULAR SONG FORM

INTRODUCTION (OPTIONAL)	TUNE OR HEAD	1ST SOLO IMPROV.	2ND SOLO IMPROV.	ETC.	LAST SOLO IMPROV.	TUNE OR HEAD
	AABA	**AABA**	**AABA**	**AABA**	**AABA**	**AABA**
		(+ repeats)				

I called the club, and the manager of the "Chez Imagination" said he didn't have a jam session scheduled at the club for today, but, of course, the musicians might get together on their own after hours. However, he did have something for us that might be interesting. He has one group playing at the 9:00 p.m. show and another playing at the 11:00 p.m. show. How about asking them both to play the same piece? That way we might hear what different musicians do with the same material. Not a bad idea, and they agree! Who are the musicians? The Dave Brubeck Quartet and Duke Ellington and His Famous Orchestra! How convenient, and how swinging! Let's go!

Here we are at our usual table. We know all about Brubeck and his musicians from the concert we just attended, so let's not waste any time discussing the group or their instruments. What's the piece? *Take the "A" Train*, naturally.

LISTEN

BRUBECK QUARTET, *TAKE THE "A" TRAIN* (CD SELECTION 1.9)

Brubeck is kind. He starts by playing the tune on the first beat, so we can learn this piece without any complications. He played the A phrase twice, Desmond came in on alto to show us the bridge (B), and Brubeck played the A for us once again to close out the first chorus. Desmond followed with five complete solo choruses on alto, Brubeck played one, and then Brubeck and Morello **traded fours** for two complete choruses. **Trading fours** means one player plays the first four measures of a phrase and the other player plays the last four measures of the phrase. The first player reenters playing the first four measures of the next phrase and the second player finishes that phrase, as well.

This continues until the end of the chorus. In this case, Brubeck and Morello **trade fours** for two complete choruses of 32 measures each, or 64 measures in all. Finally, Brubeck plays the melody of the first phrase of *Take the "A" Train* as a final **chorus,** and Desmond joins him for a teeny extension that serves as an ending.

BRUBECK QUARTET, *TAKE THE "A" TRAIN*

HEAD	ALTO SAX solo	PIANO solo	PIANO AND DRUMS play "fours"				HEAD 1st phrase only
AABA	**AABA**	**AABA**	**A**	**A**	**B**	**A**	**A plus tag**
8+8+8+8	5 times =	once	4+4	4+4	4+4	4+4	8+4
32 bars	160 bars	32 bars	2 times = 64 bars				12 bars

With the help of the Dave Brubeck Quartet, you should be able to sing the melody of *Take the "A" Train*. Brubeck played the first phrase straight, but Desmond added a touch of variation to the melody of the **bridge.** Still, it is close enough to the original that if you learn the tune from this performance you will be able to sing to yourself or hear it in your head any time you hear any performance of *Take the "A" Train*. While Desmond was playing his five choruses, were you able to hear the changes when the **bridge** interrupted the repeating pattern of the first phrase? Good, because that is one of the critical places in both performance and listening. Can the player **make the changes?** One of the trickiest spots is nearly always the **bridge.**

My, how time flies. The quartet finished its concert, and the Ellington band is all set up. What are they going to play? *Take the "A" Train*, of course.

DUKE ELLINGTON, *TAKE THE "A" TRAIN* (CD SELECTION 1.10)

Now that was no jam session; that was a full-blown concert version for full jazz orchestra and three outstanding soloists: Duke Ellington on piano, Betty Roché, vocalist, and Paul Gonsalves on tenor saxophone. You may not have noticed, but Ellington started on the first beat of the first phrase just as Brubeck did; but Ellington didn't play the melody. He started immediately with a solo, knowing that all his fans are already familiar with *Take the "A" Train* and don't need to be shown how the tune goes. After all, it is 1952 and he has been playing this number for over a decade. Also, he has used it off and on as his theme song, so a few notes is all it takes to clue the fans in on what **changes** they should be listening for. Ellington plays a solo for two complete choruses, just piano, bass, and drums. At the start of the second chorus he and the drummer, Louis Bellson, play around a bit with Ellington contributing a cute little phrase and Bellson responding with a couple of bass drum pops.

At the end of his second chorus, Ellington throws in a **quote,** the melody from another, unrelated piece, *I'm Beginning to See the Light,* partly because it fits and he can do it, and partly as an insider joke for those who can catch it. It takes good ears and a solid grasp of the repertory to pick up all the **quotes,** or quotations from other pieces, that appear in jazz. Immediately after, Ellington plays the descending note-and-chord pattern that has served as a traditional introduction to

The Duke Ellington Orchestra of 1952 on tour playing a job in what appears to be a college gymnasium. The tenor saxophonist of Take the "A" Train *recording, Paul Gonsalves, is the first saxophonist on the left. Ellington is standing by the piano and the other musicians are (left to right): Quentin Jackson, trombone; Juan Tizol, trombone; Wendell Marshall, bass; Clark Terry, trumpet. The saxophone section is comprised of (left to right) Gonsalves, Jimmy Hamilton, Hilton Jefferson, Russell Procope, and Harry Carney.*

Take the "A" Train for many years, and the band enters with the saxophones playing the now familiar melody of the piece. They do not play a full chorus; this is only a transition to set the stage for the vocal that follows.

Betty Roché improvises throughout her long vocal solo. An ordinary popular-song vocalist would most likely sing both the words and melody straight. Roché adds words, changes the melody, begins phrases in unexpected places, uses a plastic, relaxed rhythm that stretches or squeezes her vocal line, bends pitches, and dwells on certain sounds. Her first chorus, which is sung entirely with words, is uniquely her own. While she sings this chorus, notice the creative job of **comping** that Ellington does behind her vocal solo, sometimes complementing her singing, sometimes commenting on it instrumentally. Her second chorus is a **scat** chorus with a **blues riff** ("I Ain't Mad at You Pretty Baby, Don't Be Mad at Me") thrown in. She makes the **changes** of the **bridge** effortlessly and continues on into her second **scat** chorus. Did you catch the **quote** of *Yankee Doodle Dandy* thrown in just before the **bridge?** And did you notice that she started the bridge with a quote of *Sweet Georgia Brown?* Lots of fun right to the end of her solo.

Betty Roché, band vocalist with Duke Ellington in the 1950s, added her bebop vocal contributions to the repertoire of musical sounds and techniques from which Ellington might pick and choose as he composed and arranged the orchestra's music.

Then SMASH! The full band comes crashing in with **half time** chords. Feel the beat of the music as they play at this point and you will see that the beat immediately drops to half as fast, or twice as slow, as it was moving during her chorus. A great compositional device to create dramatic effect, the work of one of jazz's greatest arrangers, Billy Strayhorn. Ellington interjects a little of that transitional material we heard before, and the mellow tones of Paul Gonsalves's tenor saxophone transform the piece from a bouncing, swinging number to a romantic ballad—but the **changes** remain the same. Gonsalves is improvising to the same **pop song form changes** of *Take the "A" Train* that Brubeck, Desmond, Ellington, and Roché were improvising to. The lush arrangement in the background and the steady progress of the bass and drums provide the support for this ballad until, SMASH again! The tempo doubles, the brass herald the change of mood, and Gonsalves is on the first leg of an extended solo that builds, and continues to build, until the band halts for an out-of-time cadenza,

THE MUSICIANS SPEAK   BETTY ROCHÉ

I came to New York, and I stayed with my mother. . . . Shortly after I got out of school, I worked in a club in New York called Monroe's Uptown House. . . . and then I worked at Teddy Hill's on 118th Street. . . . And when I worked at . . . Teddy Hill's, there used to be a variety of different artists—Dizzy Gillespie, Charlie Parker. I worked with Mary Lou Williams and various musicians. Oh, then I joined the Savoy Sultans. . . . I worked with them, and we went out to Chicago. Now when we were working in Chicago, I was working at White's Emporium, and I happened to go out one night, and was standing at a bar, and this gentleman walked over to me, and he said—I mean, he was standing beside me at the bar, and he started talking to me—and he asked me, what was my name, and I told him, and he said, what did I do, and I told him I was a singer. He said, "I'm a drummer." I said, "Oh, really?" I said, "What's your name?" He said, "Sonny Greer." I said, "You're kidding! . . . Well, you know what? I would like very much . . . for you to come over to my, our, club and catch our show." He said, "Well, I just might do that. . . ."

The next night, one of the girls on the show said to me, "Betty." I said, "Yeah, baby." She said, "Get dressed, and look pretty, and sing your buns off." I said, "Why, what's happening?" She said, "You've got a hell of a guest out in the audience waiting to hear you sing." I said, "Who is it?" She said, "I'm not going to tell you." And when I went on, I sang to the

an elaborate and showy flourish that stretches to the final big band chord at the end of the piece. Throughout the work, the "tune" is alluded to—a snippet by the trombones here, a reference by the singer there—but never performed whole. In truth, *Take the "A" Train* is not about the tune but the **changes,** the harmonies of the piece that define the form and provide material for improvisation and orchestration.

ELLINGTON ORCHESTRA, *TAKE THE "A" TRAIN*

PIANO SOLO	BAND Interlude	VOCAL SOLO	TENOR SOLO	
			slow	fast
AABA + tag	**A + tag**	**AABA + transition and tag**	**AABA**	**AABA + end**
2 times		3 times	once	2 times

best of my ability. When I finished singing, the waitress took me, told me to come with her, and I went with her and went over to this table. It was Duke Ellington, Billy Strayhorn, Ivie Anderson, Sonny Greer, and Duke's manager. And I sat down and had a drink with them and conversation and he [Duke] said to me, "Before we leave," he said," are you working tomorrow night?" I said, "No, I'm not working. I'm off tomorrow night." He said, "Well, would you like to take a little bus ride with me, with the group?" I said, "I would like to." He said, "We're going to an Army camp to do a show, and maybe you might like to do a couple of numbers." I said, " That would be wonderful!"...

You know what he [Duke] would do? If he was teaching me a new song, he would teach me the melody, then he would give me a piece of paper with the lyrics on it, and I would run that through my mind. Then he would have me rehearse it with the music. . . . And whenever I did a number he'd say to me, "Don't play it—don't do it the way you hear it, just do it any way that it comes out in your mind." He said, "If you sing off, it's perfectly all right." And when I would sing, I had a fashion of holding my hand out like a person was going to give me some skin, like [sings] "Give it up, give it up, give it up, body and soul." And he said, "Don't take that gesture out. Keep it in." And he said, "Anything you feel, you do it."

Paul Gonsalves, tenor saxophone, came to prominence with his famous Take the "A" Train *solo for the Duke Ellington Orchestra. He began his career with the Count Basie band in 1946 and then briefly joined the Dizzy Gillespie group in 1949 before joining the Ellington Orchestra. Gonsalves was made famous for his 27-chorus improvised solo on Ellington's "Diminuendo and Crescendo in Blue" at the 1956 Newport Jazz Festival.*

As you can see, hearing the form and harmony is the key to understanding jazz improvisation, and hearing the **changes** of **popular song form** is the key to thoroughly enjoying Billy Strayhorn's and Duke Ellington's *Take the "A" Train*. Many practices of the **jam session** are carried into the nightclubs, recording studios, and concert stages, and you have been introduced to the essential elements that jazz musicians use to make their music. Every piece is distinctive and every performance is individual, so you are unlikely to run into exactly the same musical situation unless you are dealing with amateurs. But what you have learned has served professional and amateur musicians alike as the norm upon which they might expand their tonal world, and it will serve you well in the same manner. You have a solid nucleus, and to it you can add further layers of understanding as you gain experience.

REVIEW   7

Learn to recognize **popular song form** and improve your ability to hear the **changes** underpinning the art of jazz improvisation.

Compare the overall form of the two performances, the one by the Brubeck Quartet and the other by Duke Ellington and His Famous Orchestra, and list:

similarities
differences

1. What is **popular song form?**

2. Where did **pop song form** get its name?

3. What is the meaning of the title of this piece?

4. What is a **jam session?**

5. What is required in order to have a **jam session?**

6. Were either of these performances **jam sessions?** Why or why not? Which is closer? Why?

7. What does one find in the **basic repertory** of jazz?

8. What is a **fake book?** How does it differ from printed "classical" music?

9. What is the **bridge?**

10. What does it mean **to trade fours?**

Other Concepts

1. **Horn players** was not defined in Unit 7. What do you suppose it means? Ray Nance, an Ellington trumpeter from other times, was also a violinist. Can a violinist be a **horn player?**

2. Are there **standards** in "classical" music? If so, how are they different from **standards** in jazz?

3. If you were to hear other recordings of Paul Desmond, Charlie Parker, Benny Carter, Coleman Hawkins, and Paul Gonsalves, do you suppose you could tell them apart?

The Vocal Line

8

No instrument is more personal than the human voice, no sound more expressive than the vocal line, no medium more specific than language. Singers have the opportunity to characterize and dramatize the message of lyrics while instrumentalists explore the realm of allusion and abstraction. The medieval scholars knew that language, music, and mathematics were humanity's highest intellectual accomplishments, and they structured the original universities around these disciplines. Singers have the unique privilege of exploiting two of these domains, both language and music. The best singers, the vocal artists, have the ability to communicate directly with our feelings and sensibilities in a way that is unique to their art. As you have already observed, some singers work primarily in the realm of instrumental music. They sing wordless vocal solos and use their voices as just another instrument in the band. You heard that in the **scat singing** of Betty Roché. Other singers do little more than intone words in rhythm. This was true of Don Redman's vocal efforts in *Shakin' the African*. On the other hand, Billie Holiday and Ethel Waters are two vocal artists who bring an immediacy to their music through a blend of words and sound, who share the artful reality of their lyrics with their audience, and who, through sheer musicality, alter melodic contours and bend rhythmic units into the mode of jazz.

The year is 1939 and America is nervously watching the war clouds developing over Europe. As we enter the "Chez Imagination" this evening to hear the celebrated singer, Billie Holiday, we casually notice that the patrons of the club are primarily white, well-dressed, middle- and upper-class music lovers who can afford the luxury of name entertainment in small quarters. The **house band,** local musicians hired by the club to play those nights when name groups are not booked and to provide accompaniment for soloists when they come to the club without their own musicians, is a small group of trumpet, three saxes, and rhythm. While we finish our food and take a turn on the dance floor, they play bouncy versions of popular songs in the current jazz style, **swing.** The first show is scheduled for 10:00 p.m., and when it is time, the club manager makes the announcement, the applause begins, and a statuesque black woman in an ivory silk gown and a gardenia in her hair begins to sing.

LISTEN

BILLIE HOLIDAY, *STRANGE FRUIT* (CD SELECTION 1.11)

BILLIE HOLIDAY, *STRANGE FRUIT*

> Southern trees bear a strange fruit,
> Blood on the leaves and blood at the root,
> Black bodies swinging in the southern breeze,
> Strange fruit hanging from the poplar trees.
>
> Pastoral scene of the gallant South,
> The bulging eyes and the twisted mouth,
> Scent of magnolia, sweet and fresh,
> Then the sudden smell of burning flesh.
>
> Here is the fruit for the crows to pluck,
> For the rain to gather, for the wind to suck,
> For the sun to rot, for the tree to drop.
> Here is a strange and bitter crop.

Now what do we do? Applause seems inappropriate. Billie Holiday has pulled us into the reality of pre-World War II America, a segregated nation where black artists are recognized and paid but not allowed into white hotels; where blacks, regardless of their culture and accomplishment, watch what they say and where they say it for fear of physical reprisal. Every black jazz musician experienced the pain of unequal rights, and a few, like Billie Holiday, brought their art into the mainstream of social change. She remembered how her father had died, refused treatment for pneumonia at more than one white hospital and finally admitted to a black ward at a Veteran's Hospital, too late. When Lewis Allan, the poet of this song, showed her these lyrics, Billie Holiday made this song a personal cause. She not only wanted to bring the message to "a plush night club audience," but she

Billie Holiday's swatch of gardenias in her hair became a stage trademark. In 1938, the time of this photo, Holiday joined Artie Shaw and became one of the first black singers to be featured with a white orchestra. Holiday recorded regularly with producer John Hammond during the period 1935–42; the recordings feature studio bands comprised of some of the finest jazz musicians of the period, including Lester Young. Holiday often credited Louis Armstrong for influencing her singing style.

wanted to record it, and the major labels refused. She finally obtained a one-session release from her contract and recorded it with a new, and minor, label, Commodore.

Similar terrifying experiences for blacks were not uncommon. The great blues singer, Bessie Smith, died after an auto accident when the first hospital refused her admittance and treatment and sent the ambulance on a long, hopeless trip to a "colored facility."

One of Bessie Smith's admirers was the young black singer, dancer, and actress, Ethel Waters. She rose to great fame and celebrity in the 1930s as the star of several Broadway musicals and movies, but in the 1920s, when she was touring the South, she had an experience in Macon, Georgia, which left a permanent scar on her heart. When

Ethel Waters began her career as a singer and recorded with such jazz musicians as Fletcher Henderson, Coleman Hawkins, and Duke Ellington. In this photo, Waters rehearses a new blues song "Gone on that Guy" with the song's composer Al Moritz. The song was to be part of a variety show called "Blue Holiday."

she arrived at the theater, she noticed that the people were quiet and subdued. She soon discovered that a black boy had talked back to a white man, had been lynched by a mob, and had his body thrown into the lobby of the theater to make sure the many black patrons would see it. Waters comforted the grief-torn family, but what could she say to the mother? Ethel Waters, like most black artists, had to develop a compartmentalized life and personality not just to succeed in America but to survive. Occasionally, the mask slipped, and she sang, in 1930, *What Did I Do to Be So Black and Blue?*

ETHEL WATERS, *BLACK AND BLUE* (CD SELECTION 1.12)

ETHEL WATERS, *BLACK AND BLUE*

Out in the streets, shuffling feet,
couples passing two by two,
And here am I left high and dry,
black, because I'm black I'm blue.

All the race fellows, crave "high yellows,"
gentlemen prefer them light.
I'm just another spade who can't make the grade,
Looks like there's nothing but dark days in sight.

With a cold empty bed, springs hard as lead,
Pains in my head and I feel like Old Ned.
What did I do to be so black and blue?

No joys for me, no company,
Even the mouse scrams from my house,
All my life through I've been so black and blue.

I'm white, but it's inside,
    so that don't help my case.
'Cause I can't hide
    just what is on my face, oh.

Sad and forlorn, life's just a thorn,
My heart is torn, oh why was I born?
What did I do to be so black and blue?

Just 'cause you're black, boys think you lack
They laugh at you and scorn you too.
What did I do to be so black and blue?

When I draw near they laugh and sneer
I'm set aside, always denied.
All my life through, I've been so black and blue.

How sad I am,
        and each day the situation gets worse.
My mark of Ham
        seems to be a curse, oh.

How will it end, can't get a boyfriend
Yet my only sin lies in my skin.
What did I do to be so black and blue?

Ethel Waters was not alone in singing this song. Even the great Louis Armstrong sang it in concert and on record, but the immediacy of Waters's statement was not surpassed. Beyond the words themselves, what did she do with the music to create a living artistic organism? She took many of the artistic licenses we have studied in the music of other jazz performances and applied them to the presentation of both word and music. She stressed **blue notes,** she fit the **rhythm** of the notes to the meaning of the **words,** she chose a lyric that used **blues form** within the more common **popular song form,** and she varied the **vocal line** so that a repetitious, composed melody fitting the pattern AABA is transformed into an ever-changing **jazz melody.** The artist is a master of craft, and it is in the study of these details of craft that we discover the beauty of the finished product. The song that seems so natural an expression of real life is actually the highly polished work of a master craftsman.

This piece has two sections, a **verse** and a **chorus,** common features of most show and popular songs of the day, carried over from operatic ancestors who wrote recitatives and arias. The first section with a lot of words and little melody sets the stage for the aria, and a second section, the aria, reflects in song on the emotions and feelings of the singer. Though modified in the popular arena, *Black and Blue* has a **verse** and **chorus,** a recitative and aria; and the **chorus** is repeated with different words. Also, note that the **chorus** uses **popular song form,** AABA. Lastly, observe that each "A" of this **pop song form** is divided like the **blues,** aa'b, where the first line is expanded by the second and is answered by a **refrain** or recurring idea, the third line.

VERSE

Out in the streets, shuffling feet,
couples passing two by two,
And here am I left high and dry,
black, because I'm black I'm blue.

All the race fellows, crave "high yellows,"
gentlemen prefer them light.
I'm just another spade who can't make the grade,
Looks like there's nothing but dark days in sight.

CHORUS

With a cold empty bed, springs hard as lead,	A	a
Pains in my head and I feel like Old Ned.		a'
What did I do to be so black and blue?		b

No joys for me, no company,	A	a
Even the mouse scrams from my house,		a'
All my life through I've been so black and blue.		b

I'm white, but it's inside,	B	
so that don't help my case.		
'Cause I can't hide		
just what is on my face, oh.		

Sad and forlorn, life's just a thorn,	A	a
My heart is torn, oh why was I born?		a'
What did I do to be so black and blue?		b

SECOND CHORUS

Just 'cause you're black, boys think you lack	A	a
They laugh at you and scorn you too.		a'
What did I do to be so black and blue?		b

When I draw near they laugh and sneer	A	a
I'm set aside, always denied.		a'
All my life through, I've been so black and blue.		b

How sad I am,	B	
and each day the situation gets worse.		
My mark of Ham		
seems to be a curse, oh.		

How will it end, can't get a boyfriend	A a
Yet my only sin lies in my skin.	a'
What did I do to be so black and blue?	b

ETHEL WATERS, *BLACK AND BLUE* (CD SELECTION 1.12)

A certain duality is present in this performance that is not noticeable in Holiday's recording of *Strange Fruit.* Ten years had passed, the intellectual liberals who frequented the New York clubs were better prepared for cries of overt racism after having been educated by the

THE MUSICIANS SPEAK   ETHEL WATERS

But in the end this beloved son of hers had "talked back" to a white man. The sentence of the white man's mob had been death. And what was there to say? Should I have whispered, "Cry softly, little Negro mother. Put your work-cracked, tired hands before your face so the white men who killed your son won't be reminded of their shame and their crime. Hide your grief. Clutch tightly at your tormented heart so its wild beating will not be heard, mother of the Negro boy who has been lynched. Stifle your groans, little mother, as you follow his slashed and broken body to the Negro cemetery. Even though this boy you are burying was once the sweet little baby you fed at your breast and went hungry to feed and clothe. Yes, this is the little boy you dreamed of someday sending to college, the same boy you were so proud of. He is no more, little mother, but don't cry out loudly. Hide your grief and your outraged heart. You are a Negro, Mother, and don't count for anything in this white man's world."

I sat and prayed with the family of that lynched boy while I was in Macon. But there was little I or anyone else could do for them. At least so it seemed to me then. I never dreamed that some years later, in a gay and sparkling Broadway show, I would have the chance to tell the story of their misery and their impotence in a great song called *Supper Time.* . . .

Mamba's Daughters had its preview opening on New Year's Eve and its regular opening on January 3, 1939, which I still remember as the most thrilling and important experience of my life as a performer. And my whole

likes of Ethel Waters, many other admirable black jazz musicians, respected members of the Harlem Renaissance, and thinking people of all races. But *Black and Blue* speaks out in a day where it might be proper for a black woman to lament *her* problem but improper and unsafe for any black to speak boldly about *our* problem. In *Black and Blue*, there is a mixture of lively jazz (the trumpet interpolations between the vocal phrases, for example) and poignant minor **blues** sonorities (the lowered interval in the **vocal line** when Waters sings "black" in "What did I do to be so *black* and blue").

It is only natural, but there is very little agreement about most things in the world of jazz. After all, jazz is a world where expression and individuality are supreme accomplishments and members strive fiercely for their own unique identity. But it is a close-knit world, as well, where members care for each other and respect the work and

life, too, except for when I found God. I was the first colored woman, the first actress of my race, ever to be starred on Broadway in a dramatic play. And we opened at the Empire Theatre, which has the richest theatrical history of any showhouse in America. And the Empire's star dressing room was mine on that opening night. While the carriage trade was arriving outside, I sat at the dressing table where all the great actresses, past and present, had sat as they made up their faces and wondered what the first-night verdict would be—Maude Adams, Ethel Barrymore, Helen Hayes, Katharine Cornell, Lynn Fontanne, and all the others, now dead, who had brought the glitter of talent and beauty and grace to that old stage.

Yes, there I was, the Ethel who had never been coddled or kissed as a child, the Ethel who was too big to fit, but big enough to be scullion and laundress and bus girl while still a kid. And I could have looked back over my shoulder and blown a kiss to all my yesterdays in show business. I had been pushed on the stage and prodded into becoming Sweet Mama Stringbean and the refined singer of risqué songs in Edmond's Cellar, and on and up to best-selling records, Broadway musicals, and being the best-paid woman in all show business. That was *the* night of my professional life, sitting there in that old-fashioned dressing room that was a bower of flowers. The night I'd been born for, and God was in the room with me. I talked to God until the call boy came to say: "Five minutes, Miss Waters."

accomplishment of others. That singers as diverse as Betty Roché, Don Redman, Billie Holiday, and Ethel Waters can be a part of this world is an indication of the vast area jazz encompasses. In these first eight units we have acquired some technical vocabulary to deal with the music and the musicians, we have studied some attitudes about listening at home, in clubs, and at concerts, we have viewed and listened to instruments, studied the responsibilities of soloists, horn sections, and rhythm sections, and listened to the art of performance both improvisatory and rehearsed. We have begun to learn something about a few major figures, a little about social history that leaves vestiges in the music, and we have started to acquire a repertory of jazz works that span several styles. All in all we have attempted to fill our listener's toolbox with the necessary implements to dissect whatever jazz we hear into understandable modules that we can fit back together into truly enjoyable performances. No one ever knows it all, but you are ready to plunge into the deepest musical water and swim safely back to shore. From this point forward we will build upon what we know by the most enjoyable of means, listening to great music.

 REVIEW 8

Study some unique aspects of vocal jazz to blend text and tone, and learn to recognize the craft involved in great vocal jazz performances.

After listening to both Billie Holiday and Ethel Waters, compare and describe the following:

their diction;
their sense of rhythm;
their freedom from specified melodic contours with that of
 Betty Roché's; with that of Don Redman's;
their tone quality;
their overall success in conveying the message of the lyrics;
their use of performing devices.

Primary Goal of Unit 8

1. *Blue Rondo A La Turk* combined **blues form** with **rondo form,** and *Black and Blue* combines **blues form** with **popular song form.** How are the treatments different?

2. Are there poetic meter and rhyme schemes to the lyrics of the two songs we have studied in this unit?

3. Can you distinguish the instruments of *Strange Fruit* (trumpet, three saxophones, piano, bass, drums, and guitar)?

4. Can you distinguish the instruments of *Black and Blue* (trumpet, violin, piano, bass, and guitar)?

5. Since *Black and Blue* was sung by Louis Armstrong, what changes would be necessary in the lyrics to make the words appropriate?

Study Questions

6. Must the words of *Strange Fruit* be sung by a female vocalist? Would they be more effective sung by a woman or a man? Would the insertion of a scat solo into this piece heighten or destroy its effect?

Other Concepts

1. What is the social situation for black entertainers in America today? Are there still ghettos as well as black, white, and mixed nightclubs?

2. Of the four singers we studied, do you think any were classically trained musicians? Why?

3. What can a musician do better or more easily with an instrument other than voice? What can a singer do better or differently than a horn or other mechanical musical instrument?

4. What is the most perfect instrument? Why?

Reviewing the Basics

9

You may not be aware how much you have learned these past few weeks (first eight units), but it is considerable. We are going to sit down at our table at the "Chez Imagination" during the morning hours when the club is closed to the public and group our newly acquired information into categories. If we pull some tables and chairs around, we can dump "concepts" on one, "instruments" on another, and so on. Then, with a friend from the class, you might take turns quizzing each other on our "little" list. If it seems large, then take pride in how much you have covered and learned so far. By quizzing each other you will discover which terms remain unfamiliar, or whether you can explain a concept or describe an important musician, and you will find that by teaching each other you will both learn thoroughly and quickly. When ever you run into difficulty, mark the book, reread and relisten, and ask questions of your instructor. Then, when it comes time to prepare for a test, you can start on this marked list with the items that gave you trouble.

REVIEW LISTS

Sounds

a combo
a big band
a rhythm section
individual musicians

Time Blocks

the "Jazz Age"
the "Swing Era"

Groups

the Chocolate Dandies
the Benny Goodman Sextet
the Charlie Parker Quartet
Don Redman and His Orchestra
the Dave Brubeck Quartet
Duke Ellington and His Famous Orchestra

The Caravan of Dreams in Fort Worth, Texas, is a modern nightclub that features jazz music. The club manager is an unheralded, behind-the-scenes player who not only is responsible for selecting, booking, and paying the artists, but he or she must also see to the needs of the band, provide necessary house equipment, take care of publicity, organize and supervise a large nightclub staff, and see to it that the patrons are well cared for. Well run nightclubs are the natural environment for modern jazz.

Instruments

trumpet
trombone
tuba
clarinet
alto saxophone
tenor saxophone

piano
bass
drums
guitar
vibraphone
voice

Technical Terms

combo
big band
a set (performance) and set break
a set (percussion)
the stand (up on "the stand")
front line
rhythm section
sidemen
to double
vibrato
articulation
tone color
tone quality
solo
soli
the brass family
the reed family
the trumpet section
the trombone section
the sax section
the brass section
the trombone slide
quartet
sextet
wire brushes, sticks, mallets,
    and beater
bass drum
foot pedal

head
riff
solo chorus
fills
chords
changes
melody
tempo
measure
bar
78s
LPs
3-minute take
arranger
bandboy
fronts
charts
fake book
chord symbols
to back
rip, shake
motive
jam session
gig
standard
classic
session
trading fours

snare drum and tom-toms
hi-hat (sock cymbals)
ride cymbals
set of traps
pizzicato
arco
first chorus

the bridge
quotes
lyrics
house band
half time and double time
verse and chorus

Concepts

an identifiable voice
jazz sound
changes in recording technology
walking bass pattern and 2-beat
    bass pattern
beat, time, timekeeper, and keeping
    time
scat singing
comping, to comp
swinging, to swing
indefinite pitch and tuned
    percussion
form
harmonic framework
make the changes
structural elements of jazz
syncopation

acoustic and electric instruments
12-bar blues
popular song form
rondo form
improvise
arrangement
jazz orchestra
the stage setup of a jazz band
sweet and hot
concerts and club dates
meters, regular and irregular
blue notes and blues scale
basic repertory
relationship of jazz to American
    society

Important Musicians

Benny Carter
Coleman Hawkins
John Kirby
Fletcher Henderson
Horace Henderson
Benny Goodman
Mel Powell
Red Norvo

Al Haig
Percy Heath
Don Redman
Dave Brubeck
Paul Desmond
Joe Morello
Eugene Wright
Duke Ellington

Slam Stewart
Rufus Reid
Kenny Barron
Ron Carter
Charlie Parker
Max Roach

Billy Strayhorn
Paul Gonsalves
Betty Roché
Louis Bellson
Billie Holiday
Ethel Waters

Study Pieces

Bugle Call Rag, 1930
China Boy, 1945
Blues in F (rhythm section)
Bird Blues (rhythm section)
Now's the Time (rhythm section)
Now's the Time, 1953
Shakin' the African, 1931

Blue Rondo A La Turk, 1959
Take the "A" Train, 1959 (combo)
Take the "A" Train, 1952 (big band with vocal)
Strange Fruit, 1939
What Did I Do to Be So Black and Blue, 1930

Now, as a final exercise to put all your skills to work, listen to the following recorded example, which is presented with no commentary at this time, and put your analytical skills to use. Start your own list of elements that you heard in the performance that you think are particularly interesting, or important, or beautiful, or ugly. Your opinion carries as much weight as anyone's, especially now that you are becoming an informed listener. Once you have made up your opinion and written your notes, you may be interested in playing a listening game with some of your friends. You put on one of your favorite jazz records without telling them anything about it. Then you quiz them—what are the instruments? who do you think the players are? what form is it in? and so on. Then it's one of their turns. He or she puts on a record with no preparation for you. Then you get to test your ears. It's actually a lot of fun. I'll show you. I'll go first. Listen to this next recording and tell me what you hear.

(CD SELECTION 1.13)

PART TWO

MEN AND WOMEN OF JAZZ AND JAZZ STYLES

Two Superb Pianists: Erroll Garner and Bill Evans

10

MODIFIED POPULAR SONG FORM AND FORM GENERATED BY A ROTATING SEQUENCE OF CHORDS

No instrument in jazz has had a larger number of extraordinary practitioners than has the piano. From the early days of Jelly Roll Morton and James P. Johnson to the present day explorations of Yosuke Yamashita and Marcus Roberts, the honor roll of truly great pianists can almost carry, on its pages alone, the entire history of jazz—Jelly Roll Morton and Lil Hardin, Clarence Williams, Lovie Austin, Fletcher Henderson, and Duke Ellington, Earl Hines, Eubie Blake, and James P. Johnson, Fats Waller and Willie "The Lion" Smith, as well as Jimmy Yancey and Meade Lux Lewis—all pianists who made a name for themselves in the 1920s and virtually defined jazz before the calamitous 1929 stock market crash, before Chicago Style Jazz was clearly defined, before Kansas City Jazz was recognized as a distinct genre, and before the style Swing was invented. If there were that many great pianists before 1930, what can we do about the fact that the number of magnificent pianists after that date mushroomed exponentially—Art Tatum, Mary Lou Williams, Teddy Wilson, and on and on. What can we do? We can enjoy their music and count our lucky stars.

What is there about this instrument and its music that sets it apart from all the other instruments of jazz? Why has the piano, and now the "keyboard" (electronic keyboard), become the omnipresent instrument in nearly every jazz ensemble, been the one instrument that is capable of playing consistently good solo concerts, and ironically enough, been the one instrument that did not travel with the artist? What is so unique about this instrument? The answer lies in the fact that in the hands of a great artist, the piano can become the complete orchestra, the instrument of harmony, melody, and rhythm, the instrument that can do it all.

George Wein, the founder of the Newport and JVC Jazz Festivals and many other festivals around the world, is a fine pianist himself who once commented that Erroll Garner was the only musician he knew who could make *any* piano sound like a fine instrument. What magic did Garner have in his fingers that could transform wood, ivory, and metal into a living, breathing orchestra? Let's listen.

ERROLL GARNER, *WHERE OR WHEN* (CD SELECTION 1.14)

You noticed, of course, that Garner has a touch all his own—percussive, but not crude; subtle, but not weak; and varied. In this up-tempo **ballad** (usually a slow, sentimental love song), he played a long

Pianist Erroll Garner traveled to New York in the 1940s from his home in Pittsburgh where he had played with Leroy Brown's orchestra. By 1944, he had begun playing in the New York nightclubs; he served as Art Tatum's substitute in Tatum's trio with Slam Stewart and Tiny Grimes. Garner also recorded with Charlie Parker and composed several jazz piano pieces including the well-known ballad "Misty."

introduction before he announced the melody and let his listeners know what material he was going to work with. Garner starts the piece with an **ostinato** of four chords in his left hand, a brief repeated pattern that sounds the bass and establishes the beat, and he works with a **motive,** a short melodic figure, in the right hand that hints that this might be the **melody** of the piece he is going to play. The drums and bass are almost incidental to this performance, but you might have noticed that the drums lay down the beat at twice the speed of the **ostinato** chords and the bass line. Garner plays this very regular chordal **ostinato** introduction for 32 measures while his right hand begins to roam around melodically, and all this is meant, in a way, to deceive the listener, to set up a little ambiguity at the beginning about what piece is really going to be the subject of an improvisation. And you can literally hear the audience's tension released when the familiar strains of the Rogers and Hart *Where or When* appear as the real **head,** or **melody,** of this performance. Then, a breathtaking series of transformations begin to take place in the music. It is not his right hand that first captures my attention, but his left. Somehow, probably subconsciously, he begins to play with patterns of three that relate in ever-more complex ways to the steady four beats per measure of the right hand. At first we hear groups like those shown below as though the left hand were playing **waltz time,** three beats to a measure, without sounding the first beat.

r.h.	1	2	3	4	1	2	3	4	1	2	3	4	. . .
l.h.		2	3		2	3		2	3		2	3	. . .

Then he moves to a **rumba beat,** where the strong first-beat accent of both hands coincides, as does the last beat of the bar, but the left hand syncopates after beat 2:

r.h.	1	2	3	4	1	2	3	4	. . .
			>				>		
l.h.	1		2	3	1		2	3	. . .

Then, he moves to an honest **three-against-four** while his right hand plays an incredible melodic line:

r.h.		1	2	3	4		1	2	3	4	. . .
l.h.		1		2	3		1		2	3	. . .

Should you think playing **three-against-four** is easy, try patting your two hands so that the right does a steady four and the left does a steady three when only the first beat of each group coincides but nothing else does. It is next to impossible for mere mortals in the most straightforward manner, and Garner does it while improvising a superb melodic line. Then as if that were not enough, he picks up and elaborates an idea of repeated notes, skips up the keyboard in a brilliant display of technique, throws in two-fisted chords with both hands grabbing several notes each, goes in opposite directions up and down the keyboard at the same time, and more. Positively brilliant!

In case you overlooked the form while you were being overwhelmed by Garner's resplendent ideas and technique, it was our old favorite, **popular song form.** If you don't believe me, sing along with Garner when he sticks rather closely to the original **melody** in the first complete chorus. You'll see that it is truly an AABA' composition (the last A gets a little variation for a proper ending). I'll bet you didn't notice that the phrases are lopsided; that is, the first and second phrases are ten measures each, the third is only eight, and the last is twelve. If you picked that fact up on your own, give yourself a gold star! So, if you were going to outline the piece, the formal sketch might look like this:

FORMAL OUTLINE OF ERROLL GARNER, *WHERE OR WHEN*

INTRODUCTION	Tune or head	1st solo improvisation	2nd solo improvisation	3rd solo improvisation and ending
32 MEASURES	40 measures	40 measures	40 measures	60+ measures
	A A B A	AABA	AABA	A A B A
	10 + 10 + 8 + 12			10 + 10 + 8 + 32 +

What a great performance, and to think he kept all those things going and never got lost, never floundered around, always headed for a logical and musical middle and end.

I don't know about you, but after a performance like that I feel exhilarated. But remember, all jazz does not proceed at a furious pace. Some is contemplative, loving, tender. All the best musicians balance their repertoires with a variety of compositions for performance, not just because it is the practical thing to do, but because their own personalities are not one-sided and require many kinds of music to express the range of their moods. During the course of the evening, most performers will mix ballads along with up-tempo numbers that display their virtuosity. We can't afford to spend more time with Erroll Garner here, but perhaps the next artist will change the mood for us.

Here comes the owner of the nightclub, Mr. Imagination, to announce the next pianist. What, you didn't know the club was named after the boss? Sure, Harry Imagination is a successful biochemist with several patents on synthetic cotton fibers who also plays drums. He loves jazz and wanted an opportunity to jam with some of his heroes, so he bought this club years ago and has since earned a reputation for booking the best talent in Manhattan. He maintains a Steinway grand on the stage, pays the musicians well, respects their needs and idiosyncrasies, and subsidizes the club during hard times with money from the royalties on his patents. Most of his patrons are very loyal and have been coming here for years. Also, musicians come here on their off nights to enjoy the jazz. Harry just told me that **Bill Evans** will be the next featured piano artist. However, on this number, two other players will also solo—**Miles Davis** on muted trumpet and **John Coltrane** on tenor saxophone. Along with **Paul Chambers** on bass and **Jimmy Cobb** on drums, this group has become one of the most famous ensembles in jazz. Let's listen to their music first, and talk about it later.

BILL EVANS, *BLUE IN GREEN* (CD SELECTION 1.15)

When people refer to the piano artistry of Bill Evans they often compare it with poetry—beauty of sound, charged imagery, economy of means, elegance of expression, a distillation of feeling. Though Evans is quite capable of the brilliant virtuosic displays we expect from the best jazz pianists, he never seems to concern himself with display for its own sake. This performance conjures up a soft, ethereal experience with caressed piano **tones,** lush full **chords** that never jar note against note, a sweeping flow of revolving **melodic figures,** and a slow, dream-like **pulse.**

The leader, Miles Davis, wrote this piece in a way that contradicts everything I told you earlier about form. It fits none of the patterns I have outlined so far, and it has no real melody. It has a name, *Blue in Green*, and when one thinks about the color green as a blend of yellow and blue, the title is not inappropriate. This **improvisation,** and it truly is an **improvisation** that develops when one musician listens to his colleagues and reacts sympathetically, is based on a **loose rotation of six chords,** six different clusters of tones which sound good together and which have different relationships to each other. Other clusters appear, but they are transitory; they only pass from one of these to the next like morning mist in a mountain forest. Sometimes

A famous Miles Davis ensemble performing at the 1958 Newport Jazz Festival. While Miles solos on trumpet, Cannonball Adderley, alto saxophone (left), and John Coltrane, tenor saxophone (right), listen. In the rhythm section, Bill Evans is at the piano and Paul Chambers is on bass.

the passage of time between two of these chords is stretched slightly, but the formula dictates that each chord must come in sequence. Each chord owns the same block of time, but the walls of these time units are plastic, and the players may delay the resolution. They may slow or speed the time relationships, but they may not, however, ignore the proper sequence. This is what the players know, and this is what they hear as they improvise together. With a little repetition, the six chords are spread over ten measures and the pattern constantly repeats: 1 2 3 4 1 2 3 5 6 3 | 1 2 3 4 1 2 3 5 6 3 | 1 2 . . . with each number, or chord, representing one slow measure. When Bill Evans begins the piece, he plays an introduction that begins not with the first measure but the third, and his chord pattern for the 8-measure introduction is 3 4 1 2 3 5 6 3. Then Miles Davis enters with his muted trumpet at the beginning of the sequence. These chords have symbols meaningful to musicians, and I will show them in a simplified form with the formal scheme I draw below for anyone who might like to hum the bass notes of the chords as the piece moves along, but it is only essential for the performers to understand these chords, not the listener. The listener can sense the cohesion of this slow, revolving progression of recurring sounds without understanding the notation of the symbols. With this chordal pattern in mind, the soloists are at liberty to play one chord twice as long, or end or begin at points different from the beginning, as long as they do it together.

Harmonic Progression of *Blue in Green*

$\|B^bM^7 \quad | \quad A^7 \quad | \quad Dm^7 \quad | \quad Cm^7 \quad | \qquad 1 \quad 2 \quad 3 \quad 4$

$|B^bM^7 \quad | \quad A^7 \quad | \quad Dm^7 \quad | \qquad\qquad = \quad 1 \quad 2 \quad 3$

$| \quad E^7 \quad | \quad Am^7 \quad | \quad Dm^7 \quad \| \qquad\qquad 5 \quad 6 \quad 3$

$(B^bM^7=1; A^7=2; Dm^7=3; Cm^7=4; E^7=5; Am^7=6)$

Formal Scheme of *Blue in Green*

PIANO	TRUMPET	PIANO	TENOR	PIANO	TRUMPET	PIANO
Introduction	Statement of motive and improvisation	solo improvisation	solo improvisation	solo improvisation	Statement of motive and improvisation	Close (not in time)
8 measures	42 measures	18 measures	20 measures	12 measures	40 measures	16 measures

One reason why this performance is so compelling is that, when the musicians take liberties, they follow each other with unerring instincts. They sense each other's ideas and respond accordingly. Though Bill Evans plays the introduction one chord to the measure, Miles Davis prolongs the changes for two measures each. When Evans returns for his first solo, he follows the pattern loosely, moving with bassist Paul Chambers among the chords like a man and his shadow. John Coltrane enters to reestablish the standard of one measure, one chord; but Evans follows again with renewed freedom. Finally, Miles Davis rounds out the piece by restating the theme in his original half-time progression, and Evans closes freely, completely abandoning regular time. The chords blend blue into the green.

Pianist Bill Evans made his first recordings with his own group in 1956; two years later he joined Miles Davis, and in 1959 was a sideman for Davis's Kind of Blue *album. His playing style reflects the influence of the leading bop era musicians including Bud Powell and Horace Silver.*

Before we leave the club this evening, we should consider once again all the pianists we have heard thus far, seven great masters of their instrument: Horace Henderson, Mel Powell, Al Haig, Dave Brubeck, Duke Ellington, Erroll Garner, and Bill Evans. Did each not have his own musical personality, touch, and style? Was each not an artist unique from all the others? Did each not have something different to say musically? None came from a musical vacuum, and all were influenced by other pianists, but as they matured they developed a message and an identity that was purely their own, and they expressed their unique musical personalities through the same instrument, the piano.

Miles Davis grew up in East St. Louis, Missouri; in 1944 he left home to study in New York—officially he was to enter school, but unofficially he went to apprentice himself to Charlie Parker. Davis maintained a performing career throughout several different jazz eras. He was an innovator in bop, cool, and by the 1970s (when this photo was taken) jazz-rock and fusion.

THE MUSICIANS SPEAK   DAVE BRUBECK

I do *not* have a classical background. Get that straight, OK? . . . When I was studying with Milhaud I still couldn't read music, so that's how great a classical background I have. And people just don't want to hear that, but I'm telling you it's true. And a lot of the great jazz musicians I know have the same problem. I'm not gonna tell you all of them, and it might be a blessing, because you arrive where you arrive pretty much self-taught. Like Duke Ellington was self-taught. . . .

We were listeners, and composers, and we didn't have a great technical background, but we have our own way of doing things. And you can turn out students, out of a place, a conservatory, and they come out like Heinz tomato ketchup, you know, and they got an all-similar background. Or you can, you can have some people that are totally on their own, struggling to figure out how to do it. And you got some individuals, kind of rough—a little broken glass in the ketchup, maybe. You know what I mean?

[Duke was] constantly introducing new ideas. And the way he took individuals and formed a band by waiting to see what they did. It's never been done, I don't think, as well since or before. That's what I used to love, to see a guy develop in the band. A certain sound comes from a certain trombone player. That's almost like the lost art of, say, making a halo, that you can no longer do in painting. You get a guy in the band that had a certain sound, and it would be hard to replace him, but Duke didn't care about that. The next guy would have a certain sound . . . and [there was] a freedom, creative freedom, that he offered his musicians. And this is, was *so* important to me, because I only had a quartet, but I offered the same freedom to the members of my quartet. When I had an octet, the same thing was going on too. And if I had a big band as an adult (I had one as a kid), I would try to do the same thing Duke did. It's so hard to allow your musicians the freedom to develop, because usually a chart's thrown down in front of the band, made by somebody that's not even in the band, and they play it—again the Heinz tomatoes. You know it's gonna come out right no matter which band is playing it. But with Duke's band, you heard the individuals contributing. You didn't know how much was written, how much Duke knew that a guy would get the certain right sound. It was like a palette in painting. He wanted this color then, and he got it.

Darius Milhaud told me . . . [in] '46 he said the greatest two American composers are Duke Ellington and George Gershwin. And in that class were a lot of my friends, and we were astounded. . . . At that time . . . there was Milhaud, Stravinsky, and Bartok. You had to put him [Milhaud] up in there. Maybe Hindemith, too. But Milhaud was a giant in the world, and he still is. But when he said this to my friends . . . we couldn't believe that a man of this stature was honoring Duke Ellington.

R E V I E W   **10**

Primary Goal
of Unit 10

Learn more about solo jazz piano playing and the work of two recognized artists, Erroll Garner and Bill Evans.

After listening to both Erroll Garner and Bill Evans, compare and describe:

> their touch and tone;
> their sense of rhythm;
> their freedom from, or obligation to, specified melodic
>   contours;
> their overall success in communicating with the listener;
> their use of, or freedom from, performing devices.

Study Questions

1. *Where or When* uses a modified **popular song form**. Describe the unusual features of form in this piece.

2. *Blue in Green* has a unique form all its own. Can you describe its features?

3. The drumming in *Blue in Green* was never mentioned in the text. Did you hear what the drummer was doing and do you remember his role in the ensemble?

4. What instruments were used in the Erroll Garner Trio for *Where or When?*

5. What instruments were used in the Miles Davis Quintet for *Blue in Green?*

6. Can you make one brief descriptive statement about the playing of each of the following pianists to help you remember and distinguish

their sound: Horace Henderson, Mel Powell, Al Haig, Dave Brubeck, Duke Ellington, Erroll Garner, and Bill Evans?

1. How is the piano different from the other instruments of jazz?

Other Concepts

2. How are these terms used to describe music: ballad, up-tempo number, ostinato, introduction, motive, melody, waltz time, rumba, three-against-four, tones, chords, and melodic figures?

3. What can a musician do better or more easily with an instrument other than the piano?

Five Soloists from the Rhythm Section

11

PIANIST BOB JAMES; GUITARIST JOHN SCOFIELD;
PERCUSSIONIST HARVEY MASON; VIBRAPHONIST
DAVE SAMUELS; AND BASSIST RON CARTER

Gerry Mulligan, the great baritone saxophonist, has a passion for steam locomotives. He is not only expert about their history and construction, but he also has written music inspired by the configuration, sound, and romantic imagery of various famous trains. *K-4 Pacific* is just such a composition from an album called "The Age of Steam," but this evening's diversion is neither centered around Gerry Mulligan, nor on locomotives or compositions, but on **sidemen,** some of the most fascinating and important people in jazz.

You don't have to be male to be a **sideman,** it just happens to be the term that developed in the profession for the musicians who are hired by a **leader** to play a **job** (an **engagement** or "**gig**"). Only a very few combos, extremely few in fact, are **cooperatives;** that is, where no member serves as leader and all the musicians share equally in the labor of booking, the expenses of equipment, music, and transportation, and the profits from their "**paying gigs.**" In a **cooperative,** the players maintain equal rights in selecting music for performance and **kicking off** the pieces (setting the tempo and starting the music); and in essence, they just get together and play. The vast majority of musical organizations, however, have a **leader,** usually an older, experienced, and better known, if not famous, musician, and all the rest of the instrumentalists on the **job** are **sidemen** who work for the **leader.** The band or combo is, and has always been, the essential training ground for jazz musicians, for beyond learning an instrument and studying music in school and on records, there is the matter of **paying dues,** going through a rigorous apprentice period, usually under severe financial and artistic stress, to hone skills and finally *earn* a name in the profession.

Not all **sidemen** aspire to become leaders; most, in fact, are content to play their music and leave all the administrative headaches to their leader. Therefore, the majority of jazz musicians are part of an elite group of professional, established players who think of themselves as **sidemen.** There is a special pride, a clannish sense of loyalty, a bonding, if you will, among the best **sidemen,** for these artists and craftsmen know they might get a call this morning for a studio date next month, another call at noon for two weeks on the road starting tomorrow with a **name band** (a group fronted by a famous band-leader), and a third call this same afternoon for a concert at Carnegie Hall in three weeks, where all the **jobs** are in different styles and with **books** (the **library** or collection of music of the band) they haven't seen before. Still, the master **sideman** knows he or she can play any **job** artistically and with polished craft.

During their careers, these musicians also frequently cross paths with **sidemen** from other bands when they are called to the same **gigs,** and they not only work together and build a mutual understanding and respect for each other's playing, but they also fraternize with each other at intermissions and after the **jobs,** tell stories and jokes about the business, communicate news, and share the problems and successes that fall to their lot. **Sidemen** are the workhorses of the jazz profession, and they know it. Some move to fame, glory, and riches as leaders themselves, but most are content to play the music right, do each job well, fulfill their ensemble and accompanimental responsibilities, and occasionally get their moment in the limelight when they **solo.**

This chilly evening in November of 1974, we have tickets for a concert in Carnegie Hall. It is a reunion concert of two famous musicians who, though closely associated in the past, haven't played together for over ten years. However, tonight we are not going to pay attention to the big-name attractions, Gerry Mulligan and Chet Baker, but to the **sidemen** hired for this **gig.** The famous Gerry Mulligan Quartet featuring Chet Baker had disbanded over ten years earlier, so a Manhattan concert reuniting these giants of West Coast Jazz meant booking a band that didn't exist. Although Mulligan had led several different ensembles during the intervening years, someone, probably Mulligan himself, had to get on the phone and see if some choice jazz musicians were available for a November 24th concert and a couple of rehearsals, as well. He ended up with an expanded rhythm section of piano, bass, drums, guitar, and vibraphone.

In 1974, Mulligan was in his late 40s; the piano and bass players hired for the job, Bob James and Ron Carter, in their late 30s; and the drummer, vibraphonist, and guitarist, Harvey Mason, Dave Samuels, and John Scofield, were 27, 26, and 23, respectively. What does age have to do with this process? Three layers of age illustrate how the typical apprentice system of jazz works to train and give exposure to young, upcoming jazz musicians. Mulligan was a famous establishment figure in his prime. In the late 1950s, a decade and a half earlier, he and Baker personified West Coast Jazz, and this concert was designed to attract an audience on the basis of their name recognition and the unique reunion of these two men. In 1974, James and Carter were well known in the profession but just coming into their own publicly—James as a pianist, arranger, and composer and soon-to-be record producer, and Carter as a bass player and soloist who was bringing virtuoso cello technique to the larger instrument. Carter had already achieved his first fame as a regular sideman with Miles Davis in the 1960s, and he was about to move to even greater renown on his own as a leader of ensembles and as a recording solo artist. The younger musicians could learn from both these men. Even though jazz education at the college level has become an increasingly

An outstanding composer and arranger, Gerry Mulligan is also jazz's greatest exponent of the baritone saxophone. Mulligan wrote "K-4 Pacific" after noticing the locomotives that passed his home; he decided that the sounds of the train were as swinging as Duke Ellington's rhythm section.

important part of a jazz musician's training in recent years, the apprenticeship process is still the only way to refine your skills and pay your dues.

The other three players, especially Scofield, were just excellent young musicians who were virtually unknown and still looking to make it in the profession, young men who needed to earn the respect of their elders, acquire some important exposure, and get an opportunity to display their wares. This concert was an important step along the way for all three because playing an important **gig** with Mulligan and Baker means something in the profession, and playing in Carnegie Hall before a large audience of fans, other musicians, and critics puts your skills on the line. If you do well, someone will notice. If you do badly, everyone will know. Let's hear what happens.

The concert opens with an old standard featuring both Mulligan and Baker, and as it proceeds, we hear a variety of pieces old and new, some a solo display for the saxophonist and others designed to feature the instrumental or vocal artistry of the trumpeter. Not too long before this concert, about a year or so, Mulligan had formed a new band

Ron Carter, a leader among modern bassists, expanded the repertory of virtuoso solo techniques for this instrument. Carter played with the Miles Davis quintet from 1963–1968 and became one of the most sought-after bassists in jazz.

John Scofield, virtuosic modern master of the electric guitar, studied at the Berklee College of Music with Gary Burton and Mick Goodrick. In 1974, Goodrick recommended him for a reunion concert at Carnegie Hall featuring Gerry Mulligan and Chet Baker.

called "The Age of Steam," and his composition *K-4 Pacific*, which we will hear next, is still new and characteristic of his latest thinking.

LISTEN

GERRY MULLIGAN, *K-4 PACIFIC* (CD SELECTION 1.16)

You probably heard that this piece has a driving beat, miles and miles of wheels rolling over tracks, railroad ties, and bridges. There are also **bridges,** or B sections, in the music. As you heard, the piece has a characteristic, recurring two-note motive—long, short, rest. Whenever you hear it, if you count threes (1 2 3, 1 2 3, 1 2 3, . . .), you will notice that the long note starts on count one, the short note is syncopated and starts just before count two, and count three is silent (3 = rest). The entire piece has that driving pulse underneath, but the layer of underlying pulses gets divided into different lengths, groups of twos and groups of threes, or if you multiply these units by 2, groups of fours and groups of sixes:

beat ▲ ▲ ▲ ▲ ▲ ▲ ▲ ▲ ▲ ▲ ▲ ▲ ▲ ▲ ▲ ▲ ▲ ....

divided

1	2	1	2	1	2	1	2	1	....
1	2	3	1	2	3	1	2	3	....

or

1	2	3	4	1	2	3	4	1	2	3	4	1	2	3	4	1	....
1	2	3	4	5	6	1	2	3	4	5	6	1	2	3	4	5	6 ....

Every time the musicians switch from one pattern to another, especially at the rapid tempo of performance, the music gets a little bit tricky—extremely difficult, to be honest. Those are the points where the ensemble is most likely to fall apart, and those are the places that get the most rehearsal time. How did these **sidemen** do in performance? Near flawless execution! Absolutely exciting! If you just focus on the ensemble at those places where the **long-short-rest** (LSR) motive comes in, repeats, and exits, you will hear how precisely executed the rhythms and pitches are.

The piece has a **modal** harmonic organization. That is, there are not very many chords to follow, just a few **minor scales** to organize the notes the players use to play and improvise together. If you were to graph the piece so one might follow the progress of the sounds, you would get a series of ABA structures, very much like going up and down over a bridge or hill—a low minor scale, then a noticeable jump up to play the bridge passage with two higher minor scales, and then back down to the first lower scale and a repeat of the characteristic LSR motive:

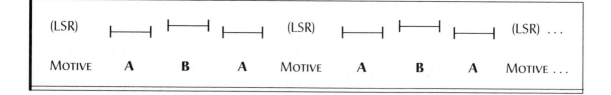

To this general pattern you surely noticed the composer added an **introduction (intro)**—some music which sets the tempo, the mood, the mode, and introduces the interruptive LSR motive—and a final chorus for full ensemble which plays the full melody of the piece:

INTRODUCTION	BARI SOLO	PIANO SOLO	GUITAR SOLO	VIBES SOLO	BASS SOLO	DRUM SOLO	ENSEMBLE ENDING
(MOTIVES INTRODUCED)	**ABABAB**	**ABAB**	**ABAB**	**ABAB**	**ABA(ba)**	**ABA**	**Head**

The full ensemble starts the introduction quietly, and one won't know until the very end of the piece that the players are introducing the motive of the **head** as well as the LSR motive. After twelve measures, a brief guitar solo line emerges. Then, the baritone saxophone moves to the foreground during the succeeding twelve measures. Four times during the introduction, the continuous progress of the beat is punctuated with the insertion of the LSR motive. If you were counting beats and measures you would notice that a pattern of twelve measures is marked at the end by the addition of the three-beat LSR motive, and this whole pattern was repeated four times in this introduction. Each successive layer adds more volume as well as more countermelody activity.

GERRY MULLIGAN, *K-4 PACIFIC* (CD SELECTION 1.16)

Separating the **intro** (introduction) from the first solo chorus, and also serving as a beginning of this next chorus, one hears the LSR motive repeated many times, one after the other, a series of three-beat measures of repeated pitches, a **drone.** This pattern becomes the A section of all the solo choruses, but in some the three-beat pattern is avoided; in others there is a **stop time** effect (chords from the rhythm section separated by long vacant spaces). Only at the very end of the work, the last Ensemble Chorus, is there a clear statement of the theme, the **head,** a tune with an ABA structure you can sing as *the* melody of the piece called *K-4 Pacific.*

We will talk about the masterful baritone saxophone solo of Gerry Mulligan later when we compare saxophonists in another unit, but while Mulligan is blowing his amazing solo, notice three important things the **sidemen** do: they maintain that ABA structure with the drone-like LSR motive for A, a higher harmonic level for B (always in straight four-beat time), and a return to the LSR drone for A. Second, they keep the beat without flagging or rushing; and third, they respond intuitively to the activity of the soloist to reinforce here, counterbalance there. Throughout the rush of this piece, these **sidemen** keep up an amazing background of swinging, informative, sensitive invention. Then, each in his turn gets an opportunity to solo. And what wonderful soloists they are.

GERRY MULLIGAN, *K-4 PACIFIC* (CD SELECTION 1.16)

Bob James, the pianist, at the end of his second A section starts a far-flung melodic pattern, follows its logical sequences, and magically ends up in the B section where he coordinates sparkling chordal rhythms with the superb drum work of Harvey Mason. John Scofield, the young guitarist, enters next for his solo and demonstrates both great melodic invention and fabulous technique. He always keeps on top of the beat, and at the end of his second B section, he gets a push from Bob James that initiates a cadential rush to a close. His solo, too, leads smoothly into the next solo, Dave Samuels's vibraphone chorus, and here we hear a combination of interesting melodic invention at the beginning and chordal, or harmonic, invention at the end.

Ron Carter's bass solo is absolutely stunning. In his solo, and even in his back-up work, one hears an incredibly rich repertory of devices—drones, ostinatos, walking bass patterns, melodies, multiple stops, single note combinations deriving from multiple stops, work high on the finger board, slides up and down, and more. What are these devices? A **drone** is a single sound repeated over and over. It might even be two or three notes played together, like strumming across two open strings, but they don't go anywhere. For a long time, it, or they, repeats over and over and over. An **ostinato** is similar, a short bass melody that repeats over and over. Today, the **walking bass pattern** is probably the most familiar bass sound in jazz. The plucked bass line moves along step by step by step from note to note to note, one pitch to every beat. Every time Mulligan or James or the melody instrument players move their solos into the B section of the piece, Carter drives them on with a **walking bass pattern.** And in addition, in his own solo, Carter creates interesting and tasteful melodies, like the point where he slows the feel of the piece by moving twice as slow as the basic beat and inserts a bluesy, relaxed bass melody.

Carter was the first jazz master of **multiple stops** on the bass. For years, concert violinists, violists, and cellists performed chords on their instruments by learning how to place the fingers of their left hand on two or three strings at a time and then bowing or plucking the strings simultaneously. Ron Carter brought this technique to jazz and vastly increased the potential of the bass instrument as a solo instrument in its own right. He also used this same left-hand technique for extremely fast melodic solos by setting up combinations of notes with

THE MUSICIANS SPEAK   GEORGE DUVIVIER

I was never really part of the bebop scene, although I used to drop in to Minton's after Teddy Hill became manager. I'd sit in and jam once in a while, but mostly I just came to listen. . . . Charlie Christian was a great influence on me because of his solo lines. He could swing you to death with just one note! By the time he moved off that note, everyone was in mid-air. The first time I heard him play was with Benny Goodman. Then they issued some earlier things from Minton's. They were recorded under the worst circumstances, but they were important because they really showed off Christian. He would play seven or eight choruses and never repeat himself. It was just amazing.

The new music affected the older guys like Coleman Hawkins. Of course, there were the so-called "moldy figs"—the staunch dixielanders or "two-fours," as we called them. There was a lot of territory in between them and the boppers which covered everything I was involved in: swing, jazz . . . whatever you want to call it. In those days bop was considered the raw edge of jazz; they were the radicals. Now the boppers are almost the moldy figs. If the moldy figs heard some of the music of today, they'd be in hysterics!

his left hand while plucking rapidly over various strings with several fingers of his right hand, something akin to the finger technique of classical guitarists. All of these devices can be heard in a careful listening to Carter's accompanimental and solo work.

Harvey Mason's drum solo is another fascinating creation. His work is almost as much melodic as it is rhythmic. There is no question in his playing that he, too, is following the formal structure of the piece, ABA. He moves from one set of patterns and devices to another to clearly indicate the bridge, and when he returns to the final A he clearly plays the LSR motive to make a smooth transition to the **head** and **final chorus.**

All in all, the **sidemen** of Mulligan's band serve well the dual function of rhythm section/ensemble performer and featured soloist. They are masters of their instruments, responsible members of the band, and exciting soloists in their own right. In the years after this concert, some will move to international prominence while others remain in the background, the world of the **sideman,** the musician who makes possible the solo flights of the great artists.

The late 1940s were a very busy time for me. I was active in many different groups at the same time, living a very full musical life. I worked in the Cafe Society Downtown with pianist Dave Martin. . . . You walked in and went downstairs to this very big room. The audiences were very attentive. Leonard Feather lived upstairs in the same building, and I used to see him all the time going up in the elevator. . . .

But we had problems coming and going. There were times we had to go to and from the subway in a convoy! It seems that some of the local hoodlum element resented musicians. I never knew the reason. I don't think it was racial, because they were equally hard on blacks and whites. It was the old "gang" syndrome. Some of the performers just took cabs from the door of the club, but I had to get the 6th Avenue subway. Mundell [Lowe] was only living a block from the club at the time, so he had to walk also. We had some pretty exciting times! These thugs weren't too smart. We always knew when they were waiting for us because they'd signal each other by whistling. That would alert us to pick up a garbage can lid or some other weapon. During one particular altercation, we got hold of a few of them and laid waste! After that, they left us alone.

REVIEW   11

Primary Goal of Unit 11

To understand the role and responsibilities of the **sideman** in jazz.

Study Questions

1. How do most successful jazz musicians receive their training in jazz? What role do formal studies in music play? What about formal training in jazz studies?

2. Can you explain the difference in the working relationship of members of two combos, one a group with **leader** and **sidemen** and the other a **cooperative**?

3. Can you define:

> **name band?**
> **book?**
> **gig?**
> **kicking off a piece?**
> **modal** playing?

4. What is the nature of the formal scheme of *K-4 Pacific?*

5. Who are:

> Bob James?
> Ron Carter?
> John Scofield?
> Gerry Mulligan?

6. In jazz music, what is:

> an **introduction?**
> a **drone?**

multiple stops?
walking bass pattern?

Other Concepts

1. In many areas of the entertainment industry we hear of men and women **paying their dues.** What is the meaning of **paying dues?** Does it have anything to do with the Musicians' Union and Union Dues?

2. Can you discuss some of the aspects of bonding in the jazz community?

3. Carnegie Hall was, and still is, a premiere center in America for classical music. Why do you suppose it has been used periodically since the 1920s for jazz concerts?

Improvising Brass I

12

LOUIS ARMSTRONG, JACK TEAGARDEN, AND BIX BEIDERBECKE
NEW ORLEANS AND CHICAGO

You know, I have been doing so well on the stock market lately, I'd like to take you out and treat you to some music at the "Chez Imagination" to celebrate my success. We've had a bull market for two or three years now, since the middle of 1926, and I can afford to put some money in the musicians' coffers. Our new president, Herbert Hoover, has assured us that this prosperity will never end, and he ought to know!

You will be pleased to learn that Mr. Imagination has arranged an impressive evening of improvising brass for us at his club tonight, and that ought to give us an excellent opportunity to listen to some of the fine points of trumpet and trombone solos. He is bringing a few players back to the club for return engagements, and he has booked a couple of new players for tonight's fare so you might have an opportunity to compare one musician's ideas and technique with another's. The object of our evening, besides having fun and toasting the bull market of 1929, is not to see which player is better or best, for all the players are truly great in their own way, but to distinguish some of each man's unique characteristics and to learn to hear some of the fine points of each man's playing.

From the origins of jazz to the present, trumpet players have played a key role. The brilliant, loud, clarion tones of this soprano brass instrument led the parades of New Orleans from the amusement park to the pleasure palace, and from the church to the graveside and back to the wake. Just as we have seen the possibility of learning jazz history by studying piano players alone, we can also trace the history of jazz through the names and accomplishments of the famous trumpet players alone—Buddy Bolden, King Oliver, Louis Armstrong, Bix Beiderbecke, Cootie Williams, Roy Eldridge, Harry James, Dizzy

Gillespie, Clifford Brown, Maynard Ferguson, Miles Davis, Wynton Marsalis, and many, many more. Wonderful players, improvising creators, and all of them distinct, one from another.

The slide trombone has just as illustrious a history, but its role in the jazz ensemble has changed more than that of the trumpet over the years. The trombone began its life in jazz as a tenor brass instrument that balanced the melodic activities of the trumpet with countermelodies that filled in the gaps, added necessary harmonies, and inserted characteristic sliding and shaking pitches that sprang naturally from the nature of the instrument itself. Over the years, it grew into a virtuoso solo instrument as player after player pushed the instrument's limits through new frontiers as they developed new techniques and acquired greater control. No need to overemphasize this point, but one can also trace the history of jazz through the music of the trombone players as well as the pianists and trumpeters, for trombones

Louis Armstrong and Jack Teagarden set new standards of virtuoso trumpet and trombone solo playing. Their innovative solos were always filled with fresh ideas, emotional content, and the critical element of swing.

were there at the beginning, to accompany the trumpeters on their musical errands in New Orleans in the early days, and they are still a vital part of the most exciting ensembles of today. From Kid Ory to George Brunis and Jack Teagarden, through Tricky Sam Nanton, Bill Rank, and Miff Mole, to J. J. Johnson, Frank Rosolino, and Slide Hampton, to Bill Watrous, Ray Anderson, and Steve Turre one can trace development, evolution, and revolution. The trombone is an instrument capable of great physical excitement, warm emotional feeling, and crackling sharp humor. The trumpet and the trombone are the two primary solo brass instruments of jazz.

Look at that marquee—Louis Armstrong, Jack Teagarden, and Bix Beiderbecke! Pretty hard to do better than that. Because the club has showcased so many name attractions from several different eras in their recent bookings, it has attracted a huge following. Mr. Imagination has a capacity house tonight. Even though I called for reservations, was willing to pay a stiff cover charge as well as a minimum, and mentioned I was friends with the boss, the lady on the phone at first told me I was too late. Said they were booked solid. However, after talking with the boss, it seems that a sizable tip for the maître d' will get us a tiny table in the far corner. We can squeeze in. No problem! It's still a good day.

Even though we are a long way from the bandstand, we shouldn't have any trouble hearing the brass; they can easily fill the hall with sound. But if you can't see, try standing up. Since we are back against the far wall, we shouldn't bother anyone by standing. Hey, look! Louis Armstrong is coming on now with his group, and he will lead off with our old favorite, *Knockin' a Jug.* That's the piece I had you listen to a while back when we were reviewing. I didn't say anything about the music then, but I will now. Do you remember it? You were supposed to listen and quiz yourself and your friends about what you heard to see how well you understood what we had covered up to that point. Ah, good! I'm glad you remember. Louis Armstrong recorded it just a few months ago, March of 1929, if I remember right, and he'd love to sell a few more copies this chilly September evening. He's here with the same group of his friends that he used to record the piece in the studio. He only just returned to Manhattan from Chicago a few months before, and two of the players, **Jack Teagarden** and **Joe Sullivan,** met and played a while in Chicago before coming here recently. The others are all New York musicians.

Notice anything unusual about the group? That's right. Armstrong is African-American, but the others are not. The rest of the world may be trying to separate black from white, but in jazz there is a camaraderie that transcends bigotry. It's how you play and what you've got to say that counts. Although it is still tough for black and white musicians to work together in most public places, especially in September, 1929, Mr. Imagination and his jazz patrons are color blind, and we're the better off for it.

They're on the bandstand, ready to go now, so let's listen.

LOUIS ARMSTRONG, *KNOCKIN' A JUG* (CD SELECTION 1.13)

The trombonist, Jack Teagarden, nods to the guitarist, Eddie Lang, and Lang starts the brief **intro** at a relaxed, strolling **tempo.** Did you notice he is not **strumming** chords, like some of the other guitarists we heard did, but **arpeggiating** them, that is, playing the notes of the chord melodically, one note after another? And isn't that a beautiful guitar sound? Even though it is soft and quiet, much like a classical guitar, it is full and rich, because this unamplified instrument, an **acoustic guitar,** has a big hollow body to act as a sound box or resonance chamber, just like violins and cellos do. Also, Eddie Lang has such a great touch. He makes the notes sound so even and smooth.

Now listen to Teagarden as he enters. The world hadn't heard beautiful solo trombone work like this before Teagarden came along. What a magnificent sound he gets, and he has such mastery of the upper range of the instrument. Did you notice he started right out on a solo improvisation rather than playing a **head?** The way he makes his trombone sing you would think he is playing a standard melody that everyone knows. How long did it take you to figure out that he was improvising to the blues? Half a chorus, more? This is one of those jazz pieces with no melody, just a series of blues choruses for the musicians to improvise. Teagarden is such a lyrical player you can easily take his solo line and sing it as a melody. Also, notice the way he makes his instrument "talk." He bends the sound, varies the articulation, changes the pace of his notes just like a person does in conversation, especially at the start of his second chorus where he repeats one pitch over and over with various inflections to tell the world what he thinks. His music is expressive on many levels. Did you know Jack

Louis Armstrong (1901–1971) was jazz's first great trumpet soloist and most prominent leader for many years. He grew up impoverished in the Storyville district of New Orleans and learned to play the cornet while in a home for juvenile delinquents. After his release, he played with King Oliver, then considered the best cornet player in New Orleans. When Oliver left for Chicago, Armstrong took his place in the band led by Kid Ory.

is a great singer, too? Sometime later you ought to hear him and Louis do their thing on *Rockin' Chair*. They'll blow you away. Minor detail that they don't record it together until 1947, but this is the year, 1929, when Louis recorded *Rockin' Chair* with the composer, Hoagy Carmichael. This is some year! When you do get a chance to hear Teagarden and Armstrong sing together, you'll know why they are considered two of the greatest singers in jazz.

By the way, did you catch the great stick work the drummer, Kaiser Marshall, played while he was **backing** Teagarden's first chorus? He was rolling and tapping those **sticks** on the solid **rim** of the drum, not on the stretched calfskin **drumheads.** Even if you can't see the drums from where you are sitting, you can tell from the sound that he was playing on the **rim** rather than on, say, a **wood block.** The **rim,** although not originally designed to make music, is high pitched and has a kind of dry, not-too-resonant wooden sound, like a table top. Who knows, maybe he was playing on the table top! If Marshall had been playing on a hollow **wood block,** however, the sound would

Jack Teagarden, one of the first great trombone soloists in jazz, had a sense of humor and personality that perfectly matched that of his friend Louis Armstrong. The warmth and beauty of Teagarden's sound was matched by the easy virtuosity of his technique and his inventive musical ideas. He was also one of the great jazz vocalists of his day.

have been lower, fuller, and more resonant. A drummer actually has a tremendous variety of percussive sound resources at his disposal in his complete drum kit that he can bring to the music if he has the imagination and taste to pull it off. Obviously, Marshall is not lacking in these categories. Now listen to what he plays behind Teagarden's second chorus. Right! He traded his sticks for **brushes,** and he rubs and pats new patterns on the head of the snare while the snare wires vibrate in sympathy against the other head on the opposite side. Pretty slick, huh?

If you were listening very carefully, you would have noticed that Joe Sullivan, the pianist, was also playing along in the background. The sound didn't carry well in this crowded club, so you may have missed it, but he was playing **stride** piano, along with the guitar and drum, to accompany the trombone. You remember this stride technique from when Mel Powell was playing *China Boy* with Benny Goodman. It's basically the same here, even at this slower **tempo.** And I am sure you know that **stride** gets its name from the jumping, or striding, left hand, which hits a bass note first and then jumps up, or strides, to a chord in the middle of the piano. That left hand continues alternating back and forth—left-right, bottom-middle—with a few variations while the right hand tinkles away, ornamenting chords or playing melodies in the right hand. Good stuff, stride piano, and hard to do, too.

Guitarist Eddie Lang was a key figure in the transference from banjo to guitar in the jazz ensembles of the 1920s. He is shown here with his unamplified, acoustic instrument in 1929.

Eddie Lang's guitar solo, which follows, is pretty, but not terribly interesting, although I do like the way he bends those pitches. Happy Caldwell's tenor sax solo, which follows Lang's, reminds me of background music for a tap dancer's "soft shoe routine." It is cute, light, and bouncy, and it is supported by the steady thumping of Kaiser Marshall's brushes on every beat of the bar. The drum lays down the beat and the tenor does the bouncing and syncopating. After the tenor finishes, Joe Sullivan throws in a respectable stride piano solo, too, but none of the three guitar, tenor, and piano solos will probably ever earn a notable place in the annals of jazz. But what follows will. Louis Armstrong's solo is superb!

LOUIS ARMSTRONG, *KNOCKIN' A JUG* (CD SELECTION 1.13)

The secret of Louis's solo is its combination of **double time** phrases along with patterns in the slow regular time of the piece. What do I mean by double time? Well, it's like this. If Louis were going to play a **phrase,** that's a complete short musical statement, like a simple sentence or a clause in English, that was going to fill this much time:

ONE COMPLETE MUSICAL THOUGHT
Louis |————————————|

along with the rest of the musicians who were also playing accompanying music to fill the same amount of time:

ACCOMPANIMENT FOR ONE COMPLETE MUSICAL THOUGHT
Band |————————————|

but played twice as fast, or with twice as many notes as would normally be expected, it would sound as if he crushed his ideas into half the space and was able to crowd in twice as many ideas into one full unit of music. Like this:

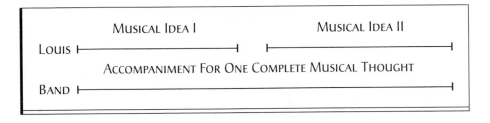

This is precisely what Armstrong does. Also, it gives the piece an unexpected surge of rhythmic fire and vitality. He plays the first four measures in double time, relaxes into regular time for the next two, then peps it up for another four of double time, and ends his first chorus with two at regular speed. This also divides the twelve measures of the blues into an interesting pattern. Normally they are played 4 + 4 + 4, and the band does just that. Louis plays 4 + 2 + 4 + 2 right on top of their three equal parts. Pretty slick. Then in his second chorus he sticks to regular time but goes up an octave to the high notes of his soprano brass instrument and begins to "talk" a solo, much as Teagarden did in his second chorus. He plays a great "high d," a kind of high note he was famous for; throws in a "rip," an upward sliding pitch to a high note; even "clams" one, (**play a clam,** play a botched note [remember that in the live recordings of 1929 you didn't have the luxury of asking a studio engineer to clean up your mistakes and substitute correct notes]); and then surprises everyone at the very end of his solo by slipping into double time again and extending the phrase into a great unaccompanied solo flight. It is this brilliance of imagination and virtuosity of technique that earned Louis Armstrong the honor of being jazz's first great, most famous, and most important jazz musician. From his apprenticeship in New Orleans in the first two decades of this century, to his spectacular work in Chicago and New York in the 1920s and '30s, to his continued leadership in the classic jazz revival of the 1940s, and his elder statesman persona and influence of the '50s and '60s, "Pops," or "Satchmo," as he was known to his millions of admirers, was probably the most influential jazz musician of all time. He is one man you will want to learn more about, and his hundreds of classic recordings will be fun for you to explore as you find the time and money.

Bix Beiderbecke, a self-taught cornetist from Iowa, developed a love of jazz despite his family's disapproval. He worked in the Chicago area until 1924, when he met Frankie Trumbauer and began a life-long association with the saxophonist.

A younger white musician who was tremendously influenced by Armstrong, Bix Beiderbecke, will play next. Perhaps we should order another round of drinks. While Bix was in high school in a suburb north of Chicago, he and his buddies would sneak out of school and go down to Chicago's South Side to hear Armstrong play. It didn't do much for Beiderbecke's school work, but he did learn a lot about jazz. Beiderbecke has his own group here tonight, Bix Beiderbecke and His New Orleans Lucky Seven (none of them are from New Orleans, but you know how Show Biz is), but he has been a sideman most of his life. He's been playing with Frankie Trumbauer, Jean Goldkette, and Paul Whiteman, but it is his work with his own Chicago Style combo, or Trumbauer's, that I like the best. Chicago Style? What's that? Well, we'll talk about **jazz styles** later, but let me just say here that the first fully developed jazz style was what we call **New Orleans Style Jazz,** because that's where it developed shortly after the beginning of the 20th century. A lot of those musicians moved to Chicago to play, including Louis Armstrong's teacher, King Oliver, and they, of course, brought their music with them. So, they were playing **New Orleans Style Jazz** in Chicago when they started playing there just before "The Roaring Twenties," the 1920s, that is. Then two things happened. Their music began to change naturally as it and the musicians matured, and it also began to change from the input of local Chicago musicians and from what they learned from music originating elsewhere, especially New York, St. Louis, and Kansas City. We'll talk about some of the differences in the sounds of the original **New Orleans Style Jazz** and the slightly later **Chicago Style Jazz,** but both of them are considered to be, and are called, **classic jazz** and **traditional jazz,** which the jazz buffs abbreviate to **trad jazz. Bix Beiderbecke** was probably the most famous of the local, Midwest-born **Chicago Style** players, and Louis Armstrong, of course, was not only the most famous **New Orleans Style Jazz** player but was also a key figure in the development of the newer, more modern **Chicago Style.** After all, his most productive years of classic recordings were spent largely in "the windy city."

Here comes Bix and his New Orleans Lucky Seven now, and they are going to play a great tune called *Goose Pimples.* Now notice that Bix plays **cornet.** Remember, it is just like a trumpet but constructed a little differently to get a more mellow tone. Oh, we are in for a treat. See that huge saxophone? That's a **bass saxophone,** and its player, **Adrian Rollini,** is a real master. The combo will use the **bass sax** in place of a string bass or tuba in the rhythm section, and this group is going to really swing. Don Murray is a good clarinetist, but not one of the greats. However, since we are focusing on brass, be sure to pay special attention to **Bill Rank** on trombone and compare his playing with that of Jack Teagarden. He, too, is good, but he lacks that special quality that sets the great player apart from the crowd. Also notice, there's a **banjo** in the rhythm section, not a guitar, and it will be played by Howdy Quicksell. A **banjo** has a long history in jazz and ragtime, and it is different from the **guitar** we just heard Eddie Lang play because it has membrane, like calf skin, stretched over a hoop for the

This group of young musicians in 1925, Bix Beiderbecke and His Rhythm Jugglers, was photographed at a recording session in the Gennett Studios. The young man with glasses and trombone on Bix's left is future bandleader Tommy Dorsey. The other musicians are (left to right): Howdy Quicksell, banjo; Tommy Gargano, drums; Paul Mertz, piano; and Don Murray, clarinet.

body of the instrument, and it used steel wire strings, even in the early days, to give it a bright, metallic sound. Once you hear it strummed and see it played, you won't forget it. And the last musician in the combo is the pianist Frank Signorelli. He's first-rate. Looks like they are ready to start. Bix is setting the tempo, and here they go.

BIX BEIDERBECKE, *GOOSE PIMPLES* (CD SELECTION 1.17)

Did you catch the **intro,** the introduction? The cornet, clarinet, and trombone played three chords, the **bass sax** answered, and the drums punctuated with a cymbal crash. Then the pattern was elaborated into a highly syncopated pattern of sounds that makes you want to get up and dance, and this music was meant to accompany the dance, the fox-trot of the 1920s. Much fun.

Tell you what, since the form of *Goose Pimples* is a little complicated, let me sketch an outline for you to help your listening. If you need it, use it; if not, don't worry about it. We're mainly supposed to be enjoying the solo brass work this evening.

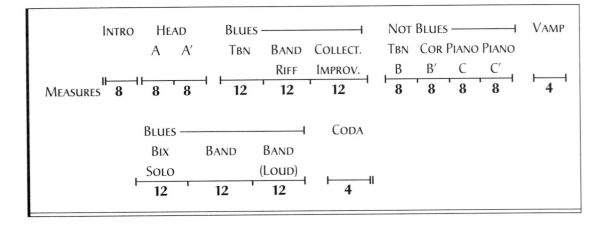

	INTRO	HEAD		BLUES ————————			NOT BLUES ————————				VAMP
		A	A′	TBN	BAND	COLLECT.	TBN	COR	PIANO	PIANO	
					RIFF	IMPROV.	B	B′	C	C′	
MEASURES	8	8	8	12	12	12	8	8	8	8	4

	BLUES ————————			CODA	
	BIX	BAND	BAND		
	SOLO		(LOUD)		
	12	12	12	4	

THE MUSICIANS SPEAK   LOUIS ARMSTRONG

By this time I was beginning to get very popular around that good old town of mine. I had many offers to leave Kid Ory's band, but for some time none of them tempted me. One day a red-headed band leader named Fate Marable came to see me. For over sixteen years he had been playing the excursion steamer *Sydney*. . . . When he asked me to join his orchestra I jumped at the opportunity. It meant a great advancement in my musical career because his musicians had to read music perfectly. Ory's men did not. Later on I found out that Fate Marable had just as many jazz greats as Kid Ory, and they were better men besides because they could read music and they could improvise. Fate's had a wide range and they played all the latest music because they could read at sight. Kid Ory's band could catch on to a tune quickly, and once they had it no one could outplay them. But I wanted to do more than fake the music all the time because there is more to music than just playing one style. I lost no time in joining the orchestra on the *Sydney*.

My last week in New Orleans while we were getting ready to go up river to Saint Louis I met a fine young white boy named Jack Teagarden. He came to New Orleans from Houston, Texas, where he had played in a

After the **intro,** did you notice that this piece is a combination of 8-bar choruses and 12-bar blues? Bix plays lead on the **head** twice through, a repeated 8-bar AA' structure, and Don Murray takes off on clarinet for the first solo chorus, which is a 12-bar blues. Then something new for us happens—the band plays a **riff,** a repeated short phrase that fits the first four measures of the blues, is played again for the second four measures of the blues, and could be repeated, although it isn't here, for the last four measures, as well. The band plays the next blues chorus in a fashion known as **collective improvisation;** that is, the rhythm section keeps pumping out the basic harmonies and rhythms while the front line of solo instruments improvises together with solos that weave in and out of each other.

Suddenly, the band is back to the shorter 8-measure phrasing, but using material from the blues **riff.** Pretty clever. Did you catch it? For the rest of the piece they keep shifting back and forth between 8- and 12-measure patterns, do a little key changing, and even throw in a 4-measure **vamp,** a musical connector. You sure don't have to catch all those things to enjoy this piece, because it swings so elementally from

band led by Peck Kelly. The first time I heard Jack Teagarden on the trombone I had goose pimples all over; in all my experience I had never heard anything so fine. Jack met all the boys in my band. Of course he met Captain Joe as well, for Captain Joe was a great music lover and he wanted to meet every good musician and have him play on one of his boats. Some of the finest white bands anyone could ever want to hear graced his bandstands, as well as the very best colored musicians. I did not see Jack Teagarden for a number of years after that first meeting, but I never ceased hearing about him and his horn and about the way he was improving all the time. We have been musically jammed buddies ever since we met.

After the first trip to Saint Louis we went up river to Davenport, Iowa, where all the Streckfus boats put up for the winter. It was there that I met the almighty Bix Beiderbecke, the great cornet genius. Every musician in the world knew and admired Bix. He made the greatest reputation possible for himself, and we all respected him as though he had been a god. Whenever we saw him our faces shone with joy and happiness, but long periods would pass when we did not see him at all.

the propulsive drive of Rollini's **bass sax** and Bix's **cornet** leadership. What I hope you did catch, however, are some of the wonderful intricacies of Bix's solo right after the **vamp.** First, his tone is so mellow, and he has such a relaxed phrasing. Then he takes the blues riff as a motivic starter for his solo, varies it in a marvelous pseudo-repetition, and follows that with a slowing down of the notes in his solo that moves them further and further behind the beat. Although Bix loves the blatant hot jazz that is characteristic of this period, which you can hear him blast away during the last chorus of the piece, he was probably the first **cool jazz** musician, the first to make a virtue out of mellow sounds and swinging lightly. The term **cool jazz** won't even be invented for another two and one-half decades, the early fifties, but it was musicians like Lester Young, listening to Bix Beiderbecke recordings for inspiration, who carved a new, cool path in jazz in the

Adrian Rollini, a master of the bass saxophone, brought this instrument to prominence through his recordings with Bix Beiderbecke.

years following. Listen to Bix play the last two measures of the piece. After all the driving bounce of Rollini's bass-propelled fox-trot, those two measures are definitely cool.

Well, it's almost time for intermission, but before we stand up and stretch, let's take a second to compare the contrasting sounds of Louis Armstrong's and Bix Beiderbecke's trumpet and cornet, and the distinctively different playing of Jack Teagarden's and Bill Rank's trombones. Recall Adrian Rollini's marvelous bass sax work, and Kaiser Marshall's inventive drumming. You might even try to compare Joe Sullivan's and Frank Signorelli's piano playing, which were similar in many regards, and then differentiate in your minds the acoustic guitar from the banjo, which is also an acoustic instrument. Lastly, if you were able to spot blues choruses and choruses which were not the blues, so much the better. Now, let's take a break while the musicians have an intermission, and we'll come back for some more brass when the show begins again.

REVIEW   12

**Primary Goal
of Unit 12**

Learn to hear and recognize the individual sound and improvisatory style of brass players Louis Armstrong, Bix Beiderbecke, and Jack Teagarden.

Study Questions

1. What are the names of the two pieces we studied? Who were the musicians in the bands? How was the makeup of the bands different? What year were both recordings made?

2. What are some of the identifiable characteristics you recognized in Louis Armstrong's solo?

3. What are some of the characteristic techniques you heard in the Jack Teagarden solo?

4. What characteristics set Bix Beiderbecke's playing apart from that of other trumpet and cornet players?

5. What is Chicago Style Jazz? What is its relationship to New Orleans Style Jazz?

6. What is classic jazz? What is trad jazz?

7. Who was Adrian Rollini? When he played, what function did he serve in the overall performance of the band?

Other Concepts

1. What is the difference between an acoustic guitar and a banjo?

2. Describe the sounds listed on page 143.

a. a trumpet
b. a slide trombone
c. a cornet
d. playing on the rim
e. using brushes on a snare

3. What is collective improvisation?

4. Can you explain a little of the concept of cool jazz that had its roots
   in the playing of Bix Beiderbecke?

5. What is a vamp?

6. What happened on Tuesday, October 29, 1929? How do you suppose this affected the band business and jazz musicians?

Improvising Brass II

13

DIZZY GILLESPIE, MILES DAVIS, J. J. JOHNSON, AND RAY ANDERSON
BEBOP AND AVANT-GARDE

This night is very special, for the show's a "triple header." We heard **early jazz** before intermission when Mr. Imagination turned back his clock to 1929. Now, for the second half of the show, he promises to reset this magic timepiece to the mid-1940s. He will then introduce some **modern jazz** musicians and finally close the evening with some younger musicians playing in the 1990s. Now isn't that a hoot? We'll have the opportunity of hearing trumpeters **Dizzy Gillespie** and **Miles Davis,** and trombonist **J. J. Johnson** in the company of their friends, most notably saxophonist **Charlie Parker;** and lastly, we'll have a chance to hear the innovations and extraordinary virtuosity of trombonist **Ray Anderson.** In one evening we'll have had the opportunity of hearing some of the founding fathers—**Satchmo, Teagarden,** and **Bix;** then a few of the men who served to catalyze the art through evolution and revolution into a new style called **bebop—Dizzy, J. J., Bird,** and **Miles;** and finally a quartet of young men working today to build on the past and shape the future with distinctive new ideas and sounds—**Ray Anderson** and his sidemen.

Since good jazz clubs don't allow chatter during the performances, perhaps you'd like to ask some questions now during the intermission, while our waitress brings us some food and drink. Why did I call these after-intermission performers **modern jazz** musicians? Good question! You know, when jazz first started, there was basically only one kind of jazz, **hot jazz,** and all the fans who liked jazz accepted it all. Jazz was that "hot," sometimes rough or earthy fun music with the syncopated beat, which contrasted with that other kind of popular music, the "sweet," usually polished and proper sound of the parlor song and the society dance orchestras. Then as time progressed, jazz began to change and people began to notice distinctions between one kind of jazz and another. Partly because of the contribution of ideas

144

from New York, Kansas City, and Chicago, and partly because of the development of larger jazz bands and the involvement of arrangers, a new style called **swing** was recognized in the 1930s as being different from the older **traditional jazz.** Of course, the critics and the record companies got involved. They were pleased to separate one kind from another, because it gave the critics something to write about, and it gave the record companies "new" products to sell. This name, **swing,** became common in the vocabulary of both the musicians and the listeners. You heard the older **hot jazz** style with the music of Louis and Bix. Louis's music is usually called **New Orleans Style Jazz,** even though he did most of his playing and recording in the 1920s in Chicago; and Bix's music is usually grouped with the music of **Chicago Style Jazz.** Both are **traditional, classic jazz.** And you heard **swing** when you listened to **Benny Goodman** and his sextet play *China Boy.* One of the things you surely noted was how all these older musicians, especially the swing soloists, played right on top of the beat. That was one of the important distinctions of their style.

Well, around the time of the Second World War, about 1939 to 1945, a new group of young musicians, especially **Dizzy Gillespie** and **Charlie Parker,** developed a way of playing that once again

One of the historic bebop concerts took place at Massey Hall in Toronto, Canada, in 1953. While Dizzy Gillespie solos on trumpet, Charlie Parker, alto saxophone, looks on. Bud Powell is at the piano, Charles Mingus is playing bass, and Max Roach is driving the set of traps.

seemed to be radically different. Eventually, all the music in this new style, and those newer styles that followed, were grouped into a general heading called **modern jazz.** Those who played the new way were **modern jazz musicians,** and their music is **modern jazz.**

It's almost time for the musicians to go on, but what's that you say? Is all modern jazz alike? Absolutely not! Modern jazz kept changing, too, but the subsequent styles or substyles are all still considered to be a part of **modern jazz.** The first style was called **bebop,** and that's what **Bird** and **Diz** will play for you on the first number after intermission. After that, **Bird, J. J.,** and **Miles** will play another **bebop** number, but where **Bird**'s and **J. J.**'s improvised solos are **bop** in nature, you will hear in **Miles**'s solo the characteristics of the next style in the progression, **cool jazz.** I'll point out some of these things as we go along and as I get the chance.

Look at that! Time for the second show, and it's 1945. The men are coming on the stand, and as you can see, the combo is a **sextet.** The musicians of the group, **Dizzy Gillespie and His All Star Sextet,** besides **Diz** and **Bird,** are Clyde Hart on piano, Slam Stewart on bass, Remo Palmieri on electric guitar, and Cozy Cole on drums. Dizzy just announced that their first number will be *Dizzy Atmosphere,* and let me just tell you before they start that this piece is based on the chords of a popular song George and Ira Gershwin wrote in 1930, *I Got Rhythm.* It has a simple AABA melody, and if you know the song, you might even try humming the Gershwin melody quietly to yourself from time to time to see if you can keep track of where the sextet or the soloists are while you listen to the piece. A graph of the form of this performance looks like this:

	INTRO	HEAD	ALTO SAX SOLO	TRUMPET SOLO	BASS SOLO
	DRUM TPT	TPT & SAX UNISON	PARKER	GILLESPIE	STEWART
FORM	a	A A B A	A A B A	A A B A	A A B A
MEASURES	4 8	8 8 8 8	8 8 8 8	8 8 8 8	8 8 8 8
	⊢—12—⊣	⊢—32—⊣	⊢—32—⊣	⊢—32—⊣	⊢—32—⊣

	NEW UNISON RIFF	CODA
	TPT & SAX UNISON	TPT
	AABA	a
	⊢—32—⊣	⊢— 8 —⊣

There are many exciting moments by all the players in this performance, including the second unison riff, but try to focus on Dizzy's trumpet work.

DIZZY GILLESPIE, *DIZZY ATMOSPHERE* (CD SELECTION 1.18)

Did you notice in Dizzy's playing that he cruised easily into the upper register of his instrument, playing long melodic ideas with great virtuosity, fire, and clarity at this very fast tempo? Did you hear him sail up to that "high f" on his horn as though playing these "atmospheric" notes should now become the norm and not the exception in trumpet playing? Did you also catch the rapid tonguing on repeated notes near the end of his solo? He used some **false fingerings,** substituting an alternate fingering for the repeat of a note so as to vary the pitch and sound ever so slightly. Through those repeated notes he was able to insert a captivating rhythmic pattern to contrast with his predominately melodic solo. Also, did you hear the wealth of ideas that spilled from his imagination as he improvised that solo? Very few trumpeters could improvise that many choice notes in so short a space of time, and virtually none of those who came before him did, not until Dizzy showed them how. It is not quite fair to say that most earlier trumpeters only played solos that usually elaborated the tune of the piece or swung happily on a few brass clichés of the **Swing Era,** but it is fair to say that Dizzy created long-line solos of great harmonic and rhythmic interest that were unprecedented at the time. His, and Charlie Parker's, solo lines were irregular or asymmetrical in their phrasing, that is, their melodic phrases would last longer than, or fall short of, the regular pattern of the chord changes; and these bebop instrumentalists emphasized the off-beat notes in their melodic lines, in contrast with the swing musicians who generally played right on top of the beat. Also, they had a fondness for chromatic notes, like flatted fifths, augmented elevenths, and the like, notes that are added to the simple chords to create dissonance and give the music spice. This new **bebop** was a music for virtuosos; not just a virtuoso soloist but an entire band of virtuosos.

In composing the head of this piece, Dizzy threw out the original tune of *I Got Rhythm,* but kept, with a few clever alterations to expand the harmonic potential, the chord structure of the piece, the **changes.**

For a melody, he develops the simple turning-pattern **riff** of the **intro-duction** into a repeated pattern for the three repeats of the A section of the **head.** He inserts an extremely difficult to play pattern for the **bridge,** or B section, and then repeats this pattern a half-step lower to make it next to impossible to play at that speed. In other words, **Diz,** with his compatriots, was making a proclamation for **modern jazz** in his music: If you want to become a jazz musician like us, you will have to become *very* proficient on your instrument. He was separating wheat from chaff.

One of the most influential musicians in the history of jazz, trumpeter Dizzy Gillespie was born and educated in the South, but his family moved to Philadelphia, where Gillespie joined them in 1935. He first worked with a band led by Frankie Fairfax, and with this group he earned his nickname, Dizzy. Like Miles Davis, his career encompassed many different styles of jazz, although he is most often referred to as a creator and innovator of the bop sound with saxophonist Charlie Parker and pianist Thelonious Monk in the 1940s.

The same thing happened in trombone playing, and **J. J. Johnson** was the man who got the job done. Up to this time, the trombone had earned respect in several categories of jazz performance that it claimed for its own—a warm and expressive melodic instrument for playing the melody of ballads, the lone sliding-pitch soloist of the jazz ensembles, the leading harmonic brass instrument of the various jazz combos and bands, and more, but it was never thought of as being capable of playing fast, articulate solos at melodic speeds common to the clarinet, saxophone, and trumpet. It was assumed the slide was too awkward to manipulate at speed, certainly not as rapidly as trumpet and reed players moved their fingers over keys, valves, and tone holes. J. J. showed this was not the case. He not only played fast, he played fascinating musical ideas at tempo.

A new band has come on the stand, the **Charlie Parker Sextet** from 1947, and it is featuring both **Miles Davis** and **J. J. Johnson**, on trumpet and trombone, as well as **Charlie Parker** on alto. They are going to play a Parker blues called *Air Conditioning* (also called *Drifting on a Reed* and *Big Foot* on some recordings), and besides **Bird**, **J. J.,** and **Miles,** the ensemble carries Duke Jordan, piano, Tommy Potter, bass, and Max Roach, drums, for a rhythm section. In spite of

Bebop saxophonist Charlie Parker is pictured here with his combo in 1947; a young Miles Davis plays trumpet in this group. Parker had returned to New York from Los Angeles in April of that year. He formed a quintet with Davis, Max Roach, Tommy Potter, and Duke Jordan. The next year, Davis would form his own bop group.

Recording sessions with Miles Davis and his nonet (nine musicians) inspired the cool-jazz period of the early 1950s, when this photo was taken. In 1954, Davis recorded with Sonny Rollins and introduced the stemless harmon mute that provided Davis with a signature sound. The harmon mute, sometimes called the wa-wa mute, fills the bell of a trumpet and focuses all the air from the mouthpiece into the mute. The center stem may be manipulated to achieve the wa-wa effect; Davis removed this stem.

the many magnificent musical events in this piece, try to keep your attention focused on the brass solos, the trombone improvisation of **J. J. Johnson** and the trumpet solo of **Miles Davis.**

CHARLIE PARKER SEXTET, *AIR CONDITIONING* (CD SELECTION 1.19)

First, did you notice that J. J.'s trombone solo was two **blues choruses** long, and that he played his instrument with a **mute** in the bell that altered and softened the sound somewhat? What everyone finds to be most impressive, of course, is his mobility on the instrument. The melodic line of his solo might have been played very effectively by a tenor saxophone, or a trumpet for that matter, and some people even

J. J. Johnson was the first trombonist to incorporate the blistering fast style of bop into his playing. Johnson first played with the Count Basie band, and he later performed in the New York jazz clubs with all the important jazz musicians of the late 1940s: Bud Powell, Charlie Parker, Dizzy Gillespie, etc. In 1954, Johnson reestablished himself as a leading jazz trombonist when he combined with jazz trombonist Kai Winding to form the duo Jay and Kai.

mistake his sound for that of a valve trombone, because the rapid passage of notes is so clear and distinct. Also, J. J. has a strong preference for a rather straight trombone tone, and he doesn't waste much effort on moving the slide on individual notes to create a **vibrato,** which earlier trombonists were prone to do. And, in his solo, you'll hear many of his favorite sounds, like the flatted fifth, and rhythm patterns, which became bebop clichés, that help identify his unique instrumental voice.

Did you like the trumpet solo of the young **Miles Davis** which immediately followed J. J.'s? **Miles** is only 21 years old this year of 1947. You say it was certainly different from **Dizzy's** trumpet solo in *Dizzy Atmosphere?* You are right; it is very unusual, especially when comparing the playing of the older **Dizzy Gillespie,** which we heard just a few minutes ago, also in the company of **Charlie Parker,** with

THE MUSICIANS SPEAK   MILES DAVIS

I love drummers. I learned so much about drums from Max Roach when we were playing together with Bird and living together on the road. . . . He taught me that the drummer is always supposed to protect the rhythm, have a beat inside, protect the groove. The way you protect the groove is to have a beat in between a beat. Like "bang, bang, sha-bang, sha-bang." The "sha" in between the "bang" is the beat in between the beat, and that little thing is the extra groove. When a drummer can't do that, then the groove is off and there ain't nothing worse in the world than to have a drummer in that no groove bag. Man, that . . . is like death. . . .

It's always been a gift with me hearing music the way I do. I don't know where it comes from, it's just there and I don't question it. Like I can hear when the time drops one beat, or I can hear when it's Prince playing the drums instead of a drum track. It's just something I've always had. I mean, I can start my tempo off and go to sleep and come back and be at the same tempo I was in before I went to sleep. I've never questioned whether I was right or wrong about things like that. Because I stop if the tempo is off, if it is wrong. I mean, it just stops me from doing anything. . . .

For me, music and life are all about style. Like if you want to look and feel rich, you wear a certain thing, a certain pair of shoes, or shirt, or coat. Styles in music produce certain kinds of feeling in people. If you want someone to feel a certain way, you play a certain style. That's all. That's

Miles's work here. In contrast, **Miles**'s playing is low-key, quiet, mid-range, and introspective, a new approach to trumpet solo work. A few years later he will be recognized as a person largely responsible for giving birth to a new **modern jazz style, cool jazz,** but today, in 1947, a lot of people think that he plays slow because he doesn't have a lot of technique, and that he plays in the lower register because he doesn't have a good lip. There may be some truth in this criticism, but I believe the truth rests in **Miles**'s real genius to hear the musical world differently. Listen to the way he carefully develops his solo. He takes the first three notes of the opening pattern of his solo and, after a brief extension, plays those same three notes, but this time slightly varied. Then almost immediately, he takes those same three notes and moves them around for a second variation. This technique of motive and development is not common in jazz. In fact, it is extremely

why it's good for me to play for different kinds of people because I pick up things from them that I can use. . . .

So, with 52nd Street open again and Bird back in town, the club owners wanted Bird. Everybody was after him. They wanted small bands again and they felt that Bird would pack them in. . . . I was really happy to be playing with Bird again, because playing with him brought out the best in me at the time. He could play so many different styles and never repeat the same musical idea. His creativity and musical ideas were endless. He used to turn the rhythm section around every night. Say we would be playing a blues. Bird would start on the eleventh bar. As the rhythm section stayed where they were, then Bird would play in such a way that it made the rhythm section sound like it was on 1 and 3 instead of 2 and 4. Nobody could keep up with Bird back in those days except maybe Dizzy. Every time he would do this, Max would scream at Duke [Jordan] not to try to follow Bird. He wanted Duke to stay where he was, because he wouldn't have been able to keep up with Bird. . . . Eventually Bird would come back to where the rhythm section was, right on time. It was like he had planned it in his mind. The only thing about this is that he couldn't explain it to nobody. You just had to ride the music out. Because anything might happen musically when you were playing with Bird. So I learned to play what I knew and extend it upwards—a little *above* what I knew.

difficult to accomplish motivic development under improvisatory conditions, but this is clearly where **Miles**'s thoughts are focused. Throughout the solo, and throughout his more than fifty-year playing career, **Miles** takes this introspective approach of listening and developing while many others follow a trail of virtuosity for its own sake.

For a proper ending to our evening, the "Chez Imagination" has moved its clock near the present, 1990, and asked the remarkable trombonist, **Ray Anderson,** to close the show. What **Ray Anderson** does on his instrument hasn't even acquired a clear stylistic label yet, but it contains a combination of motivic playing, somewhat like the work we heard with **Miles Davis,** a sampling of old and new slide trombone gestures, an incorporation of avant-garde techniques and timbral ideas, and great virtuosic display. His playing is just one of many current avant-garde styles being offered by the young virtuosos of jazz, and in this piece **Ray Anderson** will place it all in the context of a modern/old-fashioned 20-bar blues. Between the **bebop** of **Dizzy Gillespie** and **Charlie Parker,** the first **modern jazz** giants, and the new jazz styles of the present day, there were many other **modern jazz styles** that gained prominence from time to time—**progressive, cool, west coast, east coast, hard bop, funky, modal, free, fusion,** and more. We'll talk about some of these later when we hear the music, but what's important now is to firm up your knowledge of three major subdivisions with which you now have some listening experience—**early jazz, swing,** and **modern jazz.** Review in your mind who some of the innovators in these styles were; refresh in your mind's ears the sounds you would recognize to differentiate these three main categories; and, most importantly, enjoy the next performance, which borrows from and builds on the past.

L I S T E N

RAY ANDERSON, *THE GAHTOOZE* (CD SELECTION 2.1)

So many neat things to listen for. Did you hear how the single-note motive, expressed in a fascinating rhythm configuration, was gradually expanded into an extensive piece? **Miles** was thinking that way in 1947; **Ray Anderson** is doing it in the 1990s. Did you also catch the 20-measure repeated form? The first 19 measures are difficult, but the

Ray Anderson has brought the slide trombone to a new realm of improvisation, one that incorporates all that went before and adds multiphonics, new timbres, extraordinary range, disjunct melodic lines, a modern sense of humor, and more. Multiphonics is the technique which has the trombonist sing or hum through the horn as he or she plays a note. The effect is a chord-like sound achieving two or more notes simultaneously.

piano sets off measure 20 with the 4-note rising pattern in the bass notes of the left hand. How about the variety of sounds **Anderson** gets from his trombone? And the clever use of the slide to swoop notes occasionally and nail the others the rest of the time. Did you notice the fantastic range of his solo, from the low pedal tones, the lowest bass notes of the instrument, to the atmospheric range **Dizzy Gillespie** played in, which is stratospheric for the trombone? And most of all, did you enjoy the happy swing, the driving beat and clever syncopations that punctuated the whole performance? Compare **Anderson**'s performance with that of **J. J. Johnson** and **Jack Teagarden**. Do you see some similarities and differences? Good! Now you are getting the hang of it. Glad you are having a good time.

REVIEW 13

Primary Goal of Unit 13

Learn to hear and recognize the individual sound and improvisatory style of brass players Dizzy Gillespie, J. J. Johnson, Miles Davis, and Ray Anderson.

Study Questions

1. What are the names of the three pieces we studied? Who were the musicians in the bands? How was the makeup of the bands different? What years were the recordings made?

2. What are some of the identifiable characteristics you recognized in the Dizzy Gillespie solo? What makes it a bebop trumpet solo?

3. What are some of the characteristic techniques you heard in the J. J. Johnson solo? What makes it a bebop trombone solo?

4. What characteristics set Miles Davis's playing apart from that of other trumpet and cornet players? Was his solo bebop or cool? Why?

5. What are some of the characteristic techniques you heard in the Ray Anderson solo? Was his unison riff with the other members of his ensemble the same or different from the unison riffs of the Dizzy Gillespie and Charlie Parker pieces you heard? In what ways?

6. What is modern jazz? What is its relationship to New Orleans Style Jazz? to Chicago Style? to swing?

7. What is the relationship of bebop to modern jazz?

8. Who was Charlie Parker? When he played, what function did he serve in the overall performance of the two numbers you studied?

1. What is the difference between a modern jazz combo and a swing band?

2. Describe false fingerings.

3. What are "changes"?

4. What is the "bridge" of a song?

5. Of the following graphic formal schemes of jazz performances, which is:

	(answer)
a. the blues	_____
b. popular song form	_____
c. a variant of the blues	_____
d. something else	_____

1.	AABA ⊢————⊣ 32	AABA ⊢————⊣ 32	AABA ⊢————⊣ 32 . . . .
2.	AA′B ⊢————⊣ 12	AA′B ⊢————⊣ 12	AA′B ⊢————⊣ 12 . . . .
3.	AA′ ⊢————⊣ 32	AA′ ⊢————⊣ 32	AA′ ⊢————⊣ 32 . . . .
4.	AA′B ⊢————⊣ 20	AA′B ⊢————⊣ 20	AA′B ⊢————⊣ 20 . . . .

6. If three styles of jazz, bebop, swing, and traditional jazz, had their principal activities in separate decades, which decades of the 20th century would you assign to swing, trad jazz, and bebop?

Improvising Brass III: The Women 14

TINY DAVIS, MELBA LISTON, AND REBECCA COUPE FRANKS
SWING, BALLADS, MODAL JAZZ, AND MODERN BEBOP

Before we go to the club tonight, we need to sit down and talk a bit. Complex issues don't have simple answers or explanations, and the situation of women in jazz is a little complicated, to say the least. Most jazz musicians are men, and that is a simple fact. But failing to go beyond that observation distorts the real picture. The truth is that women have played important roles in jazz throughout its 100-year history, and the number of female participants is much greater, and the importance of their contributions more significant, than has been commonly assumed. Perhaps a little discussion before we leave for the club might clear the air and help us all understand what's been going down.

Although many female jazz singers are famous and a few female jazz pianists are well known, the contributions of the other women in jazz, the instrumentalists, composers, and arrangers, have been largely overlooked or ignored until recently. As in most professions historically, except those traditionally reserved for women, such as nursing, elementary school teaching, homemaking, and secretarial work, the numbers of successfully participating women have been relatively few compared with the count of participating men. In jazz, essentially an all-male profession from the first New Orleans bands to the present day, women have had to face limited access, segregation, and discrimination. For those talented women who chose to participate and compete in this very competitive field, the going was especially rough. These women musicians had to contend with a lack of encouragement, a paucity of role models, the male reluctance to accept them as equals, the problems of life on the road in otherwise all-male bands, and the stereotypical ideas that certain instruments can only be played properly by men. The brass instruments, in particular, were thought to be unsuitable for women. Male musicians and critics alike asserted women didn't have the power or stamina to master these "masculine" instruments. I brought along a little article to show you that was published in the 1930s in *down beat* magazine. Let me read a bit of it to you.

WHY WOMEN MUSICIANS ARE INFERIOR
SHOULD BE ABLE TO GET MORE OUT OF HORN THAN A MERE CRY FOR HELP

. . . women don't seem to be able to develop a lip which stymies their taking more than one chorus at a time. The mind may be willing but the flesh is weak. . . . women are as a whole emotionally unstable which prevents their being consistent performers on musical instruments. . . . gals are conscious of the facial contortions so necessary in "blowing it out" and limit their power for fear of appearing silly in the eyes of men.

These ideas are nonsense—this is sexist writing. However, it is typical of thought and writing of the time, and since this particular article appeared in what would become the leading trade journal for jazz musicians, it magnified the problem, hid reality, and in fact became but one more obstacle in the path of artistic equality.

It's certain there were not many women brass players in the early days of jazz, but still there were some, and their number is greater than we thought just a few years ago. By the 1930s, several all-women bands, like Ina Ray Hutton and Her Melodears, the Ada Leonard band, the Rita Rio orchestra, Eddie Durham's All-Star Girl Orchestra, and more, were playing for a living and obviously had women trumpet and trombone players, and good ones, too. Still, no woman brass player in jazz has achieved the fame and stature of a Satchmo, Cootie, Little Jazz, Dizzy, Miles, or Wynton, all male trumpeters who, by a first name or nickname alone, are recognized throughout the knowledgeable jazz world. Musical considerations must come first, but don't you suppose there might be some extra-musical reasons that impeded progress and help explain this situation? Think about it, and draw your own conclusions. Tonight, when we go down to the club, lend a sympathetic ear and enjoy the music of a few women who not only made the grade musically but had what it takes to succeed in this virtually all-male profession.

I just called to double check our reservations, and the maître d' said the first band has arrived and is rehearsing for the show. I heard them over the phone in the background, and they are in good form. These **International Sweethearts of Rhythm** went to Europe last summer, July of 1945, to play a USO (United States Organizations) tour for our troops, the occupation forces in France and Germany, and since their return, they have been touring and recording. I can hardly wait, so if you are ready, grab your hat and coat, and let's go have a ball.

Our table is dead center in the club, so you can see from the chairs on the bandstand, the **fronts** (**big band** music stands that look like small desks and carry the band's logo on the front), and the instruments already set up that we are going to hear a big **swing band.** Look, you can see five **fronts** set up in the front line for the reeds and three for the trombones; behind the trombones there are four **chairs** (each musician "holds a **chair**" when he or she is hired for a specific playing job in a band or orchestra—for example, Lester Young held a tenor chair in the Basie band) for four trumpets. Then there's the rhythm section of bass, guitar, and drums behind the **saxes** (the reed section), and the big grand piano is up in front of the left side of the reeds. That's sixteen instrumentalists plus the leader, **Anna Mae**

The International Sweethearts of Rhythm with leader Anna Mae Winburn. Tenor saxophone soloist Viola Burnside sits in the front row, far right, and trumpeter Ernestine "Tiny" Davis sits in the back row, far left. The group was formed in 1937 and had its origins in a swing band at a rural Mississippi boarding school.

Winburn, who will probably stand up-front-center. Not every **big band** has exactly this number of musicians or sets up the same way, but this is a typical arrangement. You might compare it with the setup Don Redman used for his band when we were listening to his music in Unit 5.

	Bass	Guitar		Drums		Trumpet Trumpet Trumpet Trumpet
Saxophone	Saxophone	Saxophone	Saxophone	Saxophone	Trombone	Trombone Trombone
	Piano			Leader		
			(Bandstand)			

The **International Sweethearts of Rhythm** began as a school band in Mississippi in 1937, and they have come a long way since then. The **sidemen** (the musicians of a band, other than the leader or vocalists [women were called **sidemen,** too]) are coming on now, warming up, tuning up, and waiting. Mr. Imagination comes to the **mike** (the microphone), says a few words about coming attractions, gives a little spiel about the band, and shouts an introduction for the leader, **Anna Mae Winburn.** She hustles on, gives a downbeat, and the band blasts through their themesong, *Galvanizing.* Much dancing, thunderous applause, and then **Anna Mae** introduces the next number, saying that their first trumpeter, **Ernestine "Tiny" Davis,** is going to sing the blues, *Jump Children,* and they are off again.

INTERNATIONAL SWEETHEARTS OF RHYTHM, *JUMP CHILDREN*
(CD SELECTION 2.2)

Did you hear the power of those brass players? They really rocked the chandeliers. And you know, it's not like modern recording orchestras where there is a mike and amplifier for every instrument and four or more for the drums. This is an acoustic band. The only **mike** they have for the band is the single stand microphone up front for

Ernestine "Tiny" Davis, an outstanding lead trumpet player, jazz vocalist, and band leader.

announcements and vocals. Occasionally a sax soloist might walk up to the **mike** for a solo, but usually those are played standing up in place in the section. These women aren't timid; they really blow!

You say you didn't get to hear much of **Tiny Davis** on the trumpet, that she sang the vocal and only wailed away on the ending of the piece? Well, that's true. There is not a satisfactory collection of her trumpet solos on record, and we have to settle for what we can get. But actually, her main area of prowess was as the **lead trumpet player** of the band, the section leader, and if you caught what she did on the end of this piece you will know that she performed that function with power, drive, and security. For the rest of the **set,** keep your ears peeled for the drum solos of Pauline Braddy and the tenor sax solos of Vi Burnside, two very well-known female swing soloists of this era who are **sidemen** in the band. If you close your eyes, there is no male or female aspect to the sound of that band, except when the women yell "yeah" during the band vocal. When they blow their horns, it is

Melba Liston was one of the few women to earn a place as a horn player in an otherwise all-male name band; she played trombone with the Dizzy Gillespie big band. She later became a leader of her own ensemble and earned fame as an arranger.

just solid, hard-driving **swing.** Incidentally, did you catch the verse where **Tiny** sang about "rock" and "roll"? You may have thought this was an invention of Bill Haley or Elvis Presley in the '50s. Now you know better.

The **Sweethearts** have finished their part of the show, and what's this? Those are men coming on the stand. I thought we were going to hear women tonight. Why, that's the **Dizzy Gillespie Orchestra** of 1956. I recognize Quincy Jones in the trumpet section and Phil Woods and Ernie Wilkins in the sax section. What's going on? The owner of "Chez Imagination" promised we would hear women brass players tonight. Oh look, there in the trombone section, that's **Melba Liston.** Now I understand.

A very few women were able to earn **chairs** in the all-male name big bands, and **Melba Liston** was one of those few. **Dizzy** is coming to the mike, and, good, he is announcing a solo for **Melba**, *My Reverie*. That's excellent! This is a great tune with fine changes. A composer of the '30s, Larry Clinton, took a classical piano piece, *Reverie* by Claude Debussy, and fashioned a popular song with English words from Debussy's original material. Tonight we'll have a **big band** arrangement of it featuring trombone lead, and **Melba Liston** is going to be the trombone soloist. Let's listen.

DIZZY GILLESPIE, *MY REVERIE* (CD SELECTION 2.3)

Such a gorgeous sound, so rich, full, and mellow. **Melba**'s phrasing is so graceful, and occasionally, with the utmost taste, she'll use that slide to pull a climactic note up into pitch from below. Not too much, just the right vibrato. An occasional lip turn for decoration. Absolutely masterful. And then, did you catch her improvisation? Her solo from the second chorus to the end of the tune was stunning. **Melba** is a great musician, and when we get home and turn our clocks to the 1990s we might consider buying a CD of her recent arrangements for Randy Westin and his band. **Melba Liston** is not only a great player, she is one of jazz's most accomplished arrangers, as well.

Why wait to turn our clocks ahead? Mr. Imagination is going to do it for us now to close the show. A young woman trumpet virtuoso is making the news as one of jazz's most promising talents of the '90s, Rebecca Coupe Franks. She did a fine album with pianist Kenny Barron and tenorist Joe Henderson not too long ago, *Suit of Armor*; and tonight she is here with another fine group. Kevin Hays is her pianist, Yoron Israel her drummer, and Scott Colley on bass to fill out the rhythm section. The group is a quintet, and Donny McCaslin is on tenor. They open with a bluesy Gospel-style piece, *All of a Sudden* and follow with a new tune, *Third Generation Suffragist*. Today's women are more open about declaring their stand on feminist issues, and **Franks** is proud of the fact that she is the third generation of women in her family to vote and have rights denied to earlier generations. Now she is telling us that for her closing number she is going to play an **up tune** (a piece played fast, or at **up tempo**) called *Serendipity*. Pay attention.

*Contemporary trumpet artist
Rebecca Coupe Franks.*

REBECCA COUPE FRANKS, *SERENDIPITY* (CD SELECTION 2.4)

How's that for trumpet playing? Range, facility, tone, ideas — all the things we've become accustomed to expect in a first-rate jazz performance. You must have noticed that this piece is in **pop song form,** our familiar 32-measure AABA structure. Right after she and Donny McCaslin ran those alternating ascending scales for an 8-measure **intro,** they played the **head** basically in unison. Kevin Hays took the first solo on piano, followed by Donny McCaslin on tenor. As we will see again and again, this pattern of **head-improvised solos-recapitulation of head** is the standard procedure of all modern groups from **bebop** on. This group is, in fact, what is known as a **straight-ahead** group, that is, they basically play a modern version of **bebop,** keeping the structure and playing the changes. **Rebecca Coupe Franks's**

trumpet solo drove right through the changes with great facility, but did you notice how it was sprinkled with nice ideas? Her opening lick was a minor version of the first eight notes of *Oh When the Saints Go Marching In.* Bebop players, even modern bebop artists, like to throw in **quotes,** little snippets of other songs that most people know, both for fun and to see if the listeners are on their toes. Then her solo flowed out of that opener, first in the low range and gradually rising into that area that excites listeners with fire and power. Before they returned to the **recap** (recapitulation or repeat) of the **head,** the melody instruments **trade fours** (play short, 4-measure solos followed by other players' 4-measure solos) with the drums. After one chorus of solo trading with the drums, the trumpet and tenor play a unison riff

THE MUSICIANS SPEAK   MARY LOU WILLIAMS

Well, my musical experience was through the men that come to the house to take me out to jam with them or show me what I was doing wrong. I've been around men all my life. Even when I was six years old, I'd be sittin' on a man's lap, playin' the piano, see; and I think my training was different than the training of other musicians . . . because men showed me everything that I know. And now this is an era of women thinking that men don't want them to play. That never happened with me. When Fletcher Henderson and all the big bands, when they came to Pittsburgh, they'd take me out on the gig with them, you know, ask my mother if I could go. And nobody stopped me; they pushed me. Like I'd be on a jam session when I was twelve or thirteen years old with Fats Waller and who else? Willie the Lion and fine famous pianists. And they'd make me play. I'd cry. They said, "Play something." And I'd cry 'cause these other guys sounded like they had 20 fingers. But I'd finally get down and play, and they loved it.

[In the '40s] Thelonious Monk, Bud Powell and I were inseparable. They'd come to the house every day around three or four if they were working nights and stay there until the next day. Thelonious is a nice guy. He's odd. *He's odd.* He doesn't talk much at all. . . . He and I and Bud were friends, very tight, you know. They'd come to the house . . . and we'd write music, play music, you know. And he [Powell] was kind of a funny guy if you asked him to do something. Like, he was working at Minton's, and the owner of the club told him to put the cover on the piano to preserve it.

in alternation with the drums, and this riff sets up a full drum solo by Yoron Israel for another chorus. Then, back to the **head** and out.

	Intro	Head	Piano Solo	Tenor Solo	Trumpet Solo	Fours with Drums	Head	Tag
Measures	⊢ 8 ⊣	⊢32⊣	⊢2 x 32⊣	⊢2 x 32⊣	⊢2 x 32⊣	⊢3 x 32⊣	⊢32⊣	⊢5⊣

This performance really smokes; they play at a blistering tempo. The style of the melodic horn solos, both **Franks**'s and McCaslin's, is that

And he said, "No, I'm not a busboy." And he walked out. He was like that. And Bud really loved Monk, you know. . . . If Bud Powell did anything wrong, I said to Bud, "I'm gonna tell Monk." Then he'd straighten up right away.

Well now, getting back to the old Andy Kirk days—really rough, you know. I've seen more deaths and accidents on the road, but we kept going. Once the cars ran out of gas and we didn't have money to buy gas and the guys were pushing the cars, you know, and Andy fell through a bridge. He has a scar on his leg now from that, you know. A slight opening in the bridge. And John Williams always saved us. In no time it seemed that he would have some money there from his mother—he would borrow from his mother. But that was really some rough days.

Jazz is way beyond the classics or any other music. If you learn how to listen to it and gather what's happening. There's so many things to make. If you were despondent, and said, "I'm going out and listen to a jazz musician," and the good ones—not any old kind—you don't know how happy that makes you. Makes you want to start out fresh the next day, you know. . . . [Jazz] heals and inspires, you know, and everything. Well, in other words, it's God's music. He didn't just claim it like this, but there was suffering, and it's the music that's very badly needed on earth now. . . . there wouldn't be any cancer or stuff like that if everybody played the truth.

of a later bebop style called **modal jazz,** a style of improvisation centered more on shifting scales than on changing chords. Although this piece has chords, with a noticeable shift in harmony at the **bridge,** the B section, there are not very many chords and the harmonies do not change frequently. This choice of **modal** structure allows soloists to focus more on **scalar improvisation,** improvising melodies within a series of acceptable scale patterns rather than melodies to fit a rapidly changing harmonic design, a key feature of **modal jazz.** Also, did you notice how skillful **Franks** and **McCaslin** were at emphasizing the off-beat eighth notes, a little push or accent on the off-beat notes of their running passages. After **Charlie Parker** popularized this technique, it became standard equipment in the performance arsenal of modern jazz players.

Well, we've had a great night. Three outstanding female brass soloists, **Tiny Davis** playing swing, **Melba Liston** blowing a beautiful ballad, and **Rebecca Coupe Franks** wailing away on a modern bebop, straight ahead, **modal jazz** number called *Serendipity.* I guess that's the feeling you get when you successfully make it through an improvised performance at an outlandishly fast tempo.

REVIEW 14

Listen to three outstanding female brass soloists of jazz: Ernestine "Tiny" Davis, Melba Liston, and Rebecca Coupe Franks. Become aware of three styles of performance—swing, ballad (in the swing and bebop big band tradition), and modal jazz.

Primary Goal of Unit 14

1. What constitutes a typical 16-piece big band?

Study Questions

2. Who were the International Sweethearts of Rhythm? What are some of the identifiable characteristics you recognized in "Tiny" Davis' vocal?

3. In music, what does it mean "to hold a chair"?

4. How would you describe Tiny Davis's lead trumpet work?

5. Was Melba Liston part of an all-woman band? What band did she play with? How would you describe her solo on *My Reverie?*

6. How is modal jazz dissimilar from earlier bebop?

7. Describe the group Rebecca Coupe Franks was leading and explain some similarities with, and differences from, traditional bebop.

8. Contrast scalar improvisation (modal jazz) with harmonic improvisation (bebop).

1. What are fronts?

Other Concepts

2. Describe the forms of *Jump Children* and *Serendipity*. The formal structure of *My Reverie* was not discussed. Do you have an opinion of the structure Liston improvised to?

3. What are sidemen?

4. Define:
   a. up tune; up tempo.
   b. straight-ahead jazz.
   c. playing fours or trading fours.
   d. quotes in jazz solos.

5. Our three performances took place in three different decades. Can you place each in an appropriate decade?

Discussion
Topic I

In what way is the role of women in jazz similar to or unlike the role of women in other walks of life?

Discussion
Topic II

In what way is the role of minorities (racial, ethnic, or religious) in jazz similar to or unlike the role of minorities in other areas of the arts, in business, in education, and so on?

Four Pianists before World War II

JELLY ROLL MORTON, JAMES P. JOHNSON, PETE JOHNSON, AND ART TATUM
EARLY PIANO STYLES: NEW ORLEANS, STRIDE, BOOGIE WOOGIE, AND SWING
A DEFINITION OF JAZZ

I love to hear the great jazz pianists, and tonight the "Chez Imagination" is featuring four soloists who span the years from jazz's beginnings through the end of the Second World War. **New Orleans Style, New York stride, boogie woogie** and **swing,** all had their pianists, and tonight we will hear one famous soloist from each of these styles. You would be hard pressed to find greater masters of the keyboard than those on tonight's show, and yet there are many more players of almost equal stature. Jazz has nurtured an incredible crop of the world's finest piano artists, and they not only combine technical mastery of the instrument with great breadth of expression, they also bring simultaneous composition and performance, that is, improvisation, to every performance.

The year is 1939, and we will have the fun of hearing artists at different stages of their careers. The oldest is **Jelly Roll Morton,** a New Orleans Creole, who was already eleven years old when Louis Armstrong was born in another part of the same city. Tonight he is 49 years old, and he has been playing professionally since he was twelve. In fact, he composed his *New Orleans Blues* and his *Jelly Roll Blues* when he was only fifteen. **Jelly Roll Morton** remembers clearly the early ragtime and barrel house piano sounds that provided musical entertainment in the sporting houses of the New Orleans Storyville district when he was a kid, and he even has vivid memories of the legendary Buddy Bolden, the man many people credit as being the first jazz cornet player and band leader. Of course, to hear **Jelly Roll** tell it, *he* invented jazz all by himself. No false modesty or ego problems here! But he is such an extraordinary musician and raconteur, I am not going to be the one to tell him some others might deserve a little of the credit.

Jelly Roll Morton, whose real name was Ferdinand Joseph Lemothe, traveled all over this country, leading jazz bands, recording, and making a living as a pool shark when the music business was slow. His story is truly fascinating, and you might want to find out more about it when you have time. Tonight, he will be first on the program, and I am sure you will be able to hear in his playing a gathering together of many different influences. He listened to classical music as a youngster at the French Opera in New Orleans, as well as to the sounds of the street bands and dance hall pianists. He is, in fact, a man who bridges the gap from **ragtime** to **jazz,** that is from the **pre-jazz syncopated popular music** called **ragtime,** to the swinging syncopated music we all know is **jazz.**

What's that you say? What is **jazz?** I thought you might have figured it out for yourself. Of course, it is all this **improvised music** we have been listening to at the club, the music with the **steady beat,** the **bluesy melodies with minor intervals,** the fascinating **syncopations,** the **changes,** the **individual performance qualities,** and the **characteristic instruments**—you know, like **rhythm sections,** muted trumpets, and the like. A person can't really put a finger on one absolute definition that holds true for every kind of jazz, from swing to free and classic to fusion, but your ears will tell you. If you are looking for a superb meal, follow your nose; when you want to find great jazz, follow your ears. And your ears will tell you that jazz is:

Definition of Jazz

improvised music,
has a steady beat,
follows harmonic patterns called changes,
prefers bluesy melodies,
uses syncopations prominently,
displays individual performer characteristics,
features particular instruments,
held together by a rhythm section.

Got a problem with that? Right, we all do, because no single definition covers all of jazz. For example, we're here to listen to solo piano players tonight. So, where's the rhythm section and the characteristic instrumental sounds? And, how can a piano lower a pitch to get a blues feel in the melody? O.K., you've got me! But I think I can explain some of this away, and if you listen carefully to tonight's music, you'll be able to decide for yourself whether or not you agree with what I say.

First, a piano, in some ways, is like an orchestra. One player can play ten different notes at once, if he or she still has all ten fingers and wants to use them that way. Actually, with a nose, elbow, and feet, a pianist can make more than ten simultaneous sounds. But it goes beyond all that. Every fine pianist develops an individual touch, a way of bringing music out of the instrument in a way unique to that pianist. Also, when playing solo, the left hand often substitutes for the rhythm section while the right hand serves as the lead instrument or some instrumental section, or vice versa. Then, each pianist has certain patterns of notes that are part of a repertory of favorite ideas and preferred sounds that crop up from time to time in different performances. And pianists can intentionally strike two adjacent keys at the same time as one possible way of suggesting the pitches that lie between the two notes, those bluesy sounds we were talking about. So, you see, a good solo pianist can take on the responsibility of an entire band, or can choose to play something sparse that suggests only a solo instrument, or can even, at least in modern music, pluck strings and kick pedals to get sounds that are new and entirely unique to this instrument and player. And if every characteristic of jazz isn't present in every performance, who cares? That's not the point. Making beautiful and exciting music is.

Now that we've got our table and ordered our drinks, let's quickly check the rest of the program before the music starts. After Jelly Roll, **James P. Johnson** is scheduled to play. You know, he is only a year younger than Jelly Roll, and he developed his **stride** jazz technique in **New York.** You'll hear many similarities between the music he plays and that which you'll hear from Jelly Roll, and that brings up a fascinating unanswered question. Was jazz being developed in New York or elsewhere in a different way about the same time as it was developing in New Orleans? **James P.** is the same age as Jelly Roll, New York is a long way from New Orleans, and both men were earning livings as "ivory ticklers" when they were teenagers. Most people don't think so and would guess that **James P. Johnson** was improvising ragtime, not jazz, before he heard the improvisations and style of the New Orleans musicians, but we really don't know. It's one of those questions that will have to remain unanswered for lack of jazz recordings before 1917. By that time, **James P. Johnson** was already 26 years old.

James P. Johnson is known as the "father of stride piano," partly because he taught the great Fats Waller, who in turn was the model for many more fine pianists, like Art Tatum and Joe Sullivan. Also, a couple of **James P.**'s really tough pieces, like *Carolina Shout* and *Keep Off the Grass* were copied note-for-note off the old piano rolls by other fine pianists, such as Duke Ellington, so that they could show off and dazzle their listeners with flying hands and fingers. Thus **James P.**'s notes and rhythms became a measure or standard for the style itself.

Now let's see, who's next? Oh yes, **Pete Johnson,** a great **boogie woogie** piano player from Kansas City. He is fifteen years younger than James P. Johnson and only came to New York three years ago. Last year, 1938, he took part in a "Spirituals to Swing" concert at Carnegie Hall and is working regularly down the street at the Café Society with a boogie woogie trio with Meade "Lux" Lewis and Albert Ammons. He slipped away for this gig at the "Chez Imagination" while his two friends are romping away at the other club. You'll hear that **boogie woogie** is a rather percussive piano style, a real African American dance music that prominently displays its African roots. **Pete Johnson** is a big man, and he really pounds those keys. For him, playing **boogie** is a physical thing, and you'll hear that volume is also a part of the style.

To close the evening, Mr. Imagination is presenting the astounding virtuosity of **Art Tatum.** He is only 30 years old tonight, the youngster of this group, and he has been playing professionally to support himself since he was seventeen. Superb classical pianists, like Vladimir Horowitz, frequent the clubs where **Tatum** plays. Sometimes they simply can't believe what his fingers can do. The technical feats of this blind African American musician are legendary among the pianists. Not just among the pianists. Charlie Parker took a job as dish washer in the New York club where **Tatum** was playing, not just because of the keyboard virtuosity but mainly to hear **Tatum**'s ideas of altered harmonies and his flow of improvisational conceptions. So, all in all, we're going to have another great evening, this cold wintry night in 1939.

Pianist Ferdinand "Jelly Roll" Morton (1890–1941) was one of the very earliest musicians to perform the kind of music that would be identified as jazz. Born in New Orleans, Louisiana, Morton developed a style that would integrate ragtime piano pieces with blues, field hollers, Protestant hymns, minstrel show tunes, spirituals, popular songs, and Caribbean influences. This synthesis formed the earliest jazz music.

Here comes **Jelly Roll Morton** to the stand, dapper as ever, to introduce himself, to tell a few anecdotes about the good old days and then to open with his slow *Buddy Bolden's Blues*. When he plays and sings, "I thought I heard Buddy Bolden say, 'You're nasty, you're dirty, take it away. You're terrible, you're awful, take it away.' I thought I heard him say . . ." we feel transported back to New Orleans in the old days. What a great song, and listen to the applause! **Jelly Roll Morton** is truly the first great composer of jazz.

Now, this next tune is another of his own compositions called *Sporting House Rag*, and it is a reworking and retitling of a virtuoso piano piece he composed and first recorded as *Perfect Rag* in 1924. Here's where you'll get a chance to see a ragtime piece transformed into a jazz composition and performance. The old ragtime composers, like Scott Joplin, wrote out their music and expected pianists to play the notes exactly as written and **not too fast**. Well, **Jelly Roll Morton**'s *Sporting House Rag* has the form of a traditional ragtime piece: introduction, first **strain**, second **strain**, **vamp**, and third **strain** in a new key. **Strain** is just another word for section, and it usually has its own melody, and **vamp** means a short transitional passage that connects one musical section with another. Here, the **vamp** connects the second **strain** with the third and makes a smooth modulation, or change, from one key to the next. You'll hear all these divisions clearly, for the **strains** are repeated, and you can count out the measures from this chart to check on your ears if you want to.

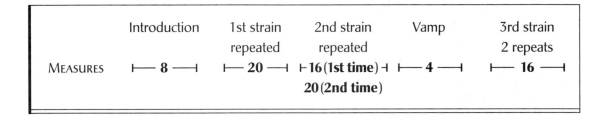

	Introduction	1st strain repeated	2nd strain repeated	Vamp	3rd strain 2 repeats
MEASURES	⊢— 8 —⊣	⊢— 20 —⊣	⊢16 (1st time)⊣ 20 (2nd time)	⊢— 4 —⊣	⊢— 16 —⊣

JELLY ROLL MORTON, *SPORTING HOUSE RAG* (CD SELECTION 2.5)

Now that was classy piano playing. The ragtime pieces were very much like the concert band and marching band marches of the day that were so popular at the turn of the century—you know, John Philip Sousa, Henry Gilmore, and those folk—with their conventions of **vamps,** key changes, and all. But the jazz players, like **Jelly Roll Morton,** gave them new life with a swinging vitality, jazz phrasing, faster tempos, and improvisation. They jazzed them up. Jazzed rags and playing the blues were two of the most important kinds of pieces these early New Orleans musicians played, and these sounds are part of the earliest style of jazz, **New Orleans Style.** If you think the repeat of the **first strain** was the same as when **Jelly Roll** played it the first time through, listen again to the left hand. The first time, he started his left hand with a pattern of descending slow notes; the second time round he bounced it all over the place. There are lots of other changes everywhere, some small and some large, like the time he added four extra bars to the repeat of the **second strain.** The improvised variation I like best appears toward the end of the piece, in the second repeat of the **third strain,** when **Morton** reharmonizes the music for a few bars. Did you catch it?

Now it is **James P. Johnson**'s turn, and he's got quite a following here tonight at the club, judging from the applause he's getting even before he's played a note. As you know, one of America's favorite

A contemporary of Jelly Roll Morton, pianist James P. Johnson is often referred to as the father of stride piano. His work combined aspects of ragtime with other African-American music styles. In 1921, when this photo was taken, Johnson began recording his own compositions for solo piano including "The Harlem Strut" and "Carolina Shout."

songs is his, *Charleston*. It came from a show he wrote, "Running Wild," and many people still dance "The Charleston." What's that he is saying into the mike? Oh super, he is going to play *The Mule Walk*, another of his own compositions. They say that both this piece and the *Charleston* were inspired by actual African American country dances that stemmed from the Southeast, in the coast lands and sea islands near the city of Charleston, South Carolina. Some of the African Americans from this region migrated to New York looking for better work, and they naturally brought their music and dance with them. **James P.** encountered these people and their entertainment and religious ceremonies in Harlem, and he often went to play rent parties in the neighborhood, parties where contributions were collected to help pay the rent, where some of these dances took place. It seems that he picked up some of his ideas for a few of his songs by adapting this American folk music to his style of **stride piano.** Now he's at the piano bench and ready to go. Let's listen.

JAMES P. JOHNSON, *THE MULE WALK* (CD SELECTION 2.6)

Now wasn't that delightful? As you noticed, the piece is really quite simple, but then, all of a sudden, he does something amazing, like in the middle chorus where it sounds like he is playing with three hands. At that point you hear the tinkling in the right hand, the bouncing **stride** in the left, and the solid melody in octaves in the middle. How did he do that? And remember when we were talking about bluesy melodies and bending pitches on the piano? Did you notice near the end of the performance how he crushed two notes together in the melody to squeeze the pitch down? I don't know if he intended to get a mule's bray out of those notes, but that's the way I hear it. Also, in the intro, you had an excellent opportunity to hear the **stride** left hand with some real clarity, because all the right hand does at the beginning is hold a few long notes. Did you notice how the first chorus was played straight, with little variation or complexity, but the second chorus not only got a "middle hand" melody but also received some great syncopations and accents? **James P.** constantly alternates something simple with something more complicated, and, of course, that's what makes the music interesting: tension and release. If everything were difficult and complicated all the time, we'd get tired and bored. That was refreshing.

Here comes **Pete Johnson,** the great **boogie woogie** pianist. All these early piano players had strong left hands, and the **boogie** piano players are certainly no exception. The left hand develops the rock-solid beat of the rhythm section in solo piano work. With **boogie,** the left-hand pattern is a different pattern from that of **stride,** but the function in the music is the same—a metronomic, unyielding beat and a regular repetition of the harmonic pattern, the **changes.** There are several melodic or chordal patterns that **boogie** piano players use in their left hand, but none of them bounce up and down the keyboard as you have heard and seen the **New Orleans** and **stride** piano play-ers use. Sometimes they employ a rhythmic chordal pattern, and other times it is a rhythmic/melodic ostinato pattern in the bass, something repeated over and over, but nearly always the left hand plays **eight-to-the-bar,** that is, a rhythm pattern that strikes twice as frequently as the **stride** pattern, which is **four-to-the-bar.** Another thing about **boogie,** it is nearly always used with the **blues,** our favorite twelve-bar repeated harmonic pattern. I'll bet that when you hear **Pete John-son**'s *Boogie Woogie*, you will think of rock 'n' roll. Where do you think Elvis, Jerry Lee Lewis, and Bill Haley, as well as the Rhythm and Blues performers before them got their ideas? It didn't spring out of thin air; it came from **boogie woogie.** Let's listen.

PETE JOHNSON, *BOOGIE WOOGIE* (CD SELECTION 2.7)

	Blues	Blues	Blues	Blues	Blues	. . . .
MEASURES	⊢—12—⊣	⊢—12—⊣	⊢—12—⊣	⊢—12—⊣	⊢—12—⊣	. . . .

I certainly appreciate Mr. Imagination taking us to 1939. It is such a vintage year; so much great music and so many different kinds. Did you get the feeling, while you were listening to **Pete Johnson**'s *Boogie Woogie*, that you were hearing party music? Actually, it is a kind of poor people's party and dance music, because when you can't afford to hire a band you can always scrape up the cash to pay the single piano player you need for **boogie.** Some of the bands of the Swing Era played **boogie woogie** tunes, but **boogie** is primarily solo piano music, a unique form of the blues, a dance and party music, a music filled with percussive energy and the rhythmic complexity of a steady left hand and a romping right.

    Art Tatum is a different kind of pianist. His music persuades with elegance and finesse. Leonard Feather, an excellent pianist and one of jazz's best critics, believes that **Art Tatum** was the greatest soloist in jazz history, regardless of instrument. That is high praise indeed!

Pete Johnson was a big man who could make a piano swing. With a rollicking left hand and a driving right, he energized his boogie solos with power and invention.

When Leonard Feather first heard **Tatum** at the "Three Deuces," a club on 52nd Street near here, he discovered Duke Ellington listening in a corner and Mary Lou Williams seated at a front table. The best working musicians lead busy lives and can't spare much time to sit in the audience for a colleague's performance. They made the time to hear **Art Tatum,** because he had a unique gift they understood and admired. Tonight, we are going to witness some of the miracle ourselves. What is it that Mr. **Tatum** is saying into the microphone? Oh yes, he is going to play the piece that was his first solo piano recording in 1933 when he was just 23 years old, *Tea for Two* by Vincent Youmans. Unlike some of the jazz musicians we have been listening to, **Art Tatum** was not a composer of original tunes. He preferred to take jazz standards and popular songs and rework them through his jazz improvisations. *Tea for Two* is a popular song of 32 measures that is divided into four 8-measure phrases. The first and third phrases are the same, but the second and fourth are different, so that is the pattern that **Tatum** will repeat over and over as he creates his fantastic elaborations and transformations: A B A C I A B A C I A B A C... In his **swing style,** he not only uses the left hand in the bouncing **stride** patterns, he sometimes shifts to a series of parallel chords in the left hand that walk up and down the keyboard stepwise. Most of the melodic virtuosity takes place in the right hand, but there is one place that **Art Tatum** throws in an incredibly fast running passage in the left hand. Don't miss it.

Art Tatum was born in 1909 and acknowledged Fats Waller as a primary inspiration. Tatum was blind in one eye and had only partial vision in the other but learned to read music at the Toledo School of Music—virtually his only formal training. Tatum incorporated both swing and stride piano into his own style, bringing improvisation to a new level through his virtuosity on the keyboard.

L I S T E N

ART TATUM, *TEA FOR TWO* (CD SELECTION 2.8)

	INTRO	1st chorus	2nd chorus	3rd chorus	4th chorus
		A B A C	A B A C	A B A C	A B A C
MEASURES	4	8 8 8 8	8 8 8 8	8 8 8 8	8 8 8 8
		⊢— 32 —⊣	⊢— 32 —⊣	⊢— 32 —⊣	⊢— 32 —⊣

Did you hear the way he threw off the rhythm at several places in the third chorus? Improvisation in jazz is not just inventing notes to fit to a chord pattern. It can also be, as it was here in the third chorus, a way of inventing new rhythm patterns that dislodge, but fit in with, the regularity of the normal rhythm of the piece. And his scales and arpeggios, chords played one note at a time in rapid succession, are impeccable. His fingers just don't miss. Of course, he's 30 years old now in 1939, but he played all those notes when he recorded this piece in 1933 at the age of 23. If you believe in talent, **Tatum** is it.

THE MUSICIANS SPEAK   BUCK CLAYTON

Lips Page was another "carver" who used to invite or, rather, I should say, dare visiting musicians to come down to the Sunset Club on 12th Street and join in a jam session. For example, if Duke Ellington [and his orchestra] would play Kansas City, Lips would find out at what hotel they would be staying and slip notes under the doors of the trumpet players, such as Cootie Williams or Rex Stewart, and dare them to come down to the Sunset Club after they had finished their engagement. Lips would sometimes get drunk and play all night in the Sunset Club until it closed. One day, shortly after Maceo [Birch] and I arrived in Kansas City from LA, Maceo said to me, "Buck, why don't you take your horn out and go jam in some of the clubs so that people will know that you're in town? It is good if all of the guys know you and you can get acquainted with all of the best musicians in Kansas City." I thought it was a good idea so I decided to go down to the Sunset Club and jam with Pete Johnson, who was playing piano there. I went down to 12th Street with my horn and started playing with Pete and pretty soon one lone trumpet player came in with his horn. I thought, "Good, I'll have somebody to jam with." Then after a few minutes about two more trumpet players came in and started jamming. That was OK with me too as I figured we'd all have a ball. Then about a half an hour later in came about three more trumpet players. I thought to myself, "Damn, there's no shortage of trumpet players in Kansas City, that's for sure." Then, as the evening went on, more and more trumpet players came in to blow. To me, it seemed as if they were coming from all directions. Soon the room was just full of trumpet players. They were coming from under the rug, out of the woodwork, behind doors, everywhere. I never saw so many trumpet players in my life. Some had even come from as far as Kansas City, Kansas, because they had heard that the new trumpet player from Los Angeles was going to be there that night, and they all had their weapons (trumpets) with them. They really had blood in their eyes. We all stayed there and jammed until about five in the morning. Then some of them started clearing out and about seven they were all gone. I really had been shown how they jammed in Kansas City. I think, though, that Maceo Birch had put out the word that I was going to be at the Sunset Club that night and from there on things just happened like they always did in Kansas City. Lips Page would have died if he knew that he missed all that. He had left for New York, thank God.

REVIEW | **15**

Primary Goal of Unit 15

Learn to recognize the individual performance characteristics of pianists Jelly Roll Morton, James P. Johnson, Pete Johnson, and Art Tatum. Get a sense of the individual achievement of each of these jazz musicians. Compare the four playing styles—**New Orleans, stride, boogie woogie,** and **swing**—as heard in solo piano playing.

Study Questions

1. What are the names of the four pieces we studied? Which were original compositions by the pianist performing, and which was a popular song composed by someone else?

2. In the performance of the popular song, what was original to the composition, and what was unique to the performance? What about the original tunes by the jazz musicians—what is played the same each time, and what is new with each performance?

3. Describe the touch, the finger technique, of each of the four pianists. Describe the left-hand technique; the right-hand technique.

4. How are these solo piano performances like some of the combo and band performances you studied? How are they different?

5. What is ragtime?

6. What is jazz?

7. Where did jazz originate? About when?

Other Concepts

1. What are "strains" and "vamps" in a ragtime piece?

2. Who was Buddy Bolden?

3. What do these "non-jazz" people have to do with this unit?
   a. Vladimir Horowitz
   b. Scott Joplin
   c. John Philip Sousa

4. Was there any collective improvisation in any of these performances? If "yes," where; if "no," why not?

5. Were there any rhythm sections in these performances?

6. Here are brief formal outlines for three pieces. Which matches:
   a. *Sporting House Rag*   _____
   b. *Boogie Woogie*   _____
   c. *Tea for Two*   _____

A.	INTRODUCTION	1st chorus	2nd chorus	3rd chorus	4th chorus
		A B A C	**A B A C**	**A B A C**	**A B A C**
B.	INTRODUCTION	1st strain repeated	2nd strain repeated	Vamp	3rd strain 2 repeats
C.	MEASURES	Blues ├—12—┤	Blues ├—12—┤	Blues ├—12—┤	Blues ├—12—┤	Blues ├—12—┤ ....

7. No formal sketch was given for James P. Johnson's *Mule Walk*. Outline one in the space below.

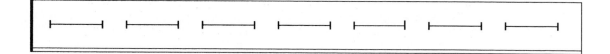

In Unit 12, we took note that the year 1929 ended a decade of economic growth and ushered in the Great Depression of the 1930s,   Extra Activity

events that had profound effects on every aspect of American life, including jazz. The final year of the '30s, 1939, not only signaled the end of the Great Depression but also the beginning of World War II in Europe, a conflict we delayed involving ourselves in until the end of 1941. What can you find out about American life and culture from library copies of 1939 editions of *Life* magazine, *The New York Times*, *down beat* magazine, the *Saturday Evening Post*, and the like? Can you construct a picture of life in your family's community, or in some metropolitan center, and share it with the class? After a little research, organize a panel discussion that addresses the issues of culture and society in 1939 with the ultimate goal of understanding jazz's place in that society.

Four Modern Masters of the Keyboard | 16

BUD POWELL, SUN RA, CECIL TAYLOR, AND JOE ZAWINUL
MODERN PIANO STYLES: BEBOP, FREE FORM, ATONAL,
AND FUSION

So far, we have sampled less than half the piano story. Even in the piano music that precedes World War II, there are literally dozens of great pianists we haven't been able to hear—Earl Hines, Lil Hardin, Fats Waller, Teddy Wilson, Willie "The Lion" Smith, and many, many more. Now we must move on and taste some of the more recent keyboard music. In the new forms of jazz since World War II, the music we have already labeled **modern jazz,** the pianists developed new approaches to playing their instrument. I was talking about this with Mr. Imagination last week, and he suggested we arrange a program of some modern players down at the club for you to hear, but we ran into a problem. You should know that he and I almost got into a fight about which musicians should be included on an evening's bill of fare. Since no more than four could be accommodated in one session, and since we needed to save the other available dates for other players we felt must be included before the holidays, like saxophonists and big bands, we had a real struggle. There are so many truly outstanding modern keyboard players—Oscar Peterson, Thelonious Monk, Marian McPartland, Nat "King" Cole, Tadd Dameron, Wynton Kelly, Lennie Tristano, George Shearing, McCoy Tyner, Mary Lou Williams, Herbie Hancock, Horace Silver, Geri Allen, Chick Corea, Keith Jarrett, and the list goes on and on. Fortunately, we have already heard a few other modern pianists in our earlier nights out at the club—**Al Haig** with Charlie Parker (CD selection 1.6), **Dave Brubeck** with his quartet (CD selection 1.9), **Erroll Garner** with his trio (CD selection 1.14), **Bill Evans** with Miles Davis (CD selection 1.15), and **Fumio Itabashi** with Ray Anderson (CD selection 2.1), so you already have some idea of the artistry and the variety of styles of performance this select group offers us music lovers. Now let's add a few more players to the list to fill in a few holes and try to bring us up to date.

No modern pianist was more influential than **Bud Powell.** He may not have been the first pianist to liberate the left hand from its rhythm section responsibilities of timekeeper, but he was in on this change at the beginning. Since he is the first acknowledged master of modern jazz keyboard who influenced all the others and then opened new possibilities for succeeding pianists, Mr. Imagination and I had no problem settling on this choice.

The next selection gave us the most trouble. "Mr. I" was correct in saying that Thelonious Monk was more influential than my suggestion and, therefore, more historically important, but I wanted to sample the more extreme fringes of the keyboard world and voted for **Sun Ra,** a musician whose idiosyncracies, both musical and personal, were way beyond the norm, even in the highly personal, idiosyncratic world of jazz. Mr. Imagination said he would only agree to book **Sun Ra** into the club for this pianist night if I would accept his choice of **Cecil Taylor** for the following set. I was quick to agree, for that was an easy concession on my part. **Cecil Taylor** is a truly great pianist, a musician of stature who could certainly have succeeded as a classical concert pianist or a mainstream jazz pianist but chose instead to chart his own new route of the integration of the most advanced avant-garde compositional thinking into the framework of African American improvisational music. Like **Sun Ra,** he, too, was scorned by many of the older jazz musicians, but his impact on younger generations has been far-reaching and long-lasting.

Then, since we only had one choice left, Mr. Imagination and I squabbled over which of our favorites, musicians for whom we would gladly dig into our pockets to pay a stiff **cover charge** and **minimum** to hear, we would ask to close the show. We finally agreed to plunge into the late 20th century with someone who controls the keyboard world of electronics, synthesizers, computers, MIDIs, and samplers. There were many fine choices, but we settled on **Joe Zawinul,** because he rose to prominence early on, is still playing today, and was the first acknowledged master of electronic keyboards and synthesizers.

You may wonder why I have worked through this litany of explanations and rationalizations about our choices, when I might just as well have picked four and invited you to join me at the club to enjoy the music. The reason is simple. It is important for you to realize that we are barely skimming the surface of outstanding jazz musicians and individual styles in these visits to the club. There is so much more out there for you to discover on your own. Jazz is such a subjective world where each artist makes a unique contribution, a world of such incredibly gifted musicians, that one lifetime, let alone one season's concerts at the club, is not sufficient to sample it all, let alone hear it all. I hoped you would bear with me through that digression so that perhaps you might see that it will be possible for you to take as much as you like from this renewable resource and never exhaust the supply.

Well, if you and your friend are ready, why don't we take that table next to the bandstand? **Bud Powell** is here with his Trio, **George Duvivier** on bass and **Art Taylor** on drums. **Powell** is going to play a popular song, *East of the Sun (West of the Moon),* so let's listen now and talk a little about it after you have heard the music.

BUD POWELL, *EAST OF THE SUN* (CD SELECTION 2.9)

Like so many bebop musicians, **Bud Powell** could amaze listeners with dazzling technique at blistering tempos, but this piece shows that fine jazz in not just playing a million notes faster than the next guy, not just happy music or only impressive performances. It is an *expressive* art form that covers the entirety of human emotions. Here, **Powell** uses his lyrical gifts and delicate touch to evoke pianistic romance from what was essentially a love song. After a brief flurry of notes that serves as a one-measure introduction, **Powell** uses two hands, essentially together, in close-voiced block chords, to harmonize the tune that he plays primarily with the top two fingers of the right hand. Did you hear the stride left hand? No, you didn't! Did you hear a boogie woogie left hand? No again! What was the left hand doing throughout the first chorus? Essentially it was locked musically with the right hand to create a **thickened melodic line** of melody on top with harmonic notes paralleling along just below. How does a piece remain in the jazz idiom if the left hand of the pianist is not functioning as part of, or in lieu of, the rhythm section? By allowing the bass and the drums to take over these responsibilities completely without duplication from the keyboard.

Bud Powell, whose classical training gave his touch a clear, almost bell-like sound, developed the new bebop technique of solo piano playing—occasional dissonant chords in the left hand to accompany swift and graceful melodic lines in the right—that became the norm for pianists of the period and thereafter.

If you were listening carefully to the drum work of **Art Taylor,** the light stick work on the cymbal, you would have noted that this part was a simple, straightforward, timekeeping assignment. Since **Taylor** was keeping time, it was not necessary for **Powell** to duplicate this function. This **freeing of the left hand from the timekeeping responsibility** is the first major innovation of modern jazz piano playing. Now, if you listen carefully to the work of bassist **George Duvivier,** you will note that his **walking bass,** one note to each beat on a melodic, rather than a skipping or jumping, bass pattern, plays the most important harmonic note, the **root,** on the first beat of every measure or plays some other critical harmonic note at those structural points when the harmonies change. In other words, the bass not only keeps the beat with the drums through its steady pizzicato motion, but **the bass sounds the harmonies through its selection of notes** played at structural points in the bass line.

Drums	I : : : I : : : I : : : I : : : I : : : I ....
Bass	**R** : : : **R** : : : **R** : : : **R** : : : **R** : : : **R** ....

(**R** = root or important harmonic note)

So, the second major innovation of modern jazz piano was the **freeing of the left hand from the rigid, bar-by-bar performance of the regular harmonies of the piece.** Since the bass and drums now keep time and imply harmonies by themselves, the pianist's left hand is free to do other things musically, such as revoicing harmonies, leaving a little open space, or adding tasteful dissonances at interesting points.

Bud Powell is a **bebop** pianist, and the usual **pattern for a bebop performance,** which you heard in this performance of *East of the Sun*, was a **complete statement of the tune** (first chorus), **improvised solos** (indefinite number of internal choruses), and a **restatement of the tune** (last chorus):

[STATEMENT—IMPROVISATION—RESTATEMENT]

The formal structure of the popular song *East of the Sun* is also simple, AA', where the first 16-measure section is followed by a similar section that has an extra four measures added for an ending:

	A	A'
measures	16	20

Since I already told you that **Powell** plays a one-measure introduction, that there is both a first chorus and a last chorus, and that there might be some improvised choruses in the middle, why don't we listen again while you outline the form of this performance, note who takes solos where, and try to determine the change in technique that **Powell** applies to his solo improvisation that is different from the description I gave you of his playing for the presentation of the tune in the first chorus.

BUD POWELL, *EAST OF THE SUN* (CD SELECTION 2.9)

Yes, that's right. **Powell**'s lyrical solo, which begins in the second chorus, is basically a single-note melody line. His left hand hardly plays at all, and when it does, it occasionally adds a scintillating harmonic cluster at varying points in the background. This is the solo technique for which **Bud Powell** became famous, and it is also the solo technique adopted by nearly all the modern pianists who followed after him.

What do you see coming to the bandstand now, musicians from another planet? Right! **Sun Ra** is dressed in 1960s intergalactic apparel with brightly colored flowing robes, amulets and charms, and a glittering hat of sparkled spandex. Followed by his fellow space travelers, the musicians of his **Arkestra** (space ark band), **Sun Ra,** the pianist, mystic, philosopher, innovator, teacher, and extraterrestrial speaks into the microphone, "I would hate to pass through a planet and not leave it a better place." In his music, **Sun Ra** is, all at once, a remnant of the past—in his eclectic performances of blues, gospel, swing, and bebop—and a pioneer in multi-media, electronics in jazz, free forms, and whatever strikes his fancy. He looks to Africa, the ghettos of Harlem, and outer space for inspiration, and he is a model of industry and self-sufficiency. He is also convinced that he is an Ark-Angel from Saturn (though earthly records indicate a Herman "Sonny" Blount was born in Birmingham, Alabama, many years ago), and that his surrealistic, free-expression music and lifestyle will clear many a musical attic of its cobwebs. Surrounded by his **Arkestra** of conventional instruments plus gongs, extra percussion, bells, flute, bass clarinet, and electronic celeste, **Sun Ra** opens with a lightly swinging modal piece, *The Others in Their World;* follows it with *Brazilian Sun*, a piano and percussion number full of tone clusters; plays a lovely,

Lined up on stage in Symphony Space in New York City in 1979, Sun Ra and His Arkestra appear almost conventional. Only the leader's costume and the series of Saturn figures beneath the keyboard hint of the extraterrestrial origins and aspirations.

tonal ballad with flute lead, *Space Mates;* and then gives us this: *Calling Planet Earth.*

SUN RA, *CALLING PLANET EARTH* (CD SELECTION 2.10)

Did you notice the electronic effects—reverberation as well as right- and left-side displacement? These were new devices in jazz when **Sun Ra** first experimented with them. Did you catch the beat? Why not? That's because there was no single, agreed-upon beat. The instructions among baritone saxophone, drums, and piano were, "play as fast as you can!" Did you catch **Sun Ra** playing the **changes?** No? Well, that's right, too. There weren't regular **changes.** This is free

Sun Ra began his performing and arranging career as Herman "Sonny" Blount playing in Fletcher Henderson's bands of 1946–47. By the mid 1950s, Blount had adopted the persona of Sun Ra; his Solar Arkestra quickly became an important part of the Chicago avant-garde music scene. In the 1970s, the group moved to the Philadelphia area and began a series of college and university lecture tours. His performances incorporated slide shows, dance, special light effects, and the Arkestra's own style of collective improvisation.

form and atonal music; that is, there is no preset form, and there is no key or tonal center, a primary pitch level that we constantly refer to and come back to, in this composition. Also, did you catch some of the **expanded performance techniques—Pat Patrick**'s baritone saxophone squeaks, squawks, double-tonguing, and slap tonguing, as well as **Sun Ra**'s repeated succession of hammered tone clusters? In case you think **Sun Ra** and his musicians are jesting or that this music lacks polish, you should know that the **Arkestra** is probably the most rehearsed band in the history of music. They practice regularly, six to eight hours a day! The audience goes wild, a standing ovation. In addition to creating interesting music, **Sun Ra** also brings a sense of fun and adventure to his music and to the audience. With a bow and a flourish, the space traveler fades from the limelight.

Now, the **Cecil Taylor** quartet has settled in on the bandstand with **Steve Lacy** on soprano saxophone, **Dennis Charles** on drums, and **Buell Neidlinger** on bass. I understand they are going to play a ballad, a lovely romantic tune composed by Billy Strayhorn, who was also a fine pianist but is best known as a composer and arranger closely associated with Duke Ellington. I'm glad we are going to have a quiet ballad. After all that excitement from **Sun Ra,** I can use some relaxing sounds.

LISTEN

CECIL TAYLOR, *JOHNNY COME LATELY* (CD SELECTION 2.11)

What happened? That wasn't a slow, romantic ballad. Well, the first thing **Cecil Taylor** did was kick off the tempo a little faster than I expected; then the band attacked the music with volume and aggressive articulations; **Taylor** also filled the piece with groups of fast rhythm patterns that are heard as recurring motives throughout the piece, and finally **Taylor** raised the level of dissonance by constantly grabbing tight clusters of notes in his fingers rather than playing the less dissonant chords the composer used to accompany the melody in the original song.

The inexperienced listener might think this performance fit into the category of atonal music, but not so. Focus your ears and listen to the bass part alone. **Neidlinger** plays the **changes** and keeps the key relationships in place. However, some of **Cecil Taylor**'s solo improvisation, especially near the end, is **atonal.** He makes a deliberate selection of notes that destroys a sense of key. One of the fascinating things about this performance is the way **Taylor** overlaps **atonal** sounds on a **tonal substructure,** much like the *collage* technique in the visual arts, where objects are layered and glued one over another to form a coherent composition. **Cecil Taylor,** who has virtually unlimited finger technique, often chooses to ignore or replace the smooth, legato technique most people associate with piano sound with a decidedly percussive stroke or attack, as you heard here. Also, he likes to dismember the smooth, long-line melodies and use groups and clusters of notes to stimulate improvisation that is disjunct and unsettling. Though he constantly struggles for a larger popular audience, at least in this country, **Cecil Taylor** has earned a devoted

Pianist and composer Cecil Taylor studied piano from an early age, but also studied with a timpanist who likely influenced his approach to the keyboard. His music was almost always a critical success, but audiences found it difficult to understand and appreciate the complexities of Taylor's approach to jazz.

following among knowledgeable performers and critics. He is a musical power to be reckoned with.

It's getting late, and we've come to the last number of the evening. The group is called **Weather Report.** It is a **collective,** and no one person serves as leader of the group. **Joe Zawinul** is the keyboardist, and **Wayne Shorter,** the composer of this piece, will play **soprano saxophone,** the same instrument **Steve Lacy** played on the last number. **Jaco Pastorius** will play **electric bass guitar, Alex Acuna** is the drummer, and **Manolo Badrena,** a percussionist, adds some vocal sounds to this performance. Before they can start, **Joe Zawinul** will have to set up and plug in his instruments. He will use the grand piano, which modern musicians now call an **acoustic piano,** as well as a Rhodes Electric Piano, an Arp 2600 Synthesizer, and an Oberheim Polyphonic Synthesizer. The Rhodes is an electric piano, not electronic piano, because, except for the amplification, the sound is produced by naturally vibrating objects. On the grand piano they are strings; on the Rhodes they are metal bars. But the Arp and the Oberheim are electronic, they are **synthesizers;** the sound is synthetically generated by electronic wave forms.

Jaco Pastorius (1951–1987) was the leader of the modern bass school, and was highly in demand both as bassist and as producer. Pastorius played a fretless bass which set him apart from most jazz and rock bass guitarists. From 1980–1983 he toured with his own group Word of Mouth.

Composer and saxophonist Wayne Shorter in 1961. Shorter met Joe Zawinul in Maynard Ferguson's band in 1958. Shorter left to play with Art Blakey's Jazz Messengers from 1959–1963, and then with Miles Davis's quintet from 1964–1970. Shorter was strongly influenced by John Coltrane, but developed his own style while composing highly original material. Shorter performed in the 1986 film Round Midnight, starring Dexter Gordon.

What's the difference and who cares? Well, the answer lies in the resulting tones, the unique sounds you hear as a final product. From the earliest days of jazz, the musicians have been fascinated by sound itself, every clarinetist trying to make his instrument sound a little different from every other clarinet, a little more beautiful or more interesting than anyone else's sound. Only recently have the jazz pianists had a variety of keyboards and tone producers to use in their music, and this allows them, as **Joe Zawinul** will do, to improvise with sound itself. He'll be ready to go in a minute, but while we wait, think about it. A piano player can vary the sound of his playing with loud and soft, hard attacks, short notes or legato playing, and the like, but basically the sound is uniform—a piano sound. With synthesizers, instruments that create new sounds electronically, and other keyboard instruments at his disposal, the modern keyboardist can have almost an infinite variety of sounds instantly available, not only synthesized instruments, like electronic saxophone or sampled string section, but

The group Weather Report included (left to right) Wayne Shorter, saxophone; Alejandro Acuña, percussion; Jaco Pastorius, electric bass; Joe Zawinul, keyboards; and Chester Thompson, drums. In 1976, when this photo was taken, the group had a critical and commercial success with their album Heavy Weather.

even such far-out sounds as dripping water, synthesized voice, mountain winds, and jet roars. Even these can be altered to create a truly infinite number of sounds. Where the older keyboardist was normally restricted to improvisations of notes and rhythms, the new keyboardist can do that plus create improvisations out of nothing but sound.

I think the group is ready, so let's see what they do. Mostly, let's pay attention to the keyboard work of **Joe Zawinul.** Of course, you can't ignore the artistry of the entire group, especially in this style, because the keyboard improvisations become part of the total mix of simultaneous improvisation and composition, but try to focus your ears on all the sounds other than saxophone, **bass guitar,** drums, and voice. These are the sounds that **Zawinul** creates at the keyboards. This piece, *Harlequin*, has no first, second, and third choruses. It is an evolving improvisation/composition that constantly recycles a relatively short series of chords.

WEATHER REPORT, *HARLEQUIN* (CD SELECTION 2.12)

L I S T E N

Did you hear how Zawinul opened with some synthesized piano chords and threw in a soft wind rush just before the **bass guitar** entered on the descending run? The percussionist added a wooden vibration and the synthesizers filled out with new sounds that cannot accurately be categorized. From this tantalizing start, which sets the tempo and the mood, the progression of sound to sound continues throughout the entire piece. One fascinating feature is the beat. The slow, steady pulse that **Zawinul** established at the beginning persists throughout the work in spite of the fact that two other very interesting rhythmic things happen. The first is that much of the inserted improvisations flow over the beat without fitting any specific metrical framework. The second occurs in the work of the drummer, who matches the beat at the beginning, doubles his time and activity after the middle, and moves at four-times-the-beat with a flurry of notes near the end, only to relax for a final cadence. This pattern of rhythmic activity is a useful musical device that creates excitement and gives direction to a composition.

Joe Zawinul was one of the first great masters of the electronic keyboards in jazz. A prolific and important composer, he emigrated from Vienna, Austria, to the United States in 1959 to play with Maynard Ferguson, Miles Davis, and others before becoming a founding member of Weather Report.

How many different kinds of sounds did you hear created by the keyboardist? Did you notice that he can change not only the **timbre,** the characteristic sound, but the **envelope** of the sound? For example, three notes in one envelope may sound "Tu Tu Tu," or "Ut Ut Ut," or "Wow Wow Wow," regardless of pitch or timbre—fast start and slow end, or slow start and abrupt end, or slow start and slow end. Pretty neat, huh? And a single run of notes can shift from a piano sound to a guitar sound and back without interruption! And vibrato can be added or deleted at will. And **Zawinul's** pitches can be raised or lowered at will by rubbing a little wheel, a feat totally impossible on a grand piano. And the last sound he made, it could have continued forever without decay (unless you had a power failure).

When **Manolo Badrena** sang his "Ah," was it something you have ever heard in the real world? The reverberation on that sound, something like that of a voice in an empty cathedral, was created with a dial and a switch and then balanced out in the mix to give the listener "presence," as though it were coming from just behind your left shoulder.

In many ways, *Harlequin* is a simple piece. It has a slow, unwavering beat, and it has a short series of chords that are repeated over and over to form a basic structure. It has no words, no "tune," and this performance only involves five players, but the range of sounds and the implications of the open form and improvised gestures is infinite, making the whole much more than the sum of its parts.

REVIEW 16

Primary Goal of Unit 16

Compare the work of four modern keyboardists—Bud Powell, Sun Ra, Cecil Taylor, and Joe Zawinul. Get a sense of their contribution to the art form as well as a sense of their individual style.

Study Questions

1. Of the four pieces we studied, three were original jazz compositions and one was a recomposition of a popular song. How did the process of composition and recomposition vary from piece to piece?

2. Outline, on paper, the general principals of performance that were operational while each of the four modern pianists performed these specific works. If another modern pianist had come to the job to substitute for Bud Powell and called the same tune, would the performance be similar? Why do you think so? What about substitutes for Sun Ra, Cecil Taylor, and Joe Zawinul?

3. Describe the touch, the finger technique, of each of the four pianists. Describe the left-hand technique; the right-hand technique as you perceived it in the sound.

4. What is a thickened melodic line?

5. What is the first major innovation of modern jazz piano playing?

6. What is the second major innovation of modern jazz piano playing?

7. Who were some of the players, other than the keyboardists, on these performances, and what did they play? Which ones played solos?

1. What do we mean by expanded performance techniques?

2. What do we mean by a walking bass pattern, and how does walking bass function in the total complex of a jazz performance? There was a bass on each performance, but was there a walking bass on each? If no, what did the bass do?

3. What is atonal music? Is jazz atonal?

4. Collective improvisation is one of the characteristics heard in the bands that played the oldest style of jazz, New Orleans Style Jazz. Was there any collective improvisation in any of these modern performances? If "yes," where; if "no," why not?

5. What is a synthesizer? What is a Rhodes Electric Piano? What is an acoustic piano?

6. What is a collective?

7. What is an Arkestra?

If you are NOT a performing musician, find yourself a piano where you can experiment for a few minutes. On the white keys, try to pick out the tune of *Mary Had a Little Lamb.* It only takes four notes, three together and one more which skips just one above this group of three. The melody will sound correct in more than one spot on the keyboard. When you get it, you will be playing in **the key** of the lowest note of the group, which is also the last note of the melody. Notice how that note focuses the sounds of all the rest and is the best note to stop on to give a feeling of rest and completion. That is what we are talking about when we refer to **the key** of a piece of music.

   After you have done this, close your eyes and play various groupings of notes randomly all over the keyboard. Unless a miracle happens, you will just have improvised an **atonal** solo; that is, a series of pitches and clusters of notes that do not relate to a key. *Mary Had a Little Lamb* was **tonal;** this random improvisation was **atonal.**

   Congratulations! You have just entered the ranks of performing musicians. Fun, huh?

Syncopating Saxophones I

17

SIDNEY BECHET, FRANKIE TRUMBAUER, LESTER YOUNG, AND SONNY ROLLINS
THE EARLY STYLES AND MODERN JAZZ: NEW ORLEANS, CHICAGO, SWING,
AND BEBOP

You might have guessed that Mr. Imagination is a history buff, at least when it comes to jazz. He pulled an old book off his shelf yesterday called *Syncopating Saxophones*, which was published in 1925. The author, Alfred Frankenstein, a well-known music critic, had a couple of fascinating things to say about this instrument, especially considering the date of his writing. He starts out with:

> It is a strange paradox in American musical affairs that the most popular instrument in the country today is the one about which the least is known by the laymen or even by the professional. When one enquires concerning the history of the saxophone in music schools one rarely gets any answer at all, for the simple reason that the teachers as a rule consider the instrument below their dignity.

Well, things haven't changed much. The saxophone is still one of the most popular instruments in American music, few people know much about it, and it still gets second-class status in most music schools. However, it was fascinating for me to learn that the sax was "the most popular instrument in the country" by 1925, because that shows how quickly jazz popularized this instrument and captivated American taste.

This critic, Frankenstein, was pretty sharp in some of his other observations, too. At the end of this brief essay, he wrote:

> let me cite the case of the piece of super-jazz of the 1925 Evanston festival. . . . This work, called an American rhapsody, "Broadway," rises to

204

a tremendous and deadly serious climax in the organ and orchestra. In the *denouement* [the final resolution; the ending of the piece] occurs an acrid, ascetic, hard-edged saxophone solo as suggestive of jazz as "no" is suggestive of "yes."

Obviously, he not only had a sense of humor but also had a feeling for what jazz is and what jazz is not. Something in the performance offended his sensibilities. What was it? Probably a mismatch of **style,** an insensitivity to the elements of **style.** All the elements of a musical performance must be in aesthetic harmony with each other. As we listen to jazz, and to other music as well, we develop our taste as well as our general knowledge of the subject. Little by little, we begin to get a feel for style—what makes for a good traditional jazz performance and what makes a swing band swing or fizzle. It's more than playing correct notes; it has to do with playing the right notes the right way in a specific style with other musicians who are also playing interesting notes correctly in the same style.

So, as Mr. Imagination and I chatted about these things, we decided that a quick trip through styles with a group of syncopating saxophones was as good a way to view this subject as any. Every instrument in jazz is important, and the saxophone is probably no better for this task than any other instrument, although we would be hard pressed to get a complete survey if we only listened to harmonica players (there is at least one great jazz artist on this instrument, by the way: Toots Thielemans!). All the major solo instruments, if traced through good performances by their most outstanding players from the early days to the present, could inform us both about the history of jazz and the evolution of jazz's various styles. To a certain extent we have been doing this as we listened to all those brass players on three successive nights at the club and made comments about their styles. We even did this to a greater degree when we followed changes of style on the two evenings we listened to keyboard players, but the solo performances (solo piano without rhythm section) don't display all the characteristics we need to be aware of. Still, if you stop to think about this, we have been doing a survey of styles with nearly every band and soloist we have heard at the "Chez Imagination" beginning with the opening night's performance of the Chocolate Dandies playing *Bugle Call Rag.* However, Mr. Imagination thought it would be worthwhile to try a systematic approach for a couple of nights, and we decided to select one great saxophone artist in each of a half a dozen or so major styles, present them in rough chronological order at the club, and ask you to pay particular attention to the style of their solo playing as well as that of the performance of the bands in which they are members. We thought we would set up our program this way: on the first night we would listen to saxophone soloists from:

New Orleans Style
Chicago Style
Swing
Bebop.

On the second night, we would complete our survey with soloists from:

Cool Jazz
Modal Jazz
Free Jazz
Jazz/Rock Fusion.

This list doesn't cover every variety or subtlety of style, but coupled with the knowledge you have gained from your other listenings, it will fill in and give structure to the total picture. No one can learn everything in a limited amount of time, and we won't pretend to teach everything here. After all, we are coming to the club primarily to learn to enjoy fully all kinds of jazz regardless of style, but these basic principles of listening and understanding will surely prove helpful in that task, as well.

Jazz styles evolved naturally in a reasonable chronological sequence, all in this century. Most styles rose to prominence, held sway and were influential for a decade or two, and then continued to a lesser extent as a new style became predominant. Most of the time, two or more styles competed for the headlines, but, in general, the pattern looks something like that shown on p. 207.

ORIGINS	ca. 1900
I. New Orleans Style	1910s and 1920s
II. Chicago Style	1920s and 1930s
III. Swing	1930s and 1940s
IV. Bebop	1940s and 1950s
V. Cool Jazz	1950s
VI. Modal Jazz	1960s and 1970s
VII. Free Jazz	1960s and 1970s
VIII. Jazz/Rock Fusion	1970s and 1980s
IX. Neoclassical Jazz	1980s and 1990s

You notice, of course, that one style, **cool jazz,** lost influence or relevance more quickly than the others, but that is because two major stylistic events occurred around 1960 that immediately set new stylistic trends, the emergence of both **modal jazz** and **free jazz.** There have been some other interesting stylistic outcroppings, such as progressive jazz, hard bop, and third stream music, but the first eight subdivisions, **New Orleans Style** through **jazz/rock fusion,** cover the main stylistic ideas of this music. Perhaps we'll see about peeking into some of these other areas later.

You are already familiar with many of the principal musicians of most of these styles, like **Bix Beiderbecke** from **Chicago Style Jazz, Charlie Parker** from **bebop,** and **Joe Zawinul** from **jazz/ rock fusion,** but Mr. Imagination and I thought it might be fun to invite to the "Chez Imagination" for your listening pleasure saxophonists you haven't heard yet who are also chief exponents of particular styles. You surely remember the work of Benny Carter, Charlie Parker, Gerry Mulligan, John Coltrane, and several other saxophonists from previous evenings at the club, so we'll have to forgo the pleasure of hearing more from these superlative artists in order to make room for a few other great jazz saxophonists. So, for the first night's show, we decided to ask **Sidney Bechet** from **New Orleans, Frankie Trumbauer** from **Chicago, Lester Young** from the great Kansas City **swing** band, the Count Basie Orchestra, and **Sonny Rollins,** a leading **bebop** tenor player, to come to the "Chez Imagination." On the second night's program, we will try to book **Stan Getz,** a pioneer of **cool jazz, Cannonball Adderley,** a supreme improviser of **modal jazz, Ornette Coleman,** the founding father of **free jazz,** and **Michael Brecker,** a great player of **jazz/rock fusion.** Let's hope they are all available for the gig.

Sidney Bechet was the first jazz musician to be the subject of serious musical criticism, and when he performed in London in 1919 as part of Will Marion Cook's Southern Syncopated Orchestra, he had already been playing jazz in his hometown of New Orleans for almost ten years. **Bechet** is a leading exponent of the earliest mature style of jazz, **New Orleans Jazz** or **traditional jazz.** Although some of the dance orchestras of New Orleans used music, most of these early **hot jazz** musicians, like **Sidney Bechet,** were not "note readers." They played totally improvised music. Although every performance in jazz is different and each jazz composition has its own idiosyncrasies, some of the characteristics you will hear in nearly every performance of **New Orleans Style Jazz** are listed below.

New Orleans Style

1. Collective improvisation in the ensemble performance interspersed with solo improvisations that are accompanied by rhythm section and occasional background support from the rest of the combo

2. Use of an original jazz repertoire primarily composed in ragtime (march) and blues forms

3. A loose rhythmic feel with four beats to the bar that generally matches the improvisatory attitude of the players and the style

4. Wind instrument sounds that frequently employ large vibratos, bent pitches, non-classical sounds (like growls and breathy tones), and energized phrasing and articulation

5. Small combos (usually two to four melodic instruments and two to four players in the rhythm section)

I should add, they also play loudly. These early **hot jazz** musicians really blew into their horns.

Whenever you listen to **collective improvisation,** you will usually hear a layered effect of a soprano instrument on top, like clarinet or soprano saxophone, playing a fast, decorative line above the lines of the other musical instruments. You will also note another soprano melody instrument in the middle, usually a cornet or trumpet, playing the melody in mid-range in a ragged, syncopated style. And you will often hear a tenor instrument on the bottom, such as a trombone, playing a slower-moving melodic line below the melody, a kind of countermelody or harmonic part. Together with these few front-line melody instruments, a rhythm section will make regular statements of the beat and harmonies to hold the performance together and support the work of the soloists.

We have already studied the song forms used in early jazz, **ragtime** or **march forms** and the **blues,** so we needn't go into that again. Also, the best way to understand the **loose rhythmic feel** of **New Orleans Jazz** is to listen to a performance of the music, so we'll not spend time talking when we could be listening. Then again, you will be able hear in performance the **unique instrumental sounds** that are so characteristic of the **New Orleans Style.** However, before we listen, let me point out a couple of typical combo makeups of **New Orleans Style Jazz** so that you will have a model of the typical instrumentation of these groups for comparison. Two of the most famous combos in this style were **Louis Armstrong**'s **Hot Five** and his **Hot Seven.** The first used clarinet, cornet, and trombone plus piano and banjo; and the **Hot Seven** used the same combination plus tuba and drums in the rhythm section. Just as we've said, these prototypical **New Orleans combo**s had a few one-of-a-kind melody instruments in the front line plus a rhythm section.

Now we're ready to take our places in the club. We have become such regular customers that the maître d' greets us by name and the waiter has our drinks ready for us at our table before we even sit down. We are beginning to recognize familiar faces among the clientele, and it is fun to engage in small talk and shop talk with fans seated near us who share our interest in this music. This is all a part of growing into and being accepted by the jazz community, a very warm and supportive group of people.

Here comes the first group now, **Clarence Williams' Blue Five.** They were among the first groups to record jazz in the 1920s, and I understand that Mr. Imagination has set the club's clock to 1924. **Clarence Williams,** the leader and pianist, introduces his colleagues, the well-known but not-yet-famous **Louis Armstrong** on cornet, Charlie Irvis on trombone, Buddy Christian on banjo, and **Sidney Bechet** on clarinet and **soprano saxophone.** I understand he will

The Clarence Williams Blue Five sometimes had as many as eight musicians and a singer. When this photo was taken (around 1927), the musicians were Ed Allen, cornet; Charlie Irvis, trombone; Ben Whittet and Arville Harris, clarinet and saxophones; Williams, piano; Leroy Harris, banjo; Cyrus St. Clair, tuba; and Floyd Casey, drums. The singer is Katherine Henderson or Evelyn Preer.

play clarinet during the ensemble sections but will use his **soprano saxophone** for his own solo. Let's listen to their rendition of *Texas Moaner Blues.*

CLARENCE WILLIAMS' BLUE FIVE, *TEXAS MOANER BLUES*
(CD SELECTION 2.13)

What can I say about **Sidney Bechet**'s saxophone solo or about the stylistic ensemble performance that you didn't hear for yourself? Certainly you noticed the **layers of instrumental sound** that result from **collective improvisation,** the **characteristic instrumental sounds** of big vibratos, bent pitches, rips (that long, upward glissando in Bechet's solo is a "rip"), and the like. Certainly the steady, equal, four-to-a-bar beat was apparent throughout, as was the outstanding quality of **Louis Armstrong**'s solo with its insertion of a double-time passage. Most importantly, the great sax solo of **Sidney Bechet** not only displays the use of the **soprano saxophone** in traditional **New Orleans Style,** but his sound is unique to himself alone. Also as a statement of his own personality, I would say this solo is full of passion and sensuality, strong emotions seemingly tinged with rage or violence. He literally attacks this solo, first working his ideas down from the top and then ripping back up with a virtuoso exhibition that focuses not on a display of notes but the expression of his inner self.

We now move to Chicago for some sounds from 1927. **Frankie Trumbauer** was one of the most important leaders of jazz bands from the Windy City, partly for the innovations and unique sound the band developed, partly for his own excellent solo performances, and certainly for the inspired solos of his friend and colleague, the cornetist **Bix Beiderbecke.** Together they have become known as **Bix and Tram.** The **Chicago Style** players were young white musicians who took inspiration from the black New Orleans jazz artists who immigrated to Chicago, men like Louis Armstrong and the clarinetists Jimmy Noone and Johnny Dodds. The young Chicagoans first tried to copy the New Orleans sounds they heard, but soon they transformed these results into music distinctively their own. Often, their music contained elements of both styles, and the piece we will hear, *Clarinet Marmalade*, is a perfect example of this mix. Some of the innovations of the new **Chicago Style** are listed below.

Chicago Style

1. A reliance on arrangements that set or fix the performance of portions of the piece for band ensemble work. These parts were often created "by ear" rather than written down, and they might use cornet or saxophone lead while the other horns fill in the harmonies. In these sections, the parts move along together rather than in the New Orleans fashion of separate, distinct, layered melodic lines.

2. A greater concentration of energy that often occurs at the end of each chorus, which contributes to a powerful forward sense of drive.

3. A reduction of volume, frequently near the end of the piece with a build-up or crescendo for a climax at the end.

Sidney Bechet, shown here with his soprano saxophone, brought the excitement of New Orleans jazz to Europe when he first toured Europe in 1919 with Will Marion Cook's Southern Syncopated Orchestra.

4. A tense series of uneven eighth notes with a pronounced accent on the longer note followed by a weak off-beat. This popular rhythm of up-tempo numbers was known as the "shuffle style."

5. An increased use of sharp tonguing in both the solos and ensemble work that tended to focus more attention on virtuosity and other purely musical features

6. An expanded instrumentation, often an extra saxophone or two

None of these features are rules etched in stone, for musicians not only display their own individual preferences but also imitate and change for variety's sake. For example, Bix Beiderbecke often favored legato-tongued solos, and not every **Chicago Style** piece has increasing volume for a final stomp at the end. As you listen to *Clarinet Marmalade*, a piece by Larry Shields from the repertoire of the white New Orleans group, the Original Dixieland Jazz Band, you will definitely be able to discern elements of both styles.

The musicians have come to the bandstand, and you can see that the ensemble is slightly enlarged over the typical combo from New Orleans. In addition to clarinet, trumpet, and trombone in the front line there are also two saxophones, **Frankie Trumbauer**'s C-melody saxophone and Doc Ryker's alto saxophone. As you listen to the ensemble work, you will hear these instruments playing in the same range as the trombone. Of course, **Trumbauer** will take a solo. **Bix Beiderbecke** plays lead on cornet, and **Bill Rank** is the trombonist. A young man, who will one day be a famous bandleader, will play clarinet, **Jimmy Dorsey.** In the rhythm section you will hear a piano, banjo, and drums. A guitar was the more usual instrument with this and other Chicago groups, but a banjo is particularly appropriate for a number that came from the New Orleans repertory. Itzy Riskin plays the piano solo, and you will probably notice that he plays in a manner similar to the Jelly Roll Morton solo we heard earlier, a performance in **New Orleans Style.**

FRANKIE TRUMBAUER AND HIS ORCHESTRA, *CLARINET MARMALADE* (CD SELECTION 2.14)

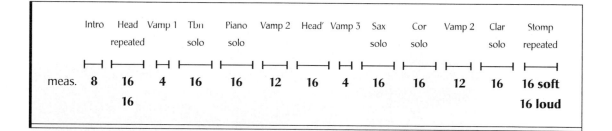

	Intro	Head	Vamp 1	Tbn	Piano	Vamp 2	Head'	Vamp 3	Sax	Cor	Vamp 2	Clar	Stomp
		repeated		solo	solo				solo	solo		solo	repeated
meas.	8	16	4	16	16	12	16	4	16	16	12	16	16 soft
		16											16 loud

The ties to **New Orleans Style** occur in at least three places: the piece from the New Orleans repertory, the collective improvisation style of the head, and the rhythm section work of the piano and banjo. The **Chicago Style** is clear in the section work of the intro, in the reworking of the head in the middle of the piece, in the vamps, in the final two band choruses (especially the hard-driving stomp at the end of the piece), and in the solos, not just **Trumbauer**'s, which bubbles happily over the notes of the chords, but also in trombonist **Bill Rank**'s solo and **Bix Beiderbecke**'s cornet solo. Although **Jimmy Dorsey**'s clarinet solo is not up to the standard of his later work, it begins with a clear example of the Chicago shuffle rhythm. The section work of the reworked head in the middle, as well as the notes at the end of the vamp that leads to this passage, also has the characteristic Chicago shuffle rhythm. And the final 32 measures, played first soft and then loud, have the drive to cadence and the chordal Chicago ensemble work so often displayed in the best of the **Chicago Style** performances.

Intermission, and time for a big band to set up, the swinging Kansas City ensemble of **Count Basie**. Tenor saxophonist **Lester Young,** known as **"Prez,"** will be the featured soloist along with trumpeter **Harry "Sweets" Edison.** We are going to be listening for characteristics of **swing** style, and some fans would claim that **swing** is the sound of the **Count Basie Orchestra.** They are right, of course, but we need some features that apply to other musicians, as well. First, we should agree that we are not talking about that rhythmic vitality, that elusive and undefinable characteristic that is present in all good jazz, regardless of style. If it is jazz, and if it is performed well, "it swings." Here, we are talking about a distinct style of jazz music that came to prominence in the 1930s and was a leading style throughout the '40s, **swing.** In **swing style:**

Photos of Bix Beiderbecke and Frankie Trumbauer are rare. This photo was taken in 1929 and shows Bix on the left and Tram on the right.

Swing Style

1. Bands enlarged and coalesced around three sections: the brass section (which quickly developed a trumpet section and a trombone section), a saxophone section (really a reed section of saxophones, clarinets, and, later, flutes, oboes, and so on), and the omnipresent rhythm section. Small combos and soloists also played in **swing** style, but the motivating force for the new style was the developing sound of the big bands.

2. Arrangements and the work of composer/arrangers become as important as the musical discourse of the improvising soloists.

3. Solos begin to change in character from those produced in earlier styles. As instrumental virtuosity progressed and soloists tended to play their regularly accented scalar or arpeggiated patterns in equally balanced units, **swing phrasing** tended to become classical—left side balances right, antecedent ideas match consequent conclusions.

4. The rhythm section standardizes on piano, string bass, and drum set with the common addition of guitar (banjo is no longer used), and these instruments develop new musical functions for themselves. The bass divides 4-beat measures in two; the guitar strums chords equally on each beat; the drums play 4-beat patterns on part of the set (for example, a stick on the ride cymbal or brushes on the snare) and 2-beat patterns on another part (usually the left foot on the newly developed foot-operated sock cymbal); and the piano begins to move away from its older rhythmic function to concentrate more on melodic and harmonic areas instead.

These are gross oversimplifications, but music is a complex art form, styles are constantly in flux, and individual musicians play what they like. One pianist will stride in the left hand, another will play a boogie beat, and a third, such as **Count Basie** tonight, will play a sparse, economical style in both hands that makes space and surprise important elements of his performance. Still, an underlying tendency and a general sense of **swing style** prevails in all good performances of **swing,** and these are some of the common features that unify the style.

Now that the **Basie** band is set up, you can see that he uses three trumpets and three trombones for a brass section, and he has four reeds in the sax section, an alto, two tenors, and a bari who doubles on alto. The rhythm section has **Walter Page** on bass, **Freddie Green** on guitar, **Jo Jones** on drums, and the **Count** at the piano, one of

The Count Basie Orchestra of the late 1930s. The standing trumpeters play with hat mutes.
The band made some of its most famous recordings during this time: One O'Clock Jump *in*
1937, Jumpin' at the Woodside *in 1938, and* Taxi War Dance *in 1939.*

jazz's truly famous rhythm sections. Although the band is similar in size to that of the International Sweethearts of Rhythm that we heard the other night, **Basie** likes to set up his men with the rhythm section grouped on the left and the hornmen lined up in three tiers, one behind the other—trumpets in back, trombones in the middle, and saxes up front. They are ready to go, and **Lester Young** is at the mike for an opening solo on *Every Tub.*

COUNT BASIE, *EVERY TUB* (CD SELECTION 2.15)

Did you notice that much of **Prez**'s solo after his dazzling introduction was a fairly steady stream of eighth notes played in a relaxed shuffle rhythm we saw developing in Chicago? This keeps most of the melodic accent on the beat, and that is part of the secret of a good horn solo in **swing style.** In the introduction, did you notice how he balanced one phrase with another? Then, as he glided up and down the various notes of different arpeggios in the solo that followed, did you

Tenor saxophonist Lester "Prez" Young is pictured here in 1958 performing at the Five Spot Cafe in New York. Young was born to a musical family and received his first fame after joining the Count Basie Orchestra in 1934. Young's style of playing influenced the younger generation of saxophonists including John Coltrane and Stan Getz. The 1986 film Round Midnight, *dedicated to Young and Bud Powell, was loosely based on Young's life.*

perceive the sense of regularity he imposed on his ideas as he improvised to the changes of the piece? His sound was not typical of most tenor players of the Swing Era, for his tone was light and buoyant compared with the full-bodied, wide-vibrato tones of many of the other leading **swing** tenor players. This personal characteristic of sound was very influential on the next generation of saxophonists. The form of the piece, of course, was popular song form, AABA, and right after the bridge of **Young**'s first chorus, did you notice how he took a brief "one-note solo," alternating regular and false fingerings for a rhythmic improvisation rather than a purely melodic one? And he dazzles us once again with his brief solo flourish at the end of the piece.

Eddie Durham's arrangement employs **riffs,** which in **swing style** mean brief melodic fragments played in unison by a section of instruments to accompany a solo. His arrangement has chordal passages at the opening, but much of the central portion of the piece organizes brass against saxophones as one riff alternates with another. When the band plays together, they are tight and loose at the same time, and they swing fiercely. They play as a cohesive musical unit, because their ensemble is precise (tight); they are relaxed in their jazz articulation and phrasing (loose); and each member supports the others with power and rhythmic vitality (swings).

Basie's piano solo was almost totally melodic; he used his left hand but once in this solo—a brief chordal interjection in the middle at the start of the bridge. And **"Sweets" Edison**'s trumpet solo employed one of his favorite devices—holding a note for a long time while tonguing lightly and gently teasing the pitch up and down. That one note *is* his solo for the bridge. While **Walter Page** and **Freddie Green** lay down the regular four beats to every measure with pizzicato bass and strummed guitar, **Jo Jones** uses a stick on cymbals as the principal percussive sound of the trap set. The stick in the other hand, when used, is reserved for accents on the snare or tom-toms of the

Harry "Sweets" Edison was one of the most distinctive trumpet soloists in jazz. Although capable of swinging at any tempo, he is best remembered for those solos that simplify and focus on an essential core of well chosen notes.

trap set. His left foot maintains a regular off-beat accentuation on the sock cymbal. Together, these are the sounds of **swing.** They are very different from **New Orleans Style Jazz** and remarkably different from **Chicago Style Jazz,** too.

To close the show, Mr. Imagination is turning his clock from 1938 to 1956 to feature one of the most advanced **bebop** bands in jazz, the **Clifford Brown-Max Roach Quintet** with **Sonny Rollins.** They are a young group. All the men are in their twenties except **Roach,** who is thirty-one. **Clifford Brown** is the trumpeter, **Max Roach** the drummer, and **Rollins,** who was close to Charlie Parker, the tenor saxophonist. They are supported by Richie Powell, **Bud Powell**'s younger brother, on piano and George Morrow on bass. Since we have talked about **bebop** style before, let's get right into the music. We can review what we hear after we have listened to this next number.

A modern timekeeper of extraordinary accomplishment, Max Roach performs, enclosed in his own space by padded studio dividers.

CLIFFORD BROWN–MAX ROACH QUINTET, *WHAT IS THIS THING CALLED LOVE?* (CD SELECTION 2.16)

As you heard, this piece used the standard **bebop** format: presentation of the tune (popular song in popular-song form AABA) at the beginning and end with lengthy solos in between. In addition, this performance added a Latin intro, a trumpet and tenor embroidery over a single droning chord, which was also brought back for a coda at the end. The piece included two **bebop riffs,** the first played in unison before the drum solo, and the second played in octaves after the trumpet and tenor "trade eights."

Intro	Head	Tpt	Tenor	Piano	Bass	Unison	Drum	Tpt & Ten	Octave	Head	Coda
	AABA	solo	solo	solo	solo	riff	solo	eights	riff	(partial)	
⊢—⊣	⊢—⊣	⊢—⊣	⊢—⊣	⊢—⊣	⊢—⊣	⊢—⊣	⊢—⊣	⊢—⊣	⊢—⊣	⊢—⊣	⊢—⊣

You noticed, of course, the following important **bebop characteristics.**

Bebop

1. Bebop articulation. The fast-running eighth notes are equalized and the off-beat eighth notes are slightly accented. This reverses the stress of the earlier swing solos, changes the on-the-beat **swing** rhythm to off-the-beat **bebop** motion:

   SWING | > u > u > u > u | > u > u > u > u | > u > u . . . .
   BEBOP | u > u > u > u > | u > u > u > u > | u > u > . . . .

2. Bebop phrasing. Instead of seeking to achieve balanced, equal phrases that fit regularly into 4- and 8-measure patterns, bebop musicians sought to create asymmetrical phrases that cross over the usual beginning and ending points. They sometimes elide one group of notes with the next by using the ending of the first as the beginning of the second. They regularly play phrases of varying lengths, interspersing short melodic passages with long melodic lines.

The incredibly gifted trumpet artist Clifford Brown inspired countless successors with the dazzling solos of his brief, meteoric career.

3. Bebop solo coherence. The statement of "ideas" in melodic solos, that is, short patterns of notes serving as musical motives, and the development of these ideas within the context of a solo, become central to improvisational thinking in bebop.

4. Bebop rhythm section work. The totality includes a walking bass, a drummer "riding the cymbal" and reserving the snare and bass drum for syncopated attacks, and a "comping" piano that intersperses infrequent chordal patterns of harmonically enriched chords.

5. Use of an expanded harmonic vocabulary. In the melodic solos, as well as in their accompaniments, more attention is paid by the soloists and the pianist to chromatic tones, altered chords, and substitute harmonies.

All the players in this performance remain true to the character of the style, and this quintet's performance of the standard tune *What Is This Thing Called Love?* by Cole Porter is a quintessential example of performance in **bebop style.**

For five decades, the great tenor saxophonist Sonny Rollins has symbolized the quest of the bebop musician. In spite of fame, acclaim, and notable achievement, he has time and again questioned his own performance in a desire to accomplish even more.

THE MUSICIANS SPEAK   BARNEY BIGARD

The main difference in a white band and a colored band was that the white band would swing, but more politely. The colored musicians, as a rule, had jazz in their soul. The white boys, they just didn't have that feeling. Nowadays they are getting that feeling though. It all comes from ethnic groups if you ask me.

If you are poor you can realize more of something than if you are rich. By just being rich you don't have to bother about things so much. A lot of life just doesn't ever come your way. But if you're born poor, you feel it. That all comes out in your music. So many of the guys that suffered because of the racial situation and the economic situation in New Orleans for instance, they can't even read music, but they play with that feeling. That's all they have to offer.

White musicians also had a better schooling on their horns. The old white teachers wouldn't teach Negroes. I was lucky and had a first-rate teacher, but a lot of those guys didn't. You take guys like Benny Goodman, Artie Shaw and Woody Herman. They all play with feeling but they were taught right. Even from the start it's easy to see how they made it, but now I'll tell you about one of the greatest instrumentalists that I ever heard in my life. This guy didn't have any knowledge about reading music but he became one of the most famous players in jazz. That's Sidney Bechet. The one and only—and I mean one and only—Sidney Bechet.

I first became acquainted with his music in New Orleans. He made a record of *Wild Cat Blues* with Clarence Williams I think it was. Everybody had that record. That was all you could hear. Every time you passed someone's house that had the door or windows open, they would be playing that song on their Victrola. When I came to New York that was when I actually met him. . . .

I guess Sidney started out with the clarinet but I know he used to fool around with oboe and bassoon a lot till he got with that soprano sax. That's what made him really to get well known and he never did go back to the clarinet. See, years before we went into the Cotton Club or before I was in Duke Ellington's Orchestra, Sidney was in Duke's band. They had six or seven pieces and Duke took them all up through the New England states. Even in later years Duke was crazy about Sidney. That sax part in Duke's *Daybreak Express* for instance. That's Sidney's part. Another one that was crazy about Sidney was Johnny Hodges. That was his idol, his early inspiration. Johnny used to take a few lessons from Sidney.

REVIEW 17

Primary Goal of Unit 17

Compare the sounds of four styles—New Orleans Style, Chicago Style, swing, and bebop. Compare the performances of four saxophonists—Sidney Bechet, Frankie Trumbauer, Lester Young, and Sonny Rollins. Learn characteristics of styles that differentiate one from another.

Study Questions

1. What were the four performances we studied, and what are the styles to which each belongs?

2. List three important distinguishing characteristics of swing.

3. What, for you, is the most distinguishing feature of New Orleans Style Jazz? Can you name two others?

4. How are Chicago Style Jazz and New Orleans Style Jazz different? How are they similar?

5. How do swing and bebop differ? What are some of the important characteristics of bebop?

6. Who are:

	Instrument	Style	Decade
Frankie Trumbauer	_____	_____	_____
Clifford Brown	_____	_____	_____
Louis Armstrong	_____	_____	_____
Lester Young	_____	_____	_____
Freddie Green	_____	_____	_____
Max Roach	_____	_____	_____
Sidney Bechet	_____	_____	_____

Jo Jones   _____   _____   _____

Sonny Rollins   _____   _____   _____

Count Basie   _____   _____   _____

Clarence Williams   _____   _____   _____

Bill Rank   _____   _____   _____

Sweets Edison   _____   _____   _____

Walter Page   _____   _____   _____

Bix Beiderbecke   _____   _____   _____

Jimmy Dorsey   _____   _____   _____

Alfred Frankenstein   _____   _____   _____

Syncopating Saxophones II

18

STAN GETZ, CANNONBALL ADDERLEY, ORNETTE COLEMAN,
AND MICHAEL BRECKER
MODERN STYLES: COOL, MODAL, FREE, AND FUSION

Remember how I said we were going to try to book four more saxophonists into the club so that we might hear some modern jazz from **cool** to **jazz/rock fusion?** We've been lucky; all the players we asked are available, and they are here with us at the club tonight. While the first group sets up, let me remind you that the four styles we will be concentrating on during this second evening's performance of saxophonists are **cool jazz, modal jazz, free jazz,** and **jazz/rock fusion.** Now that the waiter has cleared the table of our dinner dishes, why don't you look at this little chart I am drawing on the napkin? Tonight's music will fit into the overall picture of **jazz styles** something like this:

Jazz Styles

	ORIGINS	ca. 1900
I.	New Orleans Style	1910s and 1920s
II.	Chicago Style	1920s and 1930s
III.	Swing	1930s and 1940s
IV.	Bebop	1940s and 1950s
V.	**Cool Jazz**	**1950s**
VI.	**Modal Jazz**	**1960s and 1970s**
VII.	**Free Jazz**	**1960s and 1970s**
VIII.	**Jazz/Rock Fusion**	**1970s and 1980s**
IX.	Neoclassical Jazz	1980s and 1990s

Even while bebop was riding high and swing bands were still touring the country, some musicians were seeking alternatives to the hard-blowing, full-bodied sounds of swing and bop. One never really knows why styles change, but they do, and it seems that musicians, and a sizable popular audience, were looking for something different from the sometimes frenetic tempos and challenging melodies of bebop. One bandleader, Claude Thornhill, wanted an impressionistic, light, floating sound, so he added French horns to his band and got arrangers Gil Evans and Gerry Mulligan to write charts that would take advantage of these new instruments (for jazz) and lighten up the band's sound. Other groups, such as Lennie Tristano's quartet, the Miles Davis nonette, and the Modern Jazz Quartet, also got into the act, some with different approaches, and a contrasting style developed during the late 1940s that challenged the established order. Although **cool jazz** wasn't invented by any one group, didn't happen all at once or in any one location, and didn't receive a name until a few years after the fact, one thing is certain: the most popular jazz sound of the 1950s was **cool jazz.**

One of the principal exponents of **cool jazz** was tenor saxophonist **Stan Getz.** He was known as "the sound," and you will soon hear why. Although he was a superb improviser in both the swing and bebop styles, his rise to popularity during this decade was based on the perception of him as a model of **cool jazz** artistry. The essence of his playing in this style starts with his sound but goes beyond the beautiful tone he coaxes from his instrument, a **light, vibratoless sound** inspired by swing tenorman Lester Young. **Getz's** playing is also very **lyrical,** filled with **melodious** improvisations. And his **relaxed virtuosity** also produced an effect on his listeners that seemed to convince them that his music flowed from his horn seemingly without effort. He had style, and he played in a style. **Cool Jazz** is:

Cool Jazz

1. A **restrained, understated music.** It never surges to excesses of loudness or harshness and often has the light drumwork accompaniment of wire brushes on snares and cymbals. **Cool jazz** is always played at a **subdued volume** level, not necessarily soft, but never loud.

2. A music capable of brilliant moments, of fast, almost breathless playing, but when it engages in up-tempo displays, the **virtuosity must appear effortless.**

Stan Getz and Bob Brookmeyer, two leading exponents of Cool Jazz and West Coast Jazz, played and recorded together during the 1950s and 60s. Brookmeyer, pictured here with his valve trombone, was the first player of prominence to use this instrument since Juan Tizol of the Duke Ellington Orchestra.

3. A music that took a **renewed interest in counterpoint,** the fascination with producing jazz music that takes different melodies and combines them into a harmonious arrangement.

4. A **repertory** of arrangements and improvisations based primarily on **popular songs of the standard repertory (jazz standards)** and **jazz originals in popular song form.**

5. **Listening or concert music** rather than dance music. This **relaxed, refined,** and sometimes **elegant** music captured a large popular audience during the 1950s, especially among the college communities and their graduates, and this music made a lasting impression on the shape of jazz to come.

It is interesting to note that unlike bebop, where most of the players were African Americans, or swing, where the mix was probably close to 50/50 black and white, most of the **cool jazz** musicians were white. Not all, of course, for Miles Davis, who was responsible for the 1949 recording sessions that were later named "The Birth of the Cool Sessions," and the Modern Jazz Quartet, which achieved a tremendous popular following during the '50s, are notable African-American musicians who played in this style. But this perception of **cool jazz** as primarily a white man's music engendered a reaction in the black jazz community that fostered a return to the principles of bebop, a music then renamed **hard bop,** and a search for roots in blues, gospel, and soul that led to new jazz explorations sometimes called **funky jazz.** Be that as it may, the dominant new sound of the '50s was **cool jazz.**

I see that Mr. Imagination is about ready to start the show. Tonight we will hear **Stan Getz** in a sextet with **Bob Brookmeyer** on valve trombone, John Williams on piano, Jim Raney on guitar, Bill Crow on bass, and Alan Levitt on drums. **Getz** counts it out, and the drummer's brushes set the tempo for *Cool Mix.*

STAN GETZ SEXTET, *COOL MIX* (CD SELECTION 2.17)

Did you notice that the piece is in popular song form but has an extra two measures on the end (8 + 8 + 8 + 10)? Of course, you heard the

[A   A   B   A']

cool sound of both the tenor and the valve trombone, both **light and without vibrato.** And then you surely heard the **counterpoint** in the arrangement, the two **separate but simultaneous melodies** of the head. The delicate brush work on snare, with an occasional swipe on the cymbal, also added to the overall effect of the style. Just as in bebop, the walking bass sounds the harmonies and keeps the beat.

No musician in jazz pioneered more new ideas than **Miles Davis.** He learned his jazz craft as a young man in bebop when he was a sideman with Charlie Parker. After that he led the group which recorded the **Birth of the Cool** sessions, and also led the best known **bebop** or **hard bop** group of the 1950s that included, at different times, both **Sonny Rollins** and **John Coltrane** on tenor saxophone. Amazingly, he was also the leader of another historic recording session ten years after his **Birth of the Cool** sessions and was again instrumental in setting yet another trend. This 1959 session served to stimulate the next new sound in jazz, **modal jazz.**

Cannonball Adderley, along with **John Coltrane** and **Bill Evans,** was a sideman at that session, although he did not play on the number we listened to a few nights ago, *Blue in Green.* Tonight, **Cannonball** is here as a leader at the "Chez Imagination" with his friend from that 1959 session, pianist **Bill Evans,** and with the bassist and drummer from the Modern Jazz Quartet, **Percy Heath** and **Connie Kay.** At **Cannonball**'s special request, **Bill Evans** wrote this piece

Julian "Cannonball" Adderley grew up in Florida, but left in 1955 to move to New York for graduate studies at New York University; instead, after arriving in New York, he joined Oscar Pettiford's band. In 1957, Adderley replaced Sonny Rollins in Miles Davis's quintet and he remained with this group until 1959.

for him in **modal style.** You remember that when we talked about this system before, we said that **modal jazz:**

Modal Jazz

1. **Altered the focus of improvisation** from a rapidly changing series of chords, as we found in bebop, **to an interest in different scales and their new melodic possibilities.**

To that we should add that it:

2. **Slowed down the rate of change of the harmonies almost to a standstill. Modal pieces** take one chord, or vertical structure, and sustain these sounds for a relatively long time while **scalar improvisations** are layered over this supporting foundation.

3. **Created an effect of rapidly moving melodic notes over a static substructure.** In this style, the underlying vertical structure does move, it is not a drone, but it usually takes more time to move and only shifts slightly up or down. This chord climbs or descends a step or two and holds in place for a while as the **scalar improvisational process** continues.

The sound of **modal jazz** is very different from that produced by "improvising to the changes," and you will hear it clearly in this next example. **Cannonball Adderley**'s quartet, with **Bill Evans,** is ready to play **Evans**'s original for **Cannonball,** *Know What I Mean?*

CANNONBALL ADDERLEY, *KNOW WHAT I MEAN?* (CD SELECTION 2.18)

LISTEN

Wasn't that beautiful? **Evans** is truly a poet at the piano, a man who listens for every nuance of tone both in the instrument and in the chords themselves. After the brief, out-of-tempo introduction by the piano, did you notice that the pattern for the piece took a chord and held it for two measures (a long time at a slow tempo) and then shifted it to another level for another two measures? All the while, **Cannonball** played scales, not tunes, and very few motivic ideas. In their melodic solos, he and **Bill Evans** concentrated mostly on scales and the special effect of stressing one note of a scale more than another.

Connie Kay also used his drums differently in this piece from any drumming we have heard so far. He used **mallets,** drum sticks with padded tips, on his tom-toms in the first section to create a timpani, or orchestral kettle-drum, effect. It's also fascinating to hear how he changes time in this piece. The first section is in a slow four. The bass sets up a shift to double-time for the next section, and then **Cannonball** and **Connie Kay** shift the meter from **duple** to **triple,** $\frac{4}{4}$ to $\frac{3}{4}$, for the third section. All the while, the same modal principles hold sway—slowly shifting chords for a foundation and rapid melodic flights to modal scales layered above. When the group drops back to the tempo of the slow-moving original passage, **Connie Kay** returns to his mallets. A lovely and very interesting piece of **modal jazz.**

An electrifying free jazz quartet. Saxophonist, trumpeter, violinist, and composer Ornette Coleman (seated), is flanked by Billy Higgins, drums; Donald Cherry, trumpet; and Charles Haden, bass.

During this intermission, we need to talk a little about American history and the events that preceded and influenced the formation of another new style, **free jazz,** the music we are going to listen to next. Freedom was an issue very much on the mind of every black American in the late 1950s, and jazz musicians were certainly not exempt from the racial tensions that began to rock this nation. The Supreme Court declared segregation in public schools unconstitutional in 1954 and 1955, and the white-dominated southern states rebelled strongly against this ruling in 1956. As a result, blacks boycotted buses, had sit-ins at restaurants, marched, and forcibly integrated public institutions. More than a decade of civil strife followed, and it was sometimes violent—tear gas and police dogs, arrests, the bombing of a church, the assassinations of a president, an attorney general, and a civil rights leader. In this quest for real freedom, black Americans openly questioned authority and sought new means of expression in their lives and in their art. The phrase "Black is beautiful" was born, and black artists searched for new means of expression that would free them from the bondage of their recent past and connect them with the roots of their real and distant past. One jazz artist, **Ornette Coleman,** sought a new sound in jazz through free association during performance. His improvising musicians reacted to each other, and they rejected most of the previously recognized rules of jazz performance. In essence, he discarded melody, harmony, rhythm, and timbre as it was previously known and valued, and substituted spontaneous reaction and a call to "do your own thing" as the basic rules for the new music. **Free jazz** did not happen overnight, and others, such as Charles Mingus and Sun Ra, also pioneered in this endeavor, but one of the early important experiments was the performance of **Ornette Coleman's** *Free* by his quartet in 1959, the same year that **Miles Davis** made his modal recordings, including *Blue in Green.*

Here comes the group now, a quartet. **Ornette Coleman** is carrying a white, *plastic* saxophone. He originally bought it because he could not afford a new brass instrument, but he continues using it now, because the unique sound helps him express his emotion better. He thinks the tone is breathier and that he is able to continually create "his own sound" with it. His trumpeter, **Donald Cherry,** is carrying a pocket trumpet, an instrument that has many feet of a coiled brass tube compactly bent together so that it not only looks different but sounds different. The bass player, **Charlie Haden,** and the drummer, **Billy Higgins,** round out the ensemble. This group does not use a piano, but since these musicians are not going to improvise to a piece with chord changes, why would they need a piano? They are just

Donald Cherry soloing with his pocket trumpet. Cherry began his career performing with Ornette Coleman's groups in the 1950s and 1960s, and his style of free jazz is heavily influenced by Coleman. Cherry has spent a great deal of time studying the musics of other cultures, especially third world cultures, and his compositions reflect his interest in world music with many non-Western features.

about ready to go, so keep in mind these principles of **free jazz** as you listen. **Free jazz** calls for:

Free Jazz

1. The **discarding of conventional melody, harmony, rhythm, and timbre.**

2. The **freedom to play what you choose when you want to.**

3. The **requirement to listen to the other improvisers and to react to what they are playing.**

4. An **increased value on the element of surprise.**

After his original recording of this number, *Free,* **Ornette Coleman** said, "Each member goes his own way and still adds tellingly to the group endeavor. There was no predetermined chordal or time pattern. I think we got a spontaneous, free-wheeling thing going here." As you listen, keep **Coleman**'s objective in mind.

Ornette Coleman on alto saxophone is pictured here with bassist Jamaaladeen Tacuma and guitarist Charlie Ellerbe. Coleman formed the band Prime Time in 1975 and made several recordings with the electric band. Some of these recordings were made in Coleman's home town of Fort Worth, Texas, at the Caravan of Dreams recording studio where this picture was taken.

ORNETTE COLEMAN, *FREE* (CD SELECTION 3.1)

LISTEN

Did you notice that the musicians obviously worked out a pattern that they played together at the beginning and at the end? They must have felt uncomfortable leaving everything open and subject to chance, and so they imposed some external structure on this piece by using a preconceived pattern to frame the **free improvisations** of the central portion. Did you hear how the soloists tried to avoid feelings of key in their melodic solos, how they went rapidly all over their horns in an attempt to create sounds even before they had a chance to think about them? Did you also notice that often the drums, bass, and soloist (or soloists) were playing at different tempos, but that at other times they seemed to come together in some kind of agreement as a result of reacting to what the others were doing? And did you hear how the slightly different sounds of the plastic alto and the pocket trumpet, as well as a few squawks and bent pitches, also added to the effect of surprise, explosive energy, and freedom? These are the sounds of **free jazz** that set the pace for many years of experimentation and stylistic development that followed.

As you might have guessed, Miles Davis and his young sidemen once again became central figures for the introduction of yet another new style into the complex arena of jazz performance, **jazz/rock fusion.** These jazz musicians became fascinated with the electronic instruments of rock, with the return to simpler formal and harmonic schemes, especially the blues, with rock drumming, which divided each beat in four and expanded the size of the trap set, with the aesthetic principles of rock, with the amplification and the multi-track possibilities of this music, and, certainly not least of all, with the immense crowds of young people that rock concerts attracted. The result was a new style called **jazz/rock fusion** that continues to

Tenor saxophonist Michael Brecker formed the Brecker Brothers with his older brother Randy, who is a trumpet player. Brecker has been a New York session musician since 1970, and in 1987 he toured with Herbie Hancock's quartet through the United States and Japan.

evolve even today. For the last number on our Syncopating Saxophones program, Mr. Imagination has cranked his clock to 1988 and invited a tenor saxophonist who has performed with such diverse artists as Frank Zappa and Steely Dan on one side of the scale, Joni Mitchell and John Lennon in the middle, and Horace Silver, Chick Corea, and Herbie Hancock on the jazz end. Tonight he is at the "Chez Imagination" leading his own group, a sextet of five performers and one programmer. **Jazz/rock fusion** has introduced programmers and engineers into the musical equation on equal footing with the performing artists themselves. The resulting sound of most **jazz/rock fusion** performances is as much the creative act of these gifted technicians as it is the creative act of the composer/performers.

As they come on stage, notice that **Michael Brecker** is carrying not only his tenor saxophone but his Akai EWI (Electronic Wind Instrument), an eight-octave electronic device that is controlled by blowing, tonguing, fingering, and dials. **Charlie Haden,** who just played with **Ornette Coleman,** is back again on acoustic bass, and he, with **Herbie Hancock,** the virtuoso pianist, **Jack DeJohnette,**

Bassist Charlie Haden is a former sideman for Ornette Coleman. Haden formed the band Old and New Dreams in 1976 with three other former Coleman sidemen: Don Cherry, Dewey Redman, and Ed Blackwell.

Pianists Chick Corea and Herbie Hancock recorded an album together in 1978 entitled An Evening with Herbie Hancock and Chick Corea. *The two musicians both played with the Miles Davis Quintet (Hancock from 1963–1968 and Corea from 1968–1970) and each became a part of both the Cool Jazz and Fusion styles of jazz.*

the equally amazing drummer, and **Mike Stern,** the electric guitarist, will round out the rhythm section. Judd Miller, the synthesizer programmer, will see that the right sounds get mixed, separated, altered, or amplified at the right time. The tongue-in-cheek title, *Don't Try This at Home,* is actually a statement of fact: these sounds cannot be made at home. They require studio equipment *and* extraordinary musicians and technicians. " So," you ask, "what defines the style?"

Jazz/Rock fusion is:

Jazz/Rock Fusion

1. Music that **combines modern jazz improvisation with elements from rock 'n' roll.** The jazz improvisation can virtually derive from any modern jazz style, bebop, modal, free, and so on.

Jack DeJohnette helped change the old concept of drummer to that of jazz percussionist. Using the instruments of an expanded drum set for their unique sounds, or timbres, as well as for their rhythmic capabilities, he moved the sounds of percussion into a melodic domain.

2. Jazz music that **incorporates rock rhythmic drumming,** most notably the four-part division of the beat, as rhythmic accompaniment to the music. Most jazz, to this time, clung to the variations of triple division of the beat, the relaxed, shuffling rhythm so prominent in swing.

3. Music that **prominently displays the sounds of electric and electronic instruments.** Not only is a characteristic electronic timbre present when **jazz/rock** groups play, but new improvisational techniques also are apparent, for example, timbral solos, feedback solos, and so on.

4. Usually **loud.** Microphones and microphone pickups are now used to capture and transmit the sound of every instrument, including drums, and a new sense of balance for the ensembles has developed. Also, since the aesthetic of rock 'n' roll itself calls for great amplification, this aesthetic principle has been picked up by most of the **fusion** musicians, as well.

Let's see if this simple explanation is sufficient to distinguish the sound of this style from all the styles we have studied before. The group is all plugged in and ready to go, so let's listen to **Michael Brecker** as he plays *Don't Try This at Home*.

MICHAEL BRECKER, *DON'T TRY THIS AT HOME* (CD SELECTION 3.2)

The opening sounds, did you notice, appeared to be muted trumpet accompanied by strings? Obviously synthesized, since our sextet did not bring any of these players along. Did you see how **Brecker** and **Miller** made those sounds with Akai EWI and preprogrammed synthetic and sampled sounds? That's quite an arsenal for one little horn and a rack full of buttons, faders, and knobs! When **DeJohnette** entered on drums, did you notice the brilliant stick work that laid down the beat and divided it in fours? Being a great jazz drummer, and unlike most rock drummers, he did not lay down a thick, heavy beat with a strong two and four accent. Most rock drummers do this, and many **jazz/rock** drummers do, also, but **Jack DeJohnette**'s artistry is such that he can create the propulsive drive of rock and still keep the touch delicate.

Did you notice that as **Brecker** played melodies with his Akai EWI he got several tones at once moving along in parallel? He becomes, through modern electronics, a one-man sax section. Even his acoustic tenor saxophone is connected to a synthesizer via a microphone pickup, so it is possible for Brecker to play acoustic sounds, synthetic sounds, and a combination of both from his tenor. And I hope you enjoyed his brilliant acoustic tenor solo, as well. There are many great solo moments in this performance, not only by **Brecker** but by the other players, as well. I thought the **Herbie Hancock** piano solo in the middle of the piece was a knockout. I hope you did, too.

THE MUSICIANS SPEAK   BILLIE HOLIDAY

For my money Lester was the world's greatest. I loved his music, and some of my favorite recordings are the ones with Lester's pretty solos. . . . Lester sings with his horn; you listen to him and can almost hear the words. People think he's so cocky and secure, but you can hurt his feelings in two seconds. I know, because I found out once that I had. We've been hungry together, and I'll always love him and his horn.

I often think about how we used to record in those days. We'd get off a bus after a five-hundred-mile trip, go into the studio with no music, nothing to eat but coffee and sandwiches. . . . I'd say, "What'll we do, two-bar or four-bar intro?" Somebody'd say, "You play behind me the first eight, Lester," and then Harry Edison would come in or Buck Clayton and take the next eight bars. "Jo, you just brush and don't hit the cymbals too much.". . . . When I did "Night and Day" I had never seen that song before in my life. I don't read music, either. I just walked in, Teddy Wilson played it for me, and I did it.

With artists like Lester, Don Byas, Benny Carter, and Coleman Hawkins, something was always happening. No amount of preparation today is any match for them. In the old days, if we were one side short on a date, someone would say, "Try the blues in A flat," and tell me, "Go as far as you can go, honey." I'd stand up there and make up my words as I went along. . . .

I'll still remember Fox Theater in Detroit, Michigan. What Radio City is to New York, the Fox was to Detroit then. . . . But Detroit was between race riots then, and after three performances the first day, the theatre management went crazy. They claimed they had so many complaints about all those Negro men up there on the stage with those bare-legged white girls, all hell cut loose backstage.

They next thing we knew, they revamped the whole show. They cut out the girls' middle number. And when the chorus line opened the show, they'd fitted them out with special black masks and mammy dresses. They did both their numbers in blackface and those damn mammy getups.

When he saw what was happening, Basie flipped. But there was nothing he could do. We had signed the contracts to appear, and we had no control over what the panicky theatre managers did. But that wasn't the worst of it. Next they told Basie I was too yellow to sing with all the black men in his band. Somebody might think I was white if the light didn't hit me just right. So they got special dark grease paint and told me to put it on. It was my turn to flip. I said I wouldn't do it. But they had our name on the contracts and if I refused it might have played hell with bookings, not just for me, but for the future of all the cats in the band. So I had to be darkened down so the show could go on in dynamic . . . Detroit. It's like they say, there's no damn business like show business. You had to smile to keep from throwing up.

REVIEW   18

Primary Goal of Unit 18

Gain an acquaintance with the playing of four outstanding modern saxophonists: Stan Getz, Cannonball Adderley, Ornette Coleman, and Michael Brecker. Learn to distinguish the sounds of four important styles: cool jazz, modal jazz, free jazz, and jazz/rock fusion.

Study Questions

1. Might it be stylistically correct for a saxophonist to play a free jazz solo during a jazz/rock fusion performance? Why or why not? Would it be stylistically correct for a saxophonist to play a free jazz solo during a cool jazz performance? Why or why not?

2. In what ways is cool jazz a form of bebop? How does it differ from bebop?

3. In what ways is modal jazz a form of bebop? How does it differ from bebop?

4. In what ways is free jazz totally different from bebop? Are there any similarities between free jazz and bebop?

5. In the jazz/rock fusion performance we studied, *Don't Try This at Home,* what elements came from
   a. bebop
   b. cool jazz
   c. modal jazz
   d. free jazz
   e. rock 'n' roll
   f. elsewhere

6. Who are some important exponents of
   a. cool jazz
   b. modal jazz

c. free jazz
d. jazz/rock fusion
and what are their instruments? When did they play this music?

7. List three style characteristics of:
   a. jazz/rock fusion
   b. free jazz
   c. modal jazz
   d. cool jazz

1. What unusual instruments did two of the modern saxophonists in this unit play?

Other Concepts

2. What unusual instruments did two of the brass players in this unit play?

3. How did the drummer in the cool jazz ensemble, Alan Levitt, perform differently from Jack DeJohnette, the drummer in the jazz/rock fusion ensemble?

4. How did bassist Charlie Haden perform differently in his two numbers, *Free* and *Don't Try This at Home?* How was his bass played differently from that of the other fusion bassist we heard, Jaco Pastorius of Weather Report?

5. One group did not use a piano. Why? Could a piano have been incorporated successfully into the ensemble? If it could have, how might it have been played?

6. Did all these styles develop and change for purely musical reasons? How can the issue of race affect music?

7. Of the eight styles we have studied so far—New Orleans, Chicago, swing, bebop, cool, modal, free, and jazz/rock fusion, how many of them might have been heard live in New York City on the same day
   a. in 1939?
   b. in 1959?
   c. in 1979?

Extra Activity   Ask a good, professional, local jazz musician to come to class and tell you about his or her style of performance as well as his or her perception of the styles of certain key musicians, such as Louis Armstrong, Benny Goodman, Duke Ellington, Charlie Parker, Miles Davis, John Coltrane, Ornette Coleman, and Mary Lou Williams.

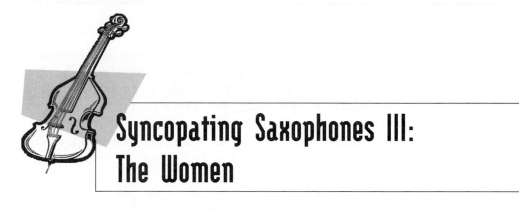

Syncopating Saxophones III: The Women

19

VI BURNSIDE, VI REDD, BARBARA THOMPSON, AND JANE IRA BLOOM
OBSERVING STYLE: SWING, BEBOP, FUSION, AND POSTMODERN

The "Chez Imagination" has booked a full roster of four outstanding soloists for tonight's show, so why don't you call some friends and see if you can get a party together for an evening out at the club? I am sure they will enjoy hearing these saxophonists, and perhaps we might have a chance to introduce your friends to one or two of the artists at intermission. We might even be able to go out for a bite to eat after the show with one of the bands. There's a bar over on Sixth Avenue and 48th Street called "Jim & Andy's" that's a favorite hangout for jazz musicians. The owner, James Koulouvaris, even keeps a postcard-covered bulletin board near the door so that road musicians can keep in touch with each other. You never know who you might see there, and if you're down on your luck you can always count on a friendly face and a helping hand.

We've heard a lot of jazz these last several weeks, and you are beginning to know your way around the music pretty well. I was impressed when I heard you explaining to that guy in the club last week why you thought the pianist in that bebop combo was a little off the mark in his solo, that he was making the changes all right but really wasn't playing any ideas. Your ears seem to be working very well now. And then you really knocked me out when that same guy asked you if you knew the name of the tune the band was playing, and you said, "It's called *Chi Chi*, but you can hear it's just a blues." Nice going! You are really becoming an astute listener.

Since our table has a good view of the bandstand, let's check out the setup and see what we can learn. By the arrangement of chairs and stands, can you predict the style? Make a guess and then let your ears tell you if you were right when the band starts playing. It is obviously a big band from what I can see: seven brasses, five saxes, and four rhythm. There's only one mike, and I don't see any amplified instruments, so that tells me something, too. Here come the musicians, and the players are taking their chairs. Since they are ready to go, I suspect they warmed up and tuned up backstage in the musicians' room. Obviously, these women are the **International Sweethearts of Rhythm.** I not only recognize some of the players from the time we heard them play before, but the band logo is plastered all over their fronts. The leader, Anna Mae Winburn, is moving to the mike to announce the tune and the soloist, *Sweet Georgia Brown* played by **Viola Burnside** on tenor saxophone. And here they go.

VI BURNSIDE, *SWEET GEORGIA BROWN* (CD SELECTION 3.3)

Didn't **Vi Burnside** wail away? She is a strong player and gets a big, powerful tone, a lot like Ben Webster. She can play a lot of notes, too. A couple of those passages moved right along. This tune, *Sweet Georgia Brown*, is a jazz standard, and not only have hundreds of arrangements, probably thousands, of this tune been made in nearly every style, but the chord progression has been lifted and used for a number of other jazz originals (such as John Eardley's *Demanton* and Bill Watrous's *Sweet Georgia Upside Down*). In the arrangement we just heard tonight, the tune got a straightforward big band treatment, with riffs, block chords, and section work for background, but it was tenor solo all the way. It is not easy for a single sax to power above all those hard-blowing instruments!

	Introduction	Head tenor lead **A A'**	1st chorus tenor solo	2nd chorus tenor solo	3rd chorus tenor solo
MEASURES	⊢ 8 ⊣	⊢ 16 + 16 ⊣	⊢ 32 ⊣	⊢ 32 ⊣	⊢ 32 ⊣

The Vi Burnside Combo: Pauline Braddy, drums; Flo Dryer, trumpet; Vi Burnside, tenor saxophone; Edna Smith, bass; and Shirley Moore, piano.

I had guessed **swing** when I saw the setup for an unamplified big band, and all the style clues were there in the music, as well—the sound, the vibrato, the phrasing, the band riffs, a tune with changes, the rhythm section work—all those things we've learned to recognize when we hear them. The style was **swing.** Did you get it? Let's see who's next.

The bandstand has been rearranged for a quintet. That alone tells us nothing. However, the piano is acoustic, and so is the bass, but the guitar is electric. They've got a mike under the lid of the piano and a second one up front for announcements, vocals, and maybe for the sax soloist if she wants to use it. Let's see who the players are. **Vi Redd** on alto saxophone and **Marian McPartland** on piano, two solid players. In fact, **McPartland** is really quite famous. And that is **Mary Osborne** on electric guitar. She is one of the best combo players and guitar soloists around. You are going to enjoy this group. Great, **Dottie Dodgion** is on drums. She keeps a terrific beat and can play swinging solos. The bass player, **Lynn Milano,** is fresh out of music school, so let's see how she does.

Alto saxophonist Vi Redd with Earl "Fatha" Hines at the piano and Ray Fisher on drums. Redd toured with Hines during 1964. As a saxophonist, she was influenced by Charlie Parker's style of playing and performed with many of the most important jazz musicians including Count Basie, Dizzy Gillespie, and Max Roach.

I just noticed that Mr. Imagination cranked his clock from 1945 to 1977 to get this group here for us tonight. I wonder what style we are going to hear now. It might be anything, because I know **Marian McPartland** can play them all, and this kind of a group can play most styles from **Chicago** to **free,** if they want to. I think I know what it is going to be, because I think I know **McPartland's** and **Redd's** preferences. Also, I think I can tell from the tune they just announced,

Marian McPartland, "First Lady of the Piano," emigrated from England to the United States in 1946. A modern pianist capable of swinging in any style, she also founded a record company, hosted a jazz radio series, and played a prominent role in jazz education.

because it came from the repertory of a certain style. Still, we'll just have to wait and see if they play this tune true to form or if they modernize it. Here they go with their version of Charlie Parker's *Now's the Time*, the same piece we studied in Unit 4 (CD selection 1.6).

VI REDD, *NOW'S THE TIME* (CD SELECTION 3.4)

The rhythm section, without guitar, started the piece, and did you catch the great bass work of **Lynn Milano** in that first chorus? I love it when bass players break the walking bass pattern and artfully throw in a little fill at the ends of phrases. And **Dodgion**'s drumming just sizzled in that opening statement. You could tell before you were two bars into the piece that a swinging performance was probably on its way. The guitar joined them about halfway through the first chorus and kept up the steady rhythm-guitar work until she and the alto played the head together starting at the third chorus.

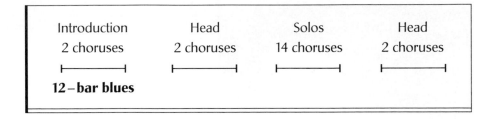

Introduction	Head	Solos	Head
2 choruses	2 choruses	14 choruses	2 choruses
⊢――――⊣	⊢――――⊣	⊢――――⊣	⊢――――⊣

12 – bar blues

You can't miss the blues, twenty choruses of a repeated 12-bar harmonic pattern.

You know something, this was an especially interesting performance for me, because I don't think everything was up to snuff. Hearing an inconsistency or an occasional mistake gives us a chance to talk about things in the music that might have gone better, that could have been more interesting, or even could have been better in tune. Don't get me wrong. These women are all superb musicians, and if they had been recording this number in a studio, they surely would have polished up every detail with another take. Since it was recorded live, a real performance for a real audience, in real time in a club, you have to realize that it is possible that occasionally a musician is tired, or sometimes a player might not have had a chance to warm up or tune up, or, as will also happen, a group is **a pick-up group,** musicians who haven't played together before. When this happens, they often don't have a chance to rehearse their numbers and call tunes they all know, like the blues, so they can **jam,** or improvise, their way through the job. Who knows? All of these possibilities are part of the realities of jazz in the real world and the art of live improvisation, and a listener needs to make the mental adjustment to hearing jazz in a way different from the way you listen to a Beethoven concert at Symphony Hall, where the notes are set, the style is rigidly fixed, there are no improvisations or spontaneous insertions of any kind, and the orchestra only plays in public after sufficient rehearsal. Imperfections must occur in real-time improvisation, but the exciting act of musical creation, not re-creation, more than makes up for this minor shortcoming. Still, I want you to be able to discriminate inventive improvisation from hackneyed playing, right notes from wrong ones, and great performances from lesser ones. I tell you what, I'll point out one thing that could have been better, and you listen again and see what other things you hear that you feel might have been done a little better. The first rough edge I heard came at the beginning of the head. The guitar and alto did not get off to a good unison start. Do you hear anything else? Describe what you heard.

VI REDD, *NOW'S THE TIME* (CD SELECTION 3.4)

Playing less than perfectly is certainly not a phenomenon restricted to female musicians. It is a byproduct of the high risk factors
involved in creating new music through improvisation. Now that you
have become knowledgeable in jazz and have developed your critical
listening skills, let me point out some rough places played by well-
known male jazz musicians in music we have studied in the past. We
did not dwell on these solos that "were not up to snuff," because we
were learning to listen to other things at the time. Now, you are a
critical listener and should be able to discern, distinguish, and corre-
late your accumulated wisdom with the musical information pouring
in your ears. What do you think of the Bobby Stark trumpet solo on
Bugle Call Rag from Unit 1? How about the Happy Caldwell tenor sax
solo on *Knockin' a Jug?* Or Jimmy Dorsey's clarinet solo on *Clarinet
Marmalade?*

CHOCOLATE DANDIES, *BUGLE CALL RAG* (CD SELECTION 1.1)

LOUIS ARMSTRONG, *KNOCKIN' A JUG* (CD SELECTION 1.13)

FRANKIE TRUMBAUER, *CLARINET MARMALADE* (CD SELECTION 2.14)

Get the idea? No one in jazz plays perfectly all the time. Improvisation
is too difficult, and if a player takes no risks, that player can only create
boring music. But now you are an accomplished listener and need to
separate the sterling from the silver plate.

Now that you have spent some time going through the music and
picking it apart, let's get back to the club and listen again for some of
the truly excellent things that happened in the performance of *Now's
the Time.* For instance, **Marian McPartland**'s solo had some great
ideas and smooth finger work, and did you catch the slick way she
threw in a quote from the introduction of Miles Davis's blues tune,
Walkin'? **Dottie Dodgion**'s drum solo created a fascinating meter shift
at the beginning, and **Vi Redd** has a great way of bending her sound
and toying with those blue notes. Good blues improvisation is more

A guitarist of legendary stature, Mary Osborne is known for her harmonic invention, smooth technique, and lyrical melodic solos.

than notes; it is soulful expression. I especially liked her second solo chorus. There is a lot there.

You were going to tell me what style you were listening to. Did you get it? Straight ahead **bebop** as far as I'm concerned.

I am so glad you were able to bring your friends to the club tonight. One of the main reasons we go out to hear jazz is to catch those great moments in improvisation when something happens musically that has never happened before and probably will never happen again. No musician, no matter how great, can improvise perfect new solos in an endless stream from his or her first year on the bandstand to retirement forty or fifty years later, but every great jazz player brings something special to each and every performance. Jazz musicians don't just rehash the same old thing night after night. Only a tiny fraction of all the great jazz that has been created in this century has been captured on record, so I think it is important that we never forget that jazz is a living art, a performing art, where musicians and audience get together to create this beautiful new music. We, the listeners, are a part of the

A versatile drummer, Dottie Dodgion can swing a big band or subtly back a combo.

performance, too. Jazz has always been a communal music that relies on a bond between artist and knowledgeable, sympathetic listener. Since the real artistic miracle only takes place in live performance, I hope this little discursion I have taken with you to work on training your ears to hear imperfections will in fact also help train your ears to hear the perfection of wonderful things new, unique, and exciting.

I am sorry we didn't have a chance to meet with the musicians during intermission, but we had better pay attention now, for the next group is ready to go. It is called **Paraphernalia,** and it is a quintet from Britain, but the first time I heard the leader, alto and soprano saxophonist **Barbara Thompson,** and her husband, drummer **Jon Hiseman,** they were playing in Warsaw, Poland, at a Jazz Festival. Jazz is definitely America's music, and I consider it America's classical music, but now it has spread worldwide, and some great players can be found everywhere. When I first heard these two in the 1980s, they were playing with the United Jazz + Rock Ensemble (UJ+RE), so I guess that gives away the likely style of the next performance.

The United Jazz + Rock Ensemble is a German-based band with international membership. This group was organized by Wolfgang Dauner in 1975 and includes: Ack van Rooyen, Ian Carr, and Kenny Wheeler on trumpet; Albert Mangelsdorff on trombone; Charlie Mariano and Barbara Thompson on saxophone; Volker Kriegel on guitar; Wolfgang Dauner on keyboards; Eberhard Weber on bass; and Jon Hiseman on drums.

Mr. Imagination has had to crank his clock from 1977 to 1991 in order to accommodate this group's appearance. They are set up and plugged in now, and you can see that it is a quintet. Besides **Barbara Thompson** and **Jon Hiseman,** that is Peter Lemer on the keyboards, Malcolm MacFarlane on the electric and acoustic guitars, and Phil Mulford on electric bass. They are going to play, *You Must Be Jokin'.*

BARBARA THOMPSON, *YOU MUST BE JOKIN'* (CD SELECTION 3.5)

The first sounds of the intro, the first eight bars, were reminiscent of one style of current American popular music, and as soon as the synthesizer added the sounds of a synthetic big band and the drummer came charging in, the next four bars of the intro, we had a Latin/Rock

Barbara Thompson, star British reed soloist, is shown tightening the ligature of her soprano saxophone. She composes for film and television, leads her own jazz group, and plays with The United Jazz + Rock Ensemble.

beat going for us. Obviously, this piece is going to be a **fusion** piece, a fusion of styles. **Thompson** played alto saxophone for the head, and it was almost in 32-measure popular song form, AABA, except the last "A" was changed to be more like "B." Then the band did some rhythmic things on a single chord for a while (I'd call it a vamp) before **Thompson** started her real solo. That she played on soprano saxophone, and what a great solo it was! She is a fine artist who lays down her ideas with certainty and clarity. The guitar and synthesizer solos which followed, as well as the bass and drum solos, were equally fine. Every once in a while we get a little recapitulation of the tune or of the vamp, devices which aid in unifying the performance, and then it's off to more solo work and a brief recap for an ending. Very nicely done!

The last performer on tonight's card is also a soprano saxophonist, but she has a little black box down by her feet that allows some beautiful electronic transformations of sound. **Jane Ira Bloom** plays her soprano sax into a microphone attached to that box, which of course

Soprano saxophonist Jane Ira Bloom modifies her acoustic instrument sound with a specially engineered electronic device which is operated by foot pedals.

goes to an amplifier and speakers. When she plays, she can not only get the acoustic sound of her instrument, but, by stepping on pedals, get varied sounds and multiple sounds. Also, her playing is almost like a dance, and as she moves her instrument around the microphone, she takes advantage of the Doppler effect, changes in sound due to motion, to create totally unique sounds. Recently she was commissioned by NASA, the space agency, to compose music inspired by our space explorations, and she wrote *Most Distant Galaxy*, an ethereal and otherworldly piece motivated by Gus Grissom's words, "There is a clarity, a brilliance to space that simply doesn't exist on earth." Perhaps we can't all experience outer space with our bodies, but through our imagination, and through our art, we may actually be able to experience even more. **Jane Ira Bloom** is here this night in 1992 with a sextet. In addition to **Bloom** on soprano saxophone and live electronics, she has two trumpet players, Kenny Wheeler and Ron Horton, Kenny Werner on piano, Rufus Reid on bass, and Jerry Granelli on drums and electro-acoustic percussion. In one way this next piece we are going to hear is **fusion** jazz, because of the electronic sounds, but in an important, fundamental way it is not; it lacks the rock drumming. Instead, the percussionist sculpts these sounds, just as **Bloom** invents timbres and articulations that take us *Further Into the Night*. If we had to put a stylistic label on this music, I would suggest **postmodern jazz** in keeping with the terminology used in art and literature. Let's listen to **Jane Ira Bloom** play her composition/improvisation, *Further Into the Night*.

JANE IRA BLOOM, *FURTHER INTO THE NIGHT* (CD SELECTION 3.6)

It's been quite a night. Before we turn back the clock and head out to "Jim & Andy's," what can you say about the music you just heard? Can you make a comment or two about the elements of music you heard in each piece that help you identify the style, such as melody, harmony, rhythm, orchestration, or instrumentation, and about the idiosyncrasies of playing that help you identify the individual players, such as tone quality, melodic devices, type of solo improvisation, and so on?

 **REVIEW** 19

Primary Goal of Unit 19

Sample the virtuosic solo playing of some women saxophone players; begin to evaluate solo and group performance; continue to make stylistic judgments of individuals and ensembles.

Study Questions

1. Name four women saxophone players, and name or describe the groups you have heard each perform with. To what decade does each performance you heard belong?

2. For the four performances you heard, assign a style and give three reasons why you think each performance appropriately belongs to the style you assigned. If any of the ensembles does not properly belong to one of the eight major styles we have studied, explain what you heard in their playing that doesn't fit into the pattern of general characteristics of a style.

3. What kinds of things might an experienced listener notice in a performance that help evaluate the success or failure of the work of a soloist or ensemble? Of those items you listed, rate their importance, using a scale of 1 (least important) to 10 (most important), and then compare your list with those of your classmates. Are the same features equally important to all?

4. One piece on this evening's concert had no regular beat. Was it jazz? Why or why not?

5. One piece on this concert had a Latin/Rock beat. Was it jazz? Why or why not?

6. One piece on this concert used a style that had faded from currency almost two decades earlier. Was it jazz? Why or why not?

7. What does it take to be "modern"? What does it take to be "post-modern"?

1. What is the difference between a "drummer" and a "percussionist"?

Other Concepts

2. What might "electro-acoustic percussion instruments" be?

3. What might "live electronics" be?

4. How does one play a synthesizer solo? Are there many ways to do this?

5. What role does the listener play in the creation of jazz? Who are the members of the jazz community?

6. What is a "pick-up group"?

7. How does one "jam," and what is a "jam session"?

Reviewing the Men and Women of Jazz

20

It is time to remind you again how much you have learned these last several weeks listening to jazz at the "Chez Imagination." It has been a genuine pleasure for me to accompany you to hear these talented musicians display their wares, and I hope it has been just as much fun for you, too. At this point, I know you have placed the sounds and names and something about many of the major players in jazz into your cerebral random access memory, and along with this included your own impression of their talent, their contribution, and their sincerity. You have experienced for yourself how each jazz artist is very much like a poet, an interpreter of the world who communicates not just words or notes but feelings and meanings, a person working to make this planet a better place to live. These gifted beings create objects of beauty that have special meaning for those who take the trouble to experience them fully and receive the expressions of joy and sorrow, pride and remorse. The great jazz men and women have all paid their dues in many ways, and in truth they did it not so much for themselves but really for you and me. So, let's take stock of who they are and review a little of what they did.

To help you, I have created a list of all the players we have emphasized in our discussions. Many more have been mentioned, and there are hundreds more you will surely learn about someday as you go off on your own explorations. But every one of these musicians has played for you at the "Chez Imagination" and received at least a modest commentary, so let's begin with these few. If first you fill in what you know without referring back to the book or to your notes, the blank spaces will tell you which areas need a little serious review. Also, if you play a "question and answer" game with a friend from the class, you can solidify and move into active recall what you already have learned in an efficient and painless manner!

IMPORTANT MUSICIANS WE HAVE STUDIED

One played tuba for you (but he also plays string bass), and a couple played electric bass or bass guitar. Many play in different styles, depending on the band with which they are working at the time. To check your memories, why don't you list a group with which they played and the style of that group. If you can add an approximate date (+ or − ten years), so much the better.

Bass Players

	Group	Style	Date
Carter, Ron			
Chambers, Paul			
Duvivier, George			
Haden, Charlie			
Heath, Percy			
Kirby, John			
Milano, Lynn			
Neidlinger, Buell			
Page, Walter			
Pastorius, Jaco			
Reid, Rufus			
Stewart, Leroy "Slam"			
Wright, Eugene			

Like bass players, most drummers play more than one style. List here the group, style, and approximate date for the performance we studied.

Drummers

	Group	Style	Date
Acuna, Alex			
Bellson, Louis			
Braddy, Pauline			
Charles, Dennis			
Cobb, Jimmy			
Cole, Cozy			
Dodgion, Dottie			

Higgins, Billy   _____   _____   _____
Hiseman, Jon   _____   _____   _____
Jones, Jo   _____   _____   _____
Kay, Connie   _____   _____   _____
Marshal, Kaiser   _____   _____   _____
Mason, Harvey   _____   _____   _____
Morello, Joe   _____   _____   _____
Roach, Max   _____   _____   _____
Taylor, Art   _____   _____   _____

Guitar Players

Until recently, guitar players, like the bass and percussion players, were primarily restricted to rhythm section work. Now, of course, the guitar is one of the most popular solo instruments in jazz, and many

Working musicians spent many hours on a band bus traveling from engagement to engagement. This photo, taken while Duke Ellington was on tour in 1962, shows screech trumpeter William "Cat" Anderson and saxophonist Johnny Hodges distracted from their card game.

bands have a guitarist for their leader. For these players, too, remember the groups they played with, the style of that performance, and the approximate date.

	Group	Style	Date
Green, Freddie	_____	_____	_____
Lang, Eddie	_____	_____	_____
Osborne, Mary	_____	_____	_____
Scofield, John	_____	_____	_____
Stern, Mike	_____	_____	_____

Pianists

The piano players of jazz have always been both soloists and ensemble players. We have listened to quite a few, all of them significant artists, and we still haven't touched on many more of my favorites, like Oscar Peterson, Earl Hines, Fats Waller, Nat "King" Cole, Thelonious Sphere Monk, and on and on. You'll have to sample these great artists later on your own. For now, try to organize what you know about those we have heard at the club.

	Group	Style	Date
Barron, Kenny	_____	_____	_____
Basie, William "Count"	_____	_____	_____
Brubeck, Dave	_____	_____	_____
Ellington, Edward "Duke"	_____	_____	_____
Evans, Bill	_____	_____	_____
Garner, Erroll	_____	_____	_____
Haig, Al	_____	_____	_____
Henderson, Fletcher	_____	_____	_____
Henderson, Horace	_____	_____	_____
James, Bob	_____	_____	_____
Johnson, James P.	_____	_____	_____
Johnson, Pete	_____	_____	_____
McPartland, Marian	_____	_____	_____
Morton, Ferdinand "Jelly Roll"	_____	_____	_____
Powell, Earl "Bud"	_____	_____	_____
Powell, Mel	_____	_____	_____

Ra, Sun ——————— ———— ————
Strayhorn, Billy ——————— ———— ————
Sullivan, Joe ——————— ———— ————
Tatum, Art ——————— ———— ————
Taylor, Cecil ——————— ———— ————
Williams, Clarence ——————— ———— ————
Zawinul, Joe ——————— ———— ————

Reed Players

For saxophonists, it is important to remember which instrument or instruments the player has achieved his or her reputation on. Most of the players you have heard at the "Chez Imagination" were playing their primary instrument, the chief exception being Jimmy Dorsey, who achieved fame as a leader and alto saxophone soloist. Nearly all the saxophonists have doubled on clarinet at one time or another, but one musician on this list has remained exclusively a clarinetist for most of his very long career. On this page, list the instrument you remember hearing at the club and relate those sounds to group, style, and approximate date.

	Instrument	Group	Style	Date
Adderley, Julian "Cannonball"	———————	———————	———————	————
Bechet, Sidney	———————	———————	———————	————
Bloom, Jane Ira	———————	———————	———————	————
Brecker, Michael	———————	———————	———————	————
Burnside, Viola	———————	———————	———————	————
Carter, Benny	———————	———————	———————	————
Coleman, Ornette	———————	———————	———————	————
Coltrane, John	———————	———————	———————	————
Desmond, Paul	———————	———————	———————	————
Dorsey, Jimmy	———————	———————	———————	————
Getz, Stan	———————	———————	———————	————
Gonsalves, Paul	———————	———————	———————	————
Goodman, Benny	———————	———————	———————	————
Hawkins, Coleman	———————	———————	———————	————
Lacy, Steve	———————	———————	———————	————
Mulligan, Gerry	———————	———————	———————	————
Parker, Charlie	———————	———————	———————	————
Patrick, Pat	———————	———————	———————	————

Redd, Elvira "Vi"	_____	_____	_____ _____
Redman, Don	_____	_____	_____ _____
Rollini, Adrian	_____	_____	_____ _____
Rollins, Sonny	_____	_____	_____ _____
Shorter, Wayne	_____	_____	_____ _____
Thompson, Barbara	_____	_____	_____ _____
Trumbauer, Frankie "Tram"	_____	_____	_____ _____
Young, Lester "Prez"	_____	_____	_____ _____

All but one of these players plays slide trombone. Which one played valve trombone at the club?

Trombone Players

	Group	Style	Date
Anderson, Ray	_____	_____	_____
Brookmeyer, Bob	_____	_____	_____
Johnson, J. J.	_____	_____	_____
Liston, Melba	_____	_____	_____
Rank, Bill	_____	_____	_____
Teagarden, Jack	_____	_____	_____

This list also includes cornet and flugelhorn players, for Louis played both trumpet and cornet at different times in his career and Miles played trumpet and flugelhorn from the 1950s on to the end of his career. Also, one player brought his pocket trumpet to the club, but none of these players came with a bass trumpet or a slide trumpet. You'll have to search these out on your own.

Trumpet Players

	Group	Style	Date
Armstrong, Louis "Satchmo"	_____	_____	_____
Beiderbecke, Leon "Bix"	_____	_____	_____
Brown, Clifford	_____	_____	_____
Cherry, Donald	_____	_____	_____
Davis, Ernestine "Tiny"	_____	_____	_____

Davis, Miles   _____ _____ _____
Edison, Harry "Sweets"   _____ _____ _____
Franks, Rebecca Coupe   _____ _____ _____
Gillespie, John "Dizzy"   _____ _____ _____

Singers

None of these categories is less representative than this one. Of course we heard Don Redman singing, and we know that Louis Armstrong and Jack Teagarden are great jazz singers, but you really must take the time to listen to some Ella Fitzgerald, Bessie Smith, Sarah Vaughan, Betty Carter, and the group Lambert, Hendricks, and Ross. Even so, that would only be the tip of the proverbial iceberg.

Progressive jazz innovator Stan Kenton expanded his jazz orchestra beyond the traditional instrumentation of rhythm section, brass, and reeds. Notice the horns (French horns) seated to the right of the saxophones and the tuba to the left of the trombones.

	Group	Style	Date
Holiday, Billie	_____	_____	_____
Roché, Betty	_____	_____	_____
Waters, Ethel	_____	_____	_____

The only instrument from the "miscellaneous instruments" category represented here is the vibraphone, and we weren't able to invite two of its most famous players to the club, Lionel Hampton and Gary Burton. Put them on your list!

Vibraphone Players

	Group	Style	Date
Norvo, Kenneth "Red"	_____	_____	_____
Samuels, Dave	_____	_____	_____

If my count is correct, there are 103 jazz musicians on this list, and there were many more who played for us in some of the bands that came to the club. Now aren't you proud of yourself? Think how much you have learned and experienced since you began patronizing the "Chez Imagination." Of course, you have learned much more than a brief "Who's Who" of jazz musicians, you have also learned many things about the music and the jazz business, as well as a great deal about style. We'll review these things in their own good time, but before we turn our attention away from the individual performers of jazz, I have a surprise for you at the club. Stan Kenton is going to lead his orchestra in a number for you that focuses on the nineteen individual members of the band. The year is 1952, and **Stan Kenton** was a leading figure in a style he called **progressive jazz.** I'm sure you will like it.

STAN KENTON, *PROLOGUE* (CD SELECTION 3.7)

Review of Concepts and Terms

21

You have learned a great deal about jazz since you started coming to the club, and I hope you agree it has been much more fun than work. We have just spent some time reviewing the major musicians you have encountered, and now we ought to do a little review of some of the useful terms and concepts you have incorporated into your vocabulary and thinking. Some questions get straightforward answers—you either know what a snare drum is or you don't. Others are equivocal—for example, where did jazz originate, or what is jazz? And a few have no agreed-upon answer; they are thought provokers meant to stimulate discussion and create a situation where one answer may be valid for one person and a totally different answer correct for a person of different persuasion—for example, what is the public's perception of jazz and has it changed over time? Or, is jazz different in different parts of the world? Or, is jazz different for people of different educational backgrounds?

So, if you are comfortable and ready to begin, I'll start with questions about the instruments. Here we go.

INSTRUMENTS

1. Describe the differences between a trumpet, a cornet, and a pocket trumpet. Who played pocket trumpet?

2. How do these instruments look and sound different: a trombone, a valve trombone, and a tuba? Who played valve trombone, and who played tuba?

3. The normal reed instruments of a sax section are saxophones and clarinet. Tell me something about all of these: the clarinet, soprano

saxophone, alto saxophone, tenor saxophone, baritone saxophone, bass saxophone, and Akai EWI (Electronic Wind Instrument). Can you name a notable player for each? One saxophonist used "live electronics." What was that all about?

4. We now refer to pianists as keyboard players. Describe the differences among these: acoustic piano, Rhodes electric piano, and keyboard synthesizer. Do you know anything about digital samplers and MIDIs?

5. Bass playing has changed, as well. What are the differences among acoustic bass, electric bass, and electric bass guitar?

6. Can you explain the differences among acoustic guitar, amplified acoustic guitar, electric guitar, and banjo?

7. What is a vibraphone (vibes)?

8. As pianists have become keyboardists, drummers have become percussionists. The simple drum set has expanded and new instruments have been invented. Describe these instruments of the trap drum set: bass drum, foot pedal, snare drum, tom-toms, ride cymbals, hi-hat or sock cymbals, sticks, mallets, wire brushes, rim, and wood block. Also, what is an electro-acoustic instrument?

9. In a big band, what instruments are typically in the brass and reed sections?

10. What instruments commonly comprise the rhythm section?

Good work! Most of that information about instruments should be second nature to you by now, and any questions that still feel insecure can be answered by asking a little help from your teacher. Now let's move on to a few of the technical terms you have learned while listening to the music. I'll write a sentence or two, putting certain words in boldface. You define those boldfaced words.

TECHNICAL TERMS

1. When I heard Coltrane's **combo** at the Jazz Showcase, he **doubled** on tenor and soprano saxophones.

2. Woody's **sidemen** included Stan Getz, Serge Chaloff, Zoot Sims, and Al Cohn. *Four Brothers* and *Early Autumn* had **arrangements** that used a **thickened melodic line** technique.

3. At the **jam session,** the trumpet and drums **traded fours** before the sax started his solo. The piano did a good job of **comping,** but the bass player couldn't get a decent **walking pattern** going. He was strictly a **two-beat** bass player.

4. What did I like best on those **LPs?** With the Brubeck **quartet** I liked the **three-against-fours;** with Miles's **quintet** I liked the **modal improvisation;** with the Coleman **octet** I liked the **free improvisation;** and with the Mulligan **nonette** I like the way Mulligan **made all those changes** at break-neck speed during his solo.

5. Did you catch all those great sounds Bechet's group added to their solos—the big sax **vibrato,** the bass switch from tuba to **pizzicato** string bass, the trombone **glissandos** and plunger **mute,** and the clarinet growls. Even the drummer threw in a **rumba rhythm** and the pianist a great **stride** solo.

6. Hey man, you won't need a **fake book** for the next tune. It is just **blues** in B♭. The tune after that is in **pop song form.** The **changes** are like *I Got Rhythm*, but the **bridge** uses the bridge **chords** from *Cherokee*.

7. In the recording studio we are going to change the **envelope of sound** and add **reverberation.** We'll use that bass **ostinato** for a **drone** during the long **intro,** and have you throw in an **out-of-tempo** keyboard solo before the band comes in with the **up-tempo head** in **triple meter.**

8. I really dig the **counterpoint** of the **collective improvisation** when the **trad jazz** groups play. Also, I think it is great when they make that key change at the **third strain** and the trumpet goes into a **stop time** solo.

9. That woman playing **boogie** piano really **swings.** I don't see how she can keep that **eight-to-the-bar** pattern going while she throws in all those **ideas** and **quotes** in her solo.

10. Lady Day liked to sing **standards,** but she had a whole **library** of original **charts,** like *God Bless the Child*. Whenever she had a **gig** with Prez, he'd **back** with some of the most lyrical **lines,** and sometimes he would play those **rhythmic figures** on one note with those **false fingerings.**

During our nights at the club, we used a lot more technical language than I called for in these ten items, and you can easily review them throughout the book by looking at the review sections at the back of each unit and by scanning the words in boldface type throughout the text. Once you have heard them used and used them once or twice yourself, they are yours forever.

Well, so much for technical terms, let's move on to concepts. These will probably receive answers that are a little vague, because sometimes they change from style to style, sometimes they can be done in more than one way, even within the same style, and some of these questions don't really have answers.

CONCEPTS

1. How have changes in recording technology affected the production and dissemination of jazz?

2. Drummers are thought of as timekeepers, but from your experiences in listening, does that accurately describe the contributions of drummers to jazz?

3. Jazz has always cut a swath through black and white America, sometimes in positive ways and other times with difficulty and negative results. From what you know, has jazz helped advance or retard the cause of equal rights in America and the world?

4. At virtually every live jazz performance, someone will "play a clam" or foul up a solo. How important is this, and why?

5. What is "the jazz community," and what roles do its various members play?

6. Jazz players are very concerned with their sound and with swinging. Why are sound and swing so important?

7. Club owners don't often get much positive attention. In fact, they often catch flack from musicians and patrons alike—musicians complain about pay and working conditions and patrons about covers, minimums, the cost of food and drink, and the quality of entertainment. For a moment, put yourself in the manager's or owner's shoes. What are your responsibilities, risks, problems, and rewards?

8. Styles change. Why? Also, what is it that tells us when a new style has emerged?

9. Some people like straight-ahead jazz, others like trad, and still others like avant-garde, experimental sounds. In fact, some people say they like jazz but only listen to innocuous background music and think they are listening to jazz. What accounts for these differences?

10. We spent a lot of time learning to hear formal structure while listening to jazz performance. Why is this an important skill, or is it?

Everyone who begins to approach expertise in some subject likes to know things that insiders share. They could live very well without these private tidbits, but it is fun to know some things the squares do not. So, here is a beginning list of trivia for you to tuck behind some cobweb in your attic.

TRIVIA

Identify:

1. Tram

2. Arkestra

3. Chocolate Dandies

4. Sweets

5. UR+JE

6. Bird

7. Fusion

8. Jim & Andy's

9. scat

10. Birth of the Cool

Jazz is filled with humor. Not only do musical jokes crop up in the music, but one of the major pastimes of musicians on the road and musicians socializing at intermission or at after-hours clubs is telling musician jokes and jokes about musicians. This next recording is pretty old, one that was issued when rock 'n' roll was just beginning to dominate the popular music market. Perhaps it might be a good way to cap off a trivia session.

STAN FREBERG, *THE GREAT PRETENDER* (CD SELECTION 3.8)

Review of Styles

22

Little by little we have been building a foundation for critical listening that is based on an understanding of jazz styles. Our ears have been our primary receptors of this information, and this book and your teacher have served as guides. Though styles overlap, have been divided into substyles, and have sometimes received transitory or conflicting names, there are clearly eight major groupings in which nearly all jazz may be categorized. To help solidify this complex body of knowledge, definitions from the preceding pages have been gathered here for systematic review.

Let's begin first with a working definition of our entire subject.

A WORKING DEFINITION OF JAZZ

Jazz is an African-American music born in the southern United States around the beginning of the 20th century, which first matured in New Orleans, Louisiana. This American music has many easily identifiable characteristics, and most of these features are present in nearly every jazz performance:

1. Improvisation;

2. A steady beat or pulse;

3. A method of performance that follows a musical structure based on a repeated series of chords, a harmonic pattern called the changes;

4. The employment of scales and melodies in improvisation that exploit blue notes;

5. The prominent use of syncopation;

6. Sounds unique to the individual performer and the individual group, sounds that feature the individual performance characteristics of jazz soloists or the distinctive group characteristics of bands and combos;

7. The varied sounds of particular instruments and their non-traditional methods of performance, which are favored by jazz musicians;

8. A rhythm section;

9. The supremacy of the improviser, which places the artistry of the improvising soloist above the usually dominant position of the composer of Western classical music; and

10. It swings!

Of course, we know by now that there are almost as many exceptions to the norm as there are jazz performers and jazz performances, but most of these rules hold true most of the time.

STYLES

We also placed the major styles of jazz into a chronological order that grouped each style roughly into a pattern of change articulated by the decades of this century.

Jazz Styles

ORIGINS	ca. 1900
I. New Orleans Style	1910s and 1920s
II. Chicago Style	1920s and 1930s
III. Swing	1930s and 1940s
IV. Bebop	1940s and 1950s
V. Cool Jazz	1950s

VI.	Modal Jazz	1960s and 1970s
VII.	Free Jazz	1960s and 1970s
VIII.	Jazz/Rock Fusion	1970s and 1980s
	Neoclassical Jazz	1980s and 1990s

We haven't dealt with origins in any detail, and that really is a subject best left to a jazz history course. Also, we have only touched on neoclassical jazz, but we will be exploring this aspect of today's music a little later. Therefore, of the eight major styles we have listened to carefully, we might point out these important characteristics that help set one apart from the other.

New Orleans Style Jazz

1. Has collective improvisation in the ensemble performance interspersed with solo improvisations that are accompanied by rhythm section and occasional background support from the rest of the combo;

2. Primarily uses an original jazz repertoire composed in ragtime (march) and blues forms;

3. Utilizes a loose rhythmic feel with four beats to the bar that generally matches the improvisatory attitude of the players and the style;

4. Employs wind instrument sounds that frequently feature large vibratos, bent pitches, non-classical sounds (like growls, rips, non-standard mutes, and breathy tones), and energized phrasing and articulation; and

5. Is a music for small combos (usually two to four melodic instruments and two to four players in the rhythm section).

Chicago Style Jazz

1. Moved toward a reliance on arrangements that set or fix the performance of portions of the piece for band ensemble work. These parts were often created "by ear" rather than written down, and they also used cornet or saxophone lead while the other horns filled in the harmonies. In these band sections, the parts move along together rather than in the New Orleans fashion of separate, distinct, layered melodic lines;

2. Often has a greater concentration of energy at the end of each chorus rather than at the beginning or evenly distributed throughout it, and this feature contributes to a powerful forward sense of drive;

3. Often reduces the volume near the end of the piece in order to facilitate a build-up of sound, or crescendo, for a climax at the end;

4. Favors a popular rhythm in its up-tempo numbers that has been called "shuffle style," a tense series of uneven eighth notes with a pronounced accent on the longer note followed by a weak off-beat;

5. Often employed an increased use of sharp tonguing in both the solos and the ensemble work, which tended to focus more attention on virtuosity and other purely musical features; and

6. Expanded the instrumentation, frequently adding an extra saxophone or two.

Swing

1. First developed as bands enlarged and coalesced around three sections: the brass section (which quickly developed a trumpet section and a trombone section), a saxophone section (really a reed section of saxophones, clarinets, and, later, flutes, oboes, and so on), and the omnipresent rhythm section. Small combos and soloists also played in **swing** style, but the motivating force for the new style was the developing sound of the big bands;

2. Called for a new partner in the creative mix: the arranger. Arrangements and the work of composer/arrangers became, at times, as important as the musical discourse of the improvising soloists;

3. Changed the character of instrumental solos produced in earlier styles. As instrumental virtuosity progressed, soloists tended to play their regularly accented scalar or arpeggiated patterns in equally balanced units. Thus, swing phrasing tended to become classical—left side balancing right, antecedent ideas matching consequent conclusions; and

4. Rhythm sections standardized on piano, string bass, and drum set with the common addition of guitar (banjo is no longer used), and these instruments developed new musical functions for themselves. The bass divided 4-beat measures in two; the guitar strummed chords equally on every beat; the drums played 4-beat patterns on part of the set (for example, a stick on the ride cymbal or brushes on the snare) and 2-beat patterns on another part (usually the left foot on the newly developed foot-operated sock cymbal); and the piano began to move away from its older rhythmic function in order to concentrate more fully on melodic and harmonic areas.

Bebop

1. Employed a distinctive new articulation. The fast-running eighth notes were equalized and the off-beat eighth notes were slightly accented. This reversed the stress of the earlier swing solos, changed the on-the-beat swing rhythm to the off-the-beat bebop motion;

SWING   ▲ u ▲ u ▲ u ▲ u | ▲ u ▲ u ▲ u ▲ u | ▲ u ▲ u ....

BEBOP   u ▲ u ▲ u ▲ u ▲ | u ▲ u ▲ u ▲ u ▲ | u ▲ u ▲ ....

2. Declassified swing phrasing (pun intended). Instead of seeking classical phrasing with its balanced, equal lengths that fit regularly into 4- and 8-measure patterns, bebop musicians sought to create asymmetrical phrases which crossed over the usual beginning and ending points, which sometimes elided one group of notes with the next, which regularly interspersed phrases of varying lengths, from very long to very short;

3. Strove to create improvised solos that had structural coherence. The statement of "ideas" in melodic solos, that is, short patterns of notes serving as musical motives, and the development of those ideas within the context of a solo, became central to improvisational thinking in bebop;

4. Changed the nature of rhythm section work. The totality included a walking bass, a drummer "riding the cymbal" and reserving the snare and bass drum for syncopated attacks, and a "comping" piano that interspersed infrequent chordal patterns of harmonically enriched chords; and

5. Highlighted an expanded harmonic vocabulary. In the melodic solos, as well as in their accompaniments, more attention was paid by the soloists and the pianist to chromatic tones, altered chords, and substitute harmonies.

Cool Jazz

1. Was a restrained, understated music. It never surged to excesses of loudness or harshness and often had the light drumwork accompaniment of wire brushes on snares and cymbals. Cool jazz was always played at a subdued volume level—not necessarily soft, but never loud;

2. Was, however, a music capable of brilliant moments, of fast, almost

breathless, playing. When cool jazz musicians engaged in up-tempo displays, their virtuosity had to appear effortless;

3. Also took a renewed interest in counterpoint, the fascination with producing jazz music that takes different melodies and combines them into a harmonious arrangement;

4. Used a **repertory** of arrangements and improvisations based primarily on popular songs of the standard repertory (jazz standards) and jazz originals in popular song form; and

5. Quickly became a listening or concert music rather than dance music. This relaxed, refined, and sometimes elegant music captured a large popular audience during the 1950s, especially among the college communities and their graduates, and this music made a lasting impression on the shape of jazz to come.

Modal Jazz

1. Altered the focus of improvisation from a rapidly changing series of chords, as we found in bebop, to an interest in different scales and their new melodic possibilities;

2. Slowed down the rate of change of the harmonies almost to a standstill. Modal pieces took one chord, or vertical structure, and sustained these sounds for relatively long durations while soloists laid scalar improvisations over this supporting foundation; and

3. Created an effect of rapidly moving melodic notes over a static substructure. In this style, the underlying vertical structure did move, it was not a drone, but it usually took more time to move and only shifted slightly up or down. A given chord climbed or descended a step or two and held in place for a while as the scalar improvisational process continued. The sound of modal jazz is very different from that produced by "improvising to the changes."

Free Jazz

1. Called for the discarding of conventional notions of melody, harmony, rhythm, and timbre;

2. Allowed soloists the freedom to play what they chose when they wanted to;

3. Only required performers to listen to the other improvisers and react spontaneously to what they were playing; and

4. Placed an increased value on the element of surprise.

Jazz/Rock Fusion

1. Combined modern jazz improvisation with elements from rock 'n' roll. The style of jazz improvisation could virtually derive from any modern jazz style, bebop, modal, free, and so on, but rock tone, phrasing, and articulation became common;

2. Produced jazz music that incorporated rock rhythmic drumming, most notably the four-part division of the beat, as rhythmic accompaniment to the music. Most jazz, to this time, clung to the variations of triple division of the beat, the relaxed, shuffling rhythm so prominent in swing, but jazz/rock fusion rarely used any beat but the quadruple sub-division of the beat;

3. Prominently displayed the sounds of electric and electronic instruments. Not only was a characteristic electronic timbre present whenever jazz/rock groups played, but new improvisational techniques also developed as a result of employing these instruments, for example, timbral solos, feedback solos, and so on; and

4. Was usually loud. Microphones and microphone pickups were newly used to capture and transmit the sound of every instrument independently, including drums, and a new sense of balance for jazz ensembles developed. Also, since the aesthetic of rock 'n' roll called for great amplification, this same aesthetic principle was picked up by most of the jazz/rock fusion musicians, as well.

Now it is time to put this newly reviewed information to work. Below is a list of the forty jazz pieces we have studied so far, excluding the rhythm section pieces and the two works inserted into this review—Stan Kenton's *Prologue* and Stan Freberg's *The Great Pretender*. They are listed here in alphabetical order by leader or group name. Photocopy these pages and cut the pages on the dotted lines to separate them into individual slips. Assign each performance a style. You will probably have to listen again to a few seconds of some performances to refresh your memory.

When every slip has your notation of a style category written on it, reorder the slips into eight groups that correspond with the eight appropriate major style categories. If some piece does not fit well, set it aside in a ninth pile and be prepared to explain to your instructor why you think it should not be classified as swing, or bebop, or whatever. Notice that every piece is listed with its year of performance. Does your new order by styles place similar pieces in the same and *correct* chronological group for the style? For those pieces that seem to be exceptions to the rule of chronological order, explain the discrepancy.

STUDY PIECES

STYLE _____   YEAR 1961

Cannonball Adderley
KNOW WHAT I MEAN?

STYLE _____   YEAR 1990

Ray Anderson
THE GAHTOOZE

STYLE _____   YEAR 1929

Louis Armstrong
KNOCKIN' A JUG

STYLE _____   YEAR 1938

Count Basie
EVERY TUB

STYLE _____   YEAR 1927

Bix Beiderbecke
GOOSE PIMPLES

STYLE _____   YEAR 1992

Jane Ira Bloom
FURTHER INTO THE NIGHT

STYLE _____   YEAR 1988

Michael Brecker
DON'T TRY THIS AT HOME

STYLE _____   YEAR 1956

Max Roach and Clifford Brown
WHAT IS THIS THING CALLED LOVE?

STYLE _____   YEAR 1959

Dave Brubeck
BLUE RONDO A LA TURK

STYLE _____   YEAR 1959

Dave Brubeck
TAKE THE "A" TRAIN

STYLE _____   YEAR 1930

Chocolate Dandies
BUGLE CALL RAG

STYLE _____   YEAR 1959

Ornette Coleman
FREE

STYLE _____   YEAR 1959

Miles Davis
BLUE IN GREEN

STYLE _____   YEAR 1952

Duke Ellington
TAKE THE "A" TRAIN

STYLE _____   YEAR 1992

Rebecca Coupe Franks
SERENDIPITY

STYLE _____   YEAR 1955

Erroll Garner
WHERE OR WHEN

STYLE _____   YEAR 1953

Stan Getz
COOL MIX

STYLE _____   YEAR 1945

Dizzy Gillespie
DIZZY ATMOSPHERE

STYLE _____　YEAR 1956

Dizzy Gillespie
MY REVERIE

STYLE _____　YEAR 1945

Benny Goodman
CHINA BOY

STYLE _____　YEAR 1939

Billie Holiday
STRANGE FRUIT

STYLE _____　YEAR 1946

International Sweethearts of Rhythm
JUMP CHILDREN

STYLE _____　YEAR 1945

International Sweethearts of Rhythm
SWEET GEORGIA BROWN

STYLE _____　YEAR 1939

James P. Johnson
THE MULE WALK

STYLE _____   YEAR 1939

Pete Johnson
BOOGIE WOOGIE

STYLE _____   YEAR 1977

Marian McPartland
NOW'S THE TIME

STYLE _____   YEAR 1939

Jelly Roll Morton
SPORTING HOUSE RAG

STYLE _____   YEAR 1974

Gerry Mulligan
K-4 PACIFIC

STYLE _____   YEAR 1947

Charlie Parker
AIR CONDITIONING

STYLE _____   YEAR 1953

Charlie Parker
NOW'S THE TIME

STYLE _____   YEAR 1955

Bud Powell
EAST OF THE SUN

STYLE _____   YEAR 1963

Sun Ra
CALLING PLANET EARTH

STYLE _____   YEAR 1931

Don Redman
SHAKIN' THE AFRICAN

STYLE _____   YEAR 1933

Art Tatum
TEA FOR TWO

STYLE _____   YEAR 1957

Cecil Taylor
JOHNNY COME LATELY

STYLE _____   YEAR 1991

Barbara Thompson
YOU MUST BE JOKIN'

STYLE _____   YEAR 1927

Frankie Trumbauer
CLARINET MARMALADE

STYLE _____   YEAR 1930

Ethel Waters
WHAT DID I DO TO BE SO BLACK AND BLUE?

STYLE _____   YEAR 1976

Weather Report
HARLEQUIN

STYLE _____   YEAR 1924

Clarence Williams
TEXAS MOANER BLUES

The poet Langston Hughes was one of the most significant writers active during the Harlem Renaissance. In addition to more than ten books of poetry, he wrote novels, plays, short stories, and more. He had an abiding love for jazz and all the music of the African-Americans and wrote lyrics for five gospel song-plays. He also wrote a children's book, *The First Book of Jazz* (1955), and narrated a recording that introduces the history of this music in a fascinating way. Here is its beginning.

LANGSTON HUGHES, *THE STORY OF JAZZ* (CD SELECTION 3.9)

Langston Hughes (1902–1967) was a distinguished American poet and writer. His work was part of the Harlem Renaissance of the 1920s. His poetry was particularly inspired by the freedom and creativity of jazz improvisation and blues rhythms. Many of his poems and stories use jazz themes explicitly while others use jazz as an influence in more subtle ways.

A MAN OF LETTERS SPEAKS

AMIRI BARAKA

Now, at the time, Howard [University] didn't allow jazz music to be played on its campus, which is interesting, because Howard, of course, is a black college.... And this was in, of course, the early '50s. Sterling Brown [a black poet and instructor] held classes in jazz and blues in the dormitories and in the lobbies of the dormitories—he would bring his collection of records and a record player and put them down on the floor, and there would be about ten people who would come and listen, and he would talk about the blues, the origins of blues, what the music meant. And I think that was the first time we discovered that the music was actually criticized in terms of its form, content, meaning and so forth and so on.

Now what I first realized in beginning to write about jazz, black music, blues, and so forth, of course, is that most of the critics were not black, and that a lot of the things that I took for granted in the music, coming at it from a purely social direction in the first place, that is, the music that you grow up with, a lot of the things that I assumed people understood from having a kind of organic relationship with the music, it would seem that in the critics, for instance, was seldom understood, you know. Now, for instance, when bebop first came on the scene, you know, that is, the music that was made in the '40s that's associated with Charlie Parker and Thelonious Monk and Dizzy Gillespie, the innovators, most of the critics—that is, the *Downbeats, Metronomes* and so forth—most of the critics put it down. In fact, it was *so* embarrassing. They had to re-review the records about six or seven years later—all the records that they initially had put down, you know, with phrases like "ill advised fanaticism"—that was one, I think, a beautiful phrase. But they had to then bring all these records back and re-review the records. That is, they had to make self criricism, or as much as they would admit, that they had been wrong-headed and then re-review all those records. Now, when we first read those criticisms, we didn't think they were accurate. You know, they didn't have anything to do with the music. But then, strangely enough, when the next wave came along—let's say the Ornette Coleman, late John Coltrane, . . . Don Cherry and the rest of those people—the same kinds of things came up. That is, John Coltrane was criticized for almost the same "ill advised fanaticism" that was laid out, you know, for Charlie Parker and the rest in the '40s.

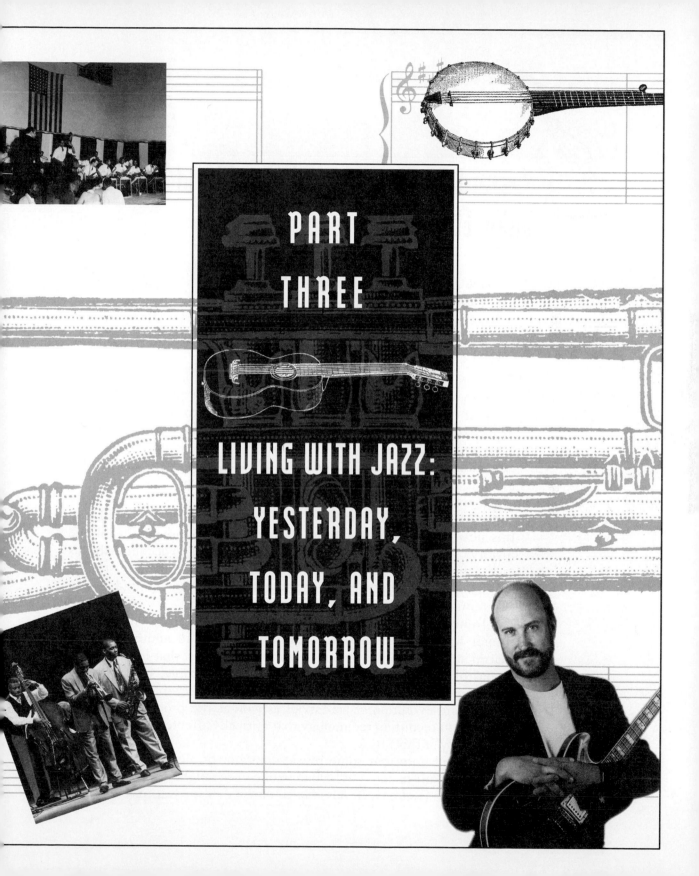

PART THREE

LIVING WITH JAZZ:

YESTERDAY, TODAY, AND TOMORROW

Yesterday: History and the World of Duke Ellington | 23

BARNEY BIGARD, JOHNNY HODGES, BUBBER MILEY,
AND DUKE ELLINGTON

Though we have not been studying the history of jazz, we have been introduced to a fairly consistent collection of primary historical sources, the recordings of jazz music from 1924 to the present. Our focus has been set on listening, enjoying, and developing our musical taste and sense of style, but if we briefly switch priorities and rearrange our listenings into an approximate chronological order, and also move those items back which were recorded at a later date but which represent an earlier style, we can hear the history of jazz in a fairly continuous and representative sequence. By listening to our CDs in this new order, we might form an interesting sound picture of the history of jazz music. It might take a few evenings to accomplish this task, especially since there is no speed-reading technique for listening to music, but it should be fun, and I would highly recommend you do this now.

To help simplify the chore of organizing the material, finding the proper track, and then shifting from one track to another, I have placed all the examples on our CDs into a single list that I think forms a sensible historical order. If you play each example, one after the other, in this new order, then I think you will be able to hear the change and evolution of jazz styles as well as the progressive developments in recording technology that critically affected the evolution and history of this music.

You will note that some music does not fit clearly into a single style; other music does not belong to one of the eight major styles; and some music is almost impossible to classify. Also, you may disagree with my categorization of certain examples, but that is all fair and good. Music is a complex art and defies categorization. You are now an experienced listener and may place more importance on certain elements you detect than I do. Another complication arises because, as time progresses, older players often continue recording in an older style long after its day of prominence has passed. Also, modern players who have all of history behind them may incorporate older stylistic elements into their new work which, of course, confuses stylistic classification. All in all, however, the following sound picture will not be too distorted.

A Listener's
History of Jazz

CD Selection	Style	Artist or Group	Years
3.9	Roots and Trad Jazz	Langston Hughes	ca.1900–30
2.5	New Orleans Style	Jelly Roll Morton	1920s
2.13	New Orleans Style	Clarence Williams	1920s
1.13	New Orleans Style	Louis Armstrong	1920s
1.12	New Orleans Style	Ethel Waters	1920s
1.17	Chicago Style	Bix Beiderbecke	1920s
2.14	Chicago Style	Frankie Trumbauer	1920s
2.6	New York Stride	James P. Johnson	1920s
3.10	(unique)	Duke Ellington	1920s
1.1	Early Swing	Chocolate Dandies	1930s
1.7	Early Swing	Don Redman	1930s
2.8	Swing	Art Tatum	1930s
2.7	Swing (boogie)	Pete Johnson	1930s
2.15	Swing	Count Basie	1930s–40s
1.11	Swing (art song)	Billie Holiday	1930s–40s
1.2	Swing	Benny Goodman	1930s–40s
3.3	Swing	Int. Sweethearts	1940s
2.2	Swing	Int. Sweethearts	1940s
1.18	Bebop	Dizzy Gillespie	1940s–50s
1.6	Bebop	Charlie Parker	1940s–50s
3.4	Bebop	Marian McPartland	1940s–50s
1.19	Bebop	Charlie Parker	1940s–50s
2.9	Bebop	Bud Powell	1940s–50s
2.3	Bebop (ballad)	Dizzy Gillespie	1940s–50s

2.16	Bebop	Roach-Brown	1950s
1.10	Swing-Bebop	Duke Ellington	1950s
1.14	Swing-Bebop	Erroll Garner	1950s
2.17	Cool	Stan Getz	1950s
1.8	Cool	Dave Brubeck	1950s
1.9	Cool	Dave Brubeck	1950s
1.16	Cool	Gerry Mulligan	1950s
3.7	Progressive	Stan Kenton	1950s
2.11	(unique)	Cecil Taylor	1950s
1.15	Modal	Miles Davis	1950s–60s
2.18	Modal	Cannonball Adderley	1950s–60s
3.1	Free Jazz	Ornette Coleman	1960s
2.10	Free Jazz	Sun Ra	1960s
3.11	(unique)	Duke Ellington	1960s
2.12	Jazz/Rock Fusion	Weather Report	1970s–80s
3.2	Jazz/Rock Fusion	Michael Brecker	1970s–80s
3.5	Jazz/Rock Fusion	Barbara Thompson	1970s–80s
2.4	Neoclassical Jazz	Rebecca Coupe Franks	1980s–90s
3.12	Neoclassical Jazz	Branford Marsalis	1980s–90s
2.1	Postmodern	Ray Anderson	1980s–90s
3.6	Postmodern	Jane Ira Bloom	1980s–90s
3.13	Postmodern	Freddie Bryant	1980s–90s

Now that you have taken the time to listen again with a new objective in mind, I need to add that even this serious review of all these recordings does some disservice to the history of this great music. This survey does not fairly present the scope and accomplishment of individual great masters. Louis Armstrong, Duke Ellington, Miles Davis, and others created exciting new music for 50-year professional careers and are sampled here with but one or two recordings. In fact, one can trace in the music of Miles Davis alone almost the entire history of modern jazz from 1945, when, at the age of nineteen, he first recorded with Charlie Parker and His Ree Boppers, through cool jazz in 1949, hard bop in the '50s, modal jazz in 1959, experiments in all these in the '60s, jazz/rock fusion in the 1970s, and constant explorations almost to 1991, the year of his death. By studying the hundreds of recordings made in his name, and then by following the thousands of recordings crafted by those musicians with whom he associated, many of whom he led, taught, and sent on their way, one might at last begin to understand the enormity of the genius and artistic accomplishment of Miles Davis.

We cannot do that here, not for Miles nor for any of the legendary masters of this great American music. However, hoping to entice you to explore the past a little more deeply, I would like to broaden the sample of one key musician and attempt to show you the fun you will surely have when you begin to follow this musical trail. Let's consider Duke Ellington. He made over 1,500 recordings under his own name; he composed over 2,000 works; he played approximately 20,000 performances during his 50-year career; and he created a band that was in itself a truly unique musical instrument. Though he was celebrated throughout the world, invited into the company of kings, queens, and presidents, and recognized by both jazz musicians and the European intellectual community as the master of his art, he was spurned by many of the established American composers. He was a champion of, as well as a role model for, his people and brought issues of race and equality to public notice through his music long before such acts were common or safe. He led a truly fascinating life, and only now, after his death, is he beginning to accumulate the recognition and stature that he truly deserved during his lifetime.

Duke Ellington and his Cotton Club Orchestra. With this band Ellington created his first masterpieces, some of the exotic "jungle" numbers, other sultry mood pieces, and still other hot, swinging dance tunes. Pictured are (left to right): Freddy Jenkins, Sam Nanton, Cootie Williams, Harry White, Arthur Whetsol, Sonny Greer, Duke Ellington, Harry Carney, Fred Guy, Johnny Hodges, Wellman Braud, and Barney Bigard.

What made his music so special? First, it is, in words he used to describe Ella Fitzgerald, "beyond category." His music literally stands alone and refuses to conform to norms. Of course, he could and did play swing arrangements for dances as he logged millions of miles on the road, but his own music was always created to satisfy his artistic needs, accommodate the sounds conceived in his mind, and utilize the singular instrumental qualities of each of the musicians in his band. He employed the New Orleans clarinetist Barney Bigard, a man with a resonant tone, a rich low register, a penetrating vibrato, and a dazzling technique. Ellington did not try to moderate these sounds and homogenize them into the section sound of the band. Instead, he capitalized on these personal musical traits and wrote music to exploit and feature them. He had the trumpet-mute virtuoso Bubber Miley, who could make his horn talk, growl, and purr. Duke created music for Miley, not just arrangements for a trumpet player but compositions for Miley's muted sounds. He had an alto saxophone virtuoso, Johnny Hodges, and Hodges possessed a unique sound and a liquid technique, a way of playing scales where one tone blended with the next. Ellington found special places for all these sounds and all his distinctive musicians in his music.

Ellington was born in Washington, D.C., in 1898 to a cultivated, middle-class family. As a young man he traveled to New York to make a name and pursue a livelihood. He soon led a band at the famous Harlem "Cotton Club," and part of the requirement for this employment, during the 1920s, was the provision of music for the exotic dances performed in an equally exotic "jungle" setting. One of the best of his "jungle" compositions was *The Mooche*. No other ensemble, then or now, ever sounded like Duke Ellington and His Cotton Club Orchestra playing, in 1928, *The Mooche*.

DUKE ELLINGTON, *THE MOOCHE* (CD SELECTION 3.10)

Mood is established immediately when the relentless, almost sinister bowed bass of Wellman Braud sets the pulse beneath high reeds in parallel harmony. In the background Miley growls and snaps with his muted trumpet. When Bigard's clarinet solo takes center stage, it never leaves the low register, never attempts a virtuoso run which might distract from the mood. The jungle is shaded, dark, heavy, and oppressive. Even the conversation between Miley's trumpet and Hodge's alto saxophone is charged with animal energy—the utterances are abrupt, biting, irregular. Duke's piano solo and Hodge's bouncy blues contrast with their primitive surroundings; perhaps they serve as musical reminders of the civilized world. They certainly serve as important elements for artistic diversity. Throughout this number the bass presses relentlessly on. How totally unlike the buoyant, swinging Duke Ellington romp of 1965, *Take the "A" Train.*

The Duke Ellington Orchestra and choir perform Ellington's Concert of Sacred Music *at Fifth Avenue Presbyterian Church in New York City.*

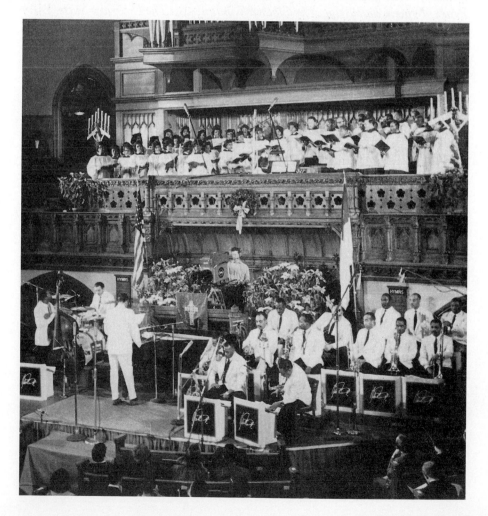

DUKE ELLINGTON, *TAKE THE "A" TRAIN* (CD SELECTION 1.10)

Many years passed between 1928 and 1965, years in which dozens of Duke Ellington compositions became household words—*Sophisticated Lady, Mood Indigo, Satin Doll,* and *Caravan;* dozens of others became classic pieces of the jazz repertoire but were primarily known among the jazz cognoscenti— *Concerto for Cootie, Black and Tan Fantasy, Diminuendo and Crescendo in Blue,* and *Cotton Tail;* and many other masterpieces slipped from view and favor—*Jump for Joy* (a musical); *Black, Brown, and Beige, The Clothed Woman,* and *The Liberian Suite.* Billy Strayhorn, Duke's friend and fellow composer/pianist/arranger, contributed *Take the "A" Train* to the Ellington library, and Duke's band

THE MUSICIANS SPEAK   DUKE ELLINGTON

Sunday night in the Cotton Club was *the* night. All the big New York stars in town, no matter where they were playing, showed up at the Cotton Club to take bows. Dan Healy was the man who staged the shows in our time, and on Sunday night he was the m.c. who introduced the stars. Somebody like Sophie Tucker would stand up, and we'd play her song, "Some of These Days" as she made her way up the floor for a bow. It was all done in pretty grand style.

Harlem had a tremendous reputation in those days, and it was a very colorful place. It was an attraction like Chinatown was in San Francisco. "When you go to New York," people said, "you mustn't miss going to Harlem!" The Cotton Club became famous nationally because of our transcontinental broadcast almost every night. A little later, something similar happened with Fatha Hines at the Grand Terrace in Chicago. But in Harlem, the Cotton Club was the top place to go.

The performers were paid high salaries, and the prices for the customers were high too. They had about twelve dancing girls and eight show girls, and they were all beautiful chicks. They used to dress so well! On Sunday nights, when celebrities filled the joint, they would rush out of the dressing room after the show in all their finery. Every time they went by, the stars and the rich people would be saying, "My, who is *that?*" They were tremendous representatives, and I'm darned if I know what hap-

still reserves a place for personal identity in the solo performances. Betty Roché sings her bebop chorus just before Paul Gonsalves blows his swing tenor chorus, and together the two of them fit harmoniously into Duke's instrumental ensemble and overriding artistic scheme that has always found unity in diversity. If there is this much contrast between *The Mooche* and *Take the "A" Train*, you may expect to find even more in the different worlds of music Duke Ellington composed, arranged, directed, and performed which we have not yet been able to sample.

During the last years of Ellington's life, he turned what must have been an inner spirituality into an overt expression of his religion through his music. These years found him engrossed with the composition of Three Sacred Concerts. Though he toured and maintained an active professional life to the end, his twilight years were spent composing, polishing, and performing sacred music in the jazz idiom.

pened to them, because you don't see anybody around like that nowadays. They were absolutely beautiful chicks, but the whole scene seems to have disappeared.

The nucleus of the band was the group I had had at the Kentucky Club. Harry Carney had joined us during the summer, and he went in with us. We also had Ellsworth Reynolds, a violinist who was supposed to be the conductor, but he really wasn't as experienced in show business as we were after playing all those shows downtown in the Kentucky Club. So I started to direct the band from the piano, without baton or any of that stuff, for I understood what they were doing more than anyone else in the band.

The music for the shows was being written by Jimmy McHugh with lyrics by Dorothy Fields. Later came Harold Arlen and that great lyric writer, Ted Koehler. They wrote some wonderful material, but this was show music and mostly popular songs. Sometimes they would use numbers that I wrote, and it would be these we played between shows and on the broadcasts. . . .

Sometimes I wonder what my music would sound like today had I not been exposed to the sounds and overall climate created by all the wonderful, and very sensitive and soulful people who were the singers, dancers, musicians, and actors in Harlem when I first came there.

His solo for Swedish soprano Alice Babs, *T.G.T.T.* (Too Good To Title), is another of his many masterpieces, another work that defies classification.

DUKE ELLINGTON, *T.G.T.T.* (CD SELECTION 3.11)

To understand an artist, one must view the years of apprenticeship, growth, and maturation as well as the highlights of artistic culmination. When you do this, you are studying the past, you are learning history, and you will discover that the past can be every bit as fascinating as the present.

R E V I E W   23

Begin to appreciate the scope, importance, and diversity of jazz's history. Gain some view of the size of a major artist's contributions. Have a first introduction to Duke Ellington.

Primary Goal of Unit 23

1. What was the form of *The Mooche?*

Study Questions

2. Who are Johnny Hodges, Barney Bigard, and Bubber Miley?

3. Are there any New Orleans Style elements in *The Mooche?* How many and which ones?

4. Are there any swing elements in *The Mooche?* Explain.

5. What instrument was Duke Ellington playing on *T.G.T.T.?*

6. How would you compare the orchestra of *The Mooche* with that of *Take the "A" Train?*

7. How would you compare the recording technology of *The Mooche* with that of *Take the "A" Train?*

1. Since some music does not fit into any particular style category, why do we study style in the first place?

Other Concepts

2. How would you describe *T.G.T.T.?* What makes it religious?

3. *T.G.T.T.* has no words. Is it a song? Why or why not? Could it be performed just as effectively on some other solo instrument? Why or why not?

Extra Activity

Organize a Duke Ellington Day for class. Everyone should select, or be assigned, a different Duke Ellington piece for home listening and preparation of a brief presentation and report. Depending on the size of the class, all presentations, or a select number, should be given before the entire class. After the reports are made, a panel of students should be chosen by the instructor to discuss this topic:

The originality and quality of Duke Ellington Compositions: the early works (to 1935); the middle period (1936-1945); and the late works (1946 on).

Second Extra Activity

Two recent publications give an outstanding introduction to the life and work of Duke Ellington. The first is a biography, and the second is a collection of essays written about Ellington and his music, which span his entire career. Why not check these out at the library:

John Edward Hasse, *Beyond Category: The Life and Genius of Duke Ellington* (New York: Simon & Schuster, 1993).

Mark Tucker, ed., *The Duke Ellington Reader* (New York: Oxford University Press, 1993).

Another Extra Activity

The next time you visit Washington, D.C., consider visiting the Duke Ellington display and archive at the Smithsonian Institution. It is the first such collection gathered for an American composer, and the holdings are extensive.

Today and Tomorrow: Neoclassical Jazz and Beyond

24

BRANFORD MARSALIS, WYNTON MARSALIS, AND FREDDIE BRYANT

We are nearing the holidays, and this will be our last night at the club. Mr. Imagination has invited some young musicians to the "Chez Imagination" to play for your send-off party. These men seem young to me, but the **Marsalis** brothers are already into their second decade of professional jazz work. **Wynton,** the trumpet player, has, in fact, been in the limelight since 1984 when two of his records were issued, one jazz and one classical, and *both* won Grammys! Before that he had already worked with Art Blakey's Jazz Messengers and Herbie Hancock's V.S.O.P. II before forming his own band. **Wynton Marsalis** did more to change both the public image of jazz and the current nature of jazz performance than any other musician of the 1980s, and he has already earned his place as a senior establishment figure of jazz and been placed in charge of the jazz programs at New York's Lincoln Center. This he does in addition to all his other multifarious activities.

Wynton Marsalis was born in New Orleans in 1961. His father is a famous jazz pianist and teacher, but he saw to it that **Wynton** studied both classical and jazz music from his youth to the present day. **Wynton**'s brother, **Branford,** the saxophonist, who is by one year **Wynton**'s elder, followed a similar path in both education and jazz performance, and he, too, is now an establishment figure of jazz and former director of NBC's "Tonight Show" band. Both brothers are phenomenal musicians, and there won't be an empty seat at the "Chez Imagination" tonight—that, I can guarantee you.

There are many fine young jazz artists entering the profession today, and choosing among them to show what is happening today and promising for tomorrow was really an overwhelming task. No one can predict who among them will become rich and famous, for that usually depends much more on luck, marketing, and public taste than sheer artistry, technique, and drive, but if success were based on merit alone, we might have selected Ryan Kiser, Cindy Blackman, Joshua Redman, Geri Allen, Wallace Roney, and many others and been assured of fame and fortune. They are all superb and dedicated artists. One player who caught Mr. Imagination's and my attention is a young guitarist whom you might not know, **Freddie Bryant,** who is also an excellent composer. He, like the **Marsalis** brothers, has a solid education in both classical music and jazz, and he will be coming to the club tonight after the release of his first CD. So, in the parlance of the stock market, we've got blue chips with the **Marsalis** brothers and a speculative issue with **Bryant.** And that, too, is part of the joy of partaking actively in the living jazz scene—watching young talent emerge, blossom, and mature. I am sure you will enjoy both groups, and I am genuinely anticipating our last night out together.

The Marsalis family of New Orleans, Louisiana, is pictured here in 1990 at a concert in Tully Hall in New York. Three of the Marsalis children—Wynton Marsalis, trumpet; Branford Marsalis, tenor saxophone; and Jason Marsalis, drums—are accompanied by their father Ellis Marsalis on piano. Reginald Veal is the bass player. Another Marsalis brother, Delfeayo, plays trombone and is also well-known as a recording producer.

As we sit down at the table, let me tell you a little bit about what seems to be going on in jazz these days. The most influential current style is that which some critics have named **neoclassical jazz.** During the 1960s and '70s, it seemed that **free jazz** and **jazz/rock fusion** were the only two avant-garde styles that might lead someday to a dominant style, a new mainstream jazz. It hasn't worked out that way, at least not yet. Some musicians and listeners turned away from **free jazz,** because they missed some key elements in the performances that they had become accustomed to and grew fond of, those same items that had been cast away or modified in **free jazz**—melody, harmony, form, and a single rhythmic pulse. Of course, those who loved **free jazz** felt these critics were simple-minded, tasteless, and old fashioned, and they might be right. Also, some musicians and listeners turned away from **jazz/rock fusion,** because of its association with rock, because of the electric instruments, and because of the volume. And of course, these are the same things that attracted some jazz musicians to the **jazz/rock fusion** style in the first place. And who is to say they were wrong? Personal taste counts a lot when it comes to music. And I would be the last to say that these styles have less aesthetic value or do not have the potential for further growth. In fact, fans of avant-garde **free jazz** or **jazz/rock fusion** do not have much patience with **neoclassical jazz** and are equally quick to criticize what they perceive to be but a regression to outdated ideas and sounds. However, they are not entirely right either, for **neoclassical jazz** is the **creation of new music** *based on modern views* of older **musical principles. Neoclassical jazz** was the new thing of the 1980s, and it continues today as a dominant force in jazz. **Wynton Marsalis,** more than any other musician, was responsible for spreading this message and popularizing the style.

In many ways, **neoclassical jazz** is a return to bebop, for the pieces have **formal structure,** the improvisers are required to **make the changes,** and the **instruments** used are **acoustic,** but it differs from bebop in significant ways: **formal structures may be expanded or compressed during performance; melodies may be modal, tonal, or highly chromatic; rhythms and meters will frequently vary** during the course of a performance; and **counterpoint and collective improvisation have increased value** in this style. What is really neat about all this, as far as you are concerned, is that you do not have to learn anything new in order to appreciate **neoclassical jazz** on first hearing. What you have learned before, all those old principles and elements of jazz improvisation, will suffice for this new style.

What you will notice, however, is how those old principles and devices can be cleverly manipulated and changed by these modern performers to give you truly exciting new music.

Now that we've finished our dinner, had our table cleared, and seen to it that we are set with a new round of drinks to last us until intermission, we can pay attention to the quartet that is coming to the bandstand. **Branford Marsalis** is serving as leader of the group tonight, and in addition to his tenor saxophone and his brother's trumpet, the group will be using only bass and drums for a rhythm section—no piano. Robert Hurst is the bassist, and Jeff "Tain" Watts is the drummer. The tune is about brothers, two of my favorite Old Testament characters, Cain and Abel. Which one do you suppose is portrayed by the tenor saxophone, and which by the trumpet?

BRANFORD MARSALIS, *CAIN & ABEL* (CD SELECTION 3.12)

Did you notice what they did to formal structure in the initial statement of the tune? It started out like a work in popular song form, AABA, but there was no return to "A," and the bridge was elided with the ending of the preceding section. Then, as the solos began, they were not played individually but together, a series of improvisational exchanges that not only created counterpoint and the sense of collective improvisation, but also included other kinds of improvisational devices—a timbral gesture here, an extended passage to develop and complete a musical idea there, a rhythmic complexity now and again. As they played, they stretched the boundaries of the limits formerly imposed by earlier styles. And best of all, you could hear they were having fun playing together, at each other, with each other. And then, in true neoclassical form, the head returned at the end. Just as in bebop, the performance is one big arch-form, ABA, head—improvisation—head, with a bit of an intro and coda added at both ends to wrap the package. What mastery!

Our last group also will use no piano, but, of course, the inclusion of a guitar might signal a chording instrument in the rhythm section. We'll just have to wait and see if this is the way the guitar will actually function in this ensemble. **Freddie Bryant** is going to use two saxophones in his group, Don Braden on tenor and Steve Wilson on alto.

To complete the rhythm section, he has hired Ira Coleman on bass and Billy Drummond on drums. All of these men are young, eager, and ready to prove themselves. The tune is a composition by **Bryant,** *Karma.* I wonder whether that refers to the Buddhist and Hindu concepts of life and fate, the totality of a person's action in any one of the successive states of existence which determine the fate of the next, or whether it is a girl's name. Maybe the music will tell us.

FREDDIE BRYANT, *KARMA* (CD SELECTION 3.13)

I am betting on philosophy and religion. What do you think?

Now wasn't that a great intro? The bass laid down a complicated ostinato while the drum established an equally complicated rhythm

Guitarist Freddie Bryant in 1994.

pattern that suggested two meters different from the one the bass was using. Did you notice that both the form of the head and the first improvisatory chorus were very similar to the pattern the **Marsalis** brothers used, an AAB for the head and a series of improvisatory interchanges for the first chorus? While the tenor and alto were going after each other, back and forth with brief improvisatory calls and responses, the guitar spoke up from the background with its own distinct message.

There is a recurring device in Baroque music called a *ritornello* that takes a bit of previously stated material and uses it periodically throughout a performance to establish formal lines of demarcation. It is a useful device that unifies a long work by bringing back something familiar every now and then. That same thing happened here with material from the bridge. It was used to separate the saxophone solo chorus from the guitar solo chorus, and separate the guitar solo from the recap of the opening material. Nice piece, polished performance, and **neoclassical jazz** through and through.

Well, where do we go from here? I hope, for you, this will be just the beginning of forty to eighty more years of enjoyable listening to jazz. You will surely want to start your own record collection, so you can savor again and again those sounds that please you most, but I hope you will never lose your love for live performance. That is the arena for spontaneous creation, and you will always be able to participate and share in that moment if you choose. Perhaps you might like to subscribe to a jazz journal, and you can hardly do better than America's own *down beat* magazine. It will keep you up-to-date on new and old players alike, report on festivals and recordings, and give you a chance to vote, once a year, for your own favorites. Perhaps you might like to form or join a jazz club, where you can get involved with bringing musicians to your community and sharing your favorite records and ideas with others of like interests. No matter where you go from here, you will find that what you have learned by listening to jazz and thinking about quality and value will help you in everything you do. As you listen to, look at, and think about the other concerns that come your way throughout your life in your own public and private worlds, jazz will not let you down. Jazz is not just an idle pastime; it is a metaphor for life. It teaches us to work hard, to do our best, to develop our talents, to respect and cooperate with others, and to pursue beauty, meaning, and fulfillment. That's what living with jazz is all about.

REVIEW   24

Learn the principles of neoclassical jazz. Study the work of Branford Marsalis, Wynton Marsalis, and Freddie Bryant. Set a goal for a continuing future living with jazz.

Primary Goal of Unit 24

Study Questions

1. In what ways is neoclassical jazz like swing or bebop?

2. In what ways is neoclassical jazz different from swing and bebop?

3. What principles of free jazz and jazz/rock fusion are rejected by adherents of neoclassical jazz?

4. The Marsalis Quartet did not use a piano. Was there a chord progression which was followed by the players during the head? During the solos? If yes, was it the same for both? Was it ever modified?

5. The Bryant Quintet also did not use a piano. Did the guitar replace the piano? If "yes," describe how. If "no," also describe how.

6. Were all the instruments of these two ensembles acoustic? If "no," which one (or ones) was not? If "no," does that invalidate accepting this music as part of the neoclassical jazz style?

7. Compare the work of the bass and drum players of the two ensembles. How were they alike, and how were they different?

Other Concepts

1. Some say jazz is America's classical music. What do you think?

2. Some say jazz is popular music. What do you think?

3. Some say jazz cannot be learned in school. What do you think?

Extra Activity   Discover who your local jazz musicians are, where they play, what kind of music they play, where they hang out, and even what their lives are like. Find one that particularly interests you and interview that person. Think about what you have learned from this interview and write it up. Then, share this information with your class.

APPENDIX A

WORKSHEET FOR

LISTENING

ASSIGNMENTS

Appendix A

LIVING WITH JAZZ

WORKSHEET FOR THE ASSIGNED LISTENINGS

_____
(name)

_____
(date)

Assignment No. _____   CD Selection _____

Recording: Leader or Group Name _____

Title of Work _____

Date of Recording _____

Performers:

Rhythm Section: _____

_____

_____

Brass: _____

_____

_____

Reeds: _____

_____

_____

Other: _____

_____

Order of solos, by instrument: _____

_____

Observations and overall impressions: _____

_____

Style: _____

Photocopy this page as necessary. Turn in filled-out worksheets to the instructor as required. Use the back to take notes, outline form, or write questions for your instructor.

APPENDIX B

DISCOGRAPHY

Appendix B

DISCOGRAPHY

DISC 1

Track	Title	Composer	Artist	Time
1.1	*Bugle Call Rag*	Pettis, Meyers, and Schoebel	The Chocolate Dandies	2:46
1.2	*China Boy*	Boutelja and Winfree	The Benny Goodman Sextet	2:38
1.3	*Fast Blues in F*		Dan Haerle, piano; Rufus Reid, bass; Mike Hyman, drums	0:33
1.4	*Bird Blues*		Dan Haerle, piano; Rufus Reid, bass; Mike Hyman, drums	0:39
1.5	*Now's the Time*	Charlie Parker	Kenny Barron, piano; Ron Carter, bass; Ben Riley, drums	0:45
1.6	*Now's the Time*	Charlie Parker	Charlie Parker Quartet	3:05
1.7	*Shakin' the African*		Don Redman and his Orchestra	2:33
1.8	*Blue Rondo A La Turk*	Dave Brubeck	Dave Brubeck Quartet	5:21
1.9	*Take the "A" Train*	Strayhorn and Ellington	Dave Brubeck Quartet	5:10
1.10	*Take the "A" Train*	Strayhorn and Ellington	Duke Ellington and His Orchestra	7:55
1.11	*Strange Fruit*	Allan	Billie Holiday	3:04
1.12	*(What Did I Do to Be So) Black and Blue*	Razaf, Waller, and Brooks	Ethel Waters	2:55
1.13	*Knockin' A Jug*	Louis Armstrong and Eddie Condon	Louis Armstrong and his Orchestra	3:23
1.14	*Where or When*	R. Rogers and L. Hart	Erroll Garner Trio	3:11
1.15	*Blue in Green*	Miles Davis	Miles Davis Quintet	5:26
1.16	*K-4 Pacific*	Gerry Mulligan	Gerry Mulligan Ensemble	11:42

1.17	*Goose Pimples*	Trent and Henderson	Bix Beiderbecke and His New Orleans Lucky Seven	3:15
1.18	*Dizzy Atmosphere*	Dizzy Gillespie	Dizzy Gillespie Sextet	2:46
1.19	*Air Conditioning*	Charlie Parker	Charlie Parker Sextet	3:00

Track	Title	Composer	Artist	Time
2.1	*The Gahtooze*	Ray Anderson	Ray Anderson Quartet	6:25
2.2	*Jump Children*	Taub and Witherspoon	International Sweethearts of Rhythm	3:00
2.3	*My Reverie*	Debussy; arr. Clinton	Dizzy Gillespie and His Orchestra	3:20
2.4	*Serendipity*	Rebecca Coupe Franks	Rebecca Coupe Franks Quintet	3:04
2.5	*Sporting House Rag*	Ferdinand "Jelly Roll" Morton	Jelly Roll Morton	3:00
2.6	*The Mule Walk*	James P. Johnson	James P. Johnson	2:26
2.7	*Boogie Woogie*	Pete Johnson	Pete Johnson	2:40
2.8	*Tea for Two*	I. Caesar and V. Youmans	Art Tatum	3:00
2.9	*East of the Sun (West of the Moon)*	Bowman	Bud Powell Trio	3:51
2.10	*Calling Planet Earth*	Sun Ra	Sun Ra and his Arkestra	5:30
2.11	*Johnny Come Lately*	Strayhorn	Cecil Taylor Quartet	6:45
2.12	*Harlequin*	Wayne Shorter	Weather Report	4:00
2.13	*Texas Moaner Blues*	Williams and Barnes	Clarence Williams Blue Five	3:10
2.14	*Clarinet Marmalade*	Shields	Frankie Trumbauer and His Orchestra	3:00
2.15	*Every Tub*	Basie, Durham, and Hendricks	Count Basie Orchestra	3:14
2.16	*What Is This Thing Called Love?*	Cole Porter	Clifford Brown-Max Roach Quintet	7:31
2.17	*Cool Mix*		Stan Getz Sextet	3:00
2.18	*Know What I Mean (take 12)*	Bill Evans	Cannonball Adderley with Bill Evans	6:59

	Track	Title	Composer	Artist	Time
DISC 3	3.1	*Free*	Ornette Coleman	Ornette Coleman Quartet	6:20
	3.2	*Don't Try This at Home*	Brecker and Grolnick	Michael Brecker Quintet	9:30
	3.3	*Sweet Georgia Brown*	Bernie, Pinkard, and Casey	International Sweethearts of Rhythm	3:00
	3.4	*Now's the Time*	Charlie Parker	Marian McPartland Quintet	6:02
	3.5	*You Must Be Jokin'*	Barbara Thompson	Barbara Thompson Quartet	6:00
	3.6	*Further into the Night*	Jane Ira Bloom	Jane Ira Bloom Sextet	6:48
	3.7	*Prologue*	Kenton and Richards	Stan Kenton Orchestra	10:00
	3.8	*The Great Pretender*	B. Ram	Stan Freberg with the Toads and Billy May's Music	3:00
	3.9	*The Story of Jazz*		Langston Hughes, narrator	5:00
	3.10	*The Mooche*	Duke Ellington	Duke Ellington and His Cotton Club Orchestra	3:00
	3.11	*T.G.T.T.*	Duke Ellington	Duke Ellington, electric piano; Alice Babs, soprano	2:55
	3.12	*Cain & Abel*	Branford Marsalis	Branford Marsalis Quartet	7:34
	3.13	*Karma*	Freddie Bryant	Freddie Bryant Quintet	5:43

Notes

P. 8   "I wouldn't tell all this": Sidney Bechet, *Treat It Gentle* (New York: Hill and Wang, 1960), pp. 201 and 212f.

P. 18   "My grandmother. She was a hard-shell Baptist": Jack V. Buerkle and Danny Barker, *Bourbon Street Black: The New Orleans Jazzman* (New York: Oxford University Press, 1973), p. 72. "This is what it was like": Nat Shapiro and Nat Hentoff, *Hear Me Talkin' To Ya: The Story of Jazz as Told by the Men Who Made It* (New York: Dover Publications, 1966), p. 66f.

P. 32   "I arrived in New York City": Shapiro and Hentoff, *ibid.*, pp. 173ff.

P. 46   "In those days we had several means of access": Dizzy Gillespie with Al Fraser, *to BE, or not . . . to BOP: Memoirs* (New York: Doubleday and Company, 1979; reprinted, New York: Da Capo Press, 1985), pp. 134, 202, and 231.

P. 78   "I came to New York": Betty Roché, interview by Harriett Milnes, November 19, 1982, on file in the Oral History American Music Collection, Yale University School of Music.

P. 90   "But in the end this beloved son": Ethel Waters and Charles Samuels, *His Eye is On the Sparrow: An Autobiography* (Garden City, New Jersey: Doubleday and Company, Inc., 1951), pp. 159f. and 246f.

P. 111   "I do *not* have a classical background": Dave Brubeck, an interview by D. Friedheim, October 14, 1977, on file in the Oral History American Music Collection, Yale University School of Music.

P. 122   "I was never really part of the bebop scene": Edward Berger, *Bassically Speaking: An Oral History of George Duvivier* (Metuchen, New Jersey: The Scarecrow Press, 1993), pp. 77–79.

P. 138   "By this time I was beginning": Louis Armstrong, *Satchmo: My Life in New Orleans* (New York: Prentice Hall, 1954), pp. 181f., 188, and 209.

P. 152   "I love drummers": Miles Davis with Quincy Troupe, *Miles: The Autobiography* (New York: Simon and Schuster, 1989), pp. 96–98 and 100f.

P. 159   "Why Women Musicians Are Inferior": Reprinted in the 55th anniversary issue of *down beat*, vol. 56, no. 9 (September 1990), p. 24.

P. 166   "Well, my musical experience": Mary Lou Williams, interview with Martha Oneppo, March 16 and 17, 1981, on file in the Oral History American Music Collection, Yale University School of Music.

P. 183   "Lips Page was another 'carver'": Buck Clayton, assisted by Nancy Miller Elliott, *Buck Clayton's Jazz World* (New York: Oxford University Press, 1986), p. 89f.

P. 204   "It is a strange paradox": Alfred V. Frankenstein, *Syncopating Saxophones* (Chicago: Robert O. Ballou, 1925), p. 51f.

P. 204   "Let me cite the case": *ibid.*, p. 59f.

P. 223   "The main difference in a white band":
Barney Bigard, *With Louis and the
Duke: The Autobiography of a Jazz
Clarinetist*, ed. by Barry Martyn (New
York: Oxford University Press, 1986),
pp. 70–72.

P. 234   "Each member goes his own way":
From the liner notes of *Change of the
Century*, Atlantic Records 1327.

P. 241   "For my money Lester was the world's
greatest": Billie Holiday with William
Dufty, *Lady Sings the Blues* (Garden City,
New York: Doubleday and Company,
1956; reprinted New York: Penguin
Books, 1984), pp. 59–61.

P. 289   "Now, at the time, Howard [University]
didn't allow jazz": Amiri Baraka,
interview by members of Vivian Perlis'
Ellington Seminar, October 4, 1977, on
file in the Oral History American Music
Collection, Yale University School of
Music.

P. 298   "Sunday night in the Cotton Club":
Edward Kennedy Ellington, *Music Is
My Mistress* (Garden City, New York:
Doubleday and Company, Inc., 1973;
reprinted New York: Da Capo Press,
n.d.), p. 80f.

Index